NEW YORK, N. Y.   Proposed Office and Convocation Building.
Bertram G. Goodhue, Architect.

THE
AMERICAN ARCHITECTURE
OF TO-DAY

G. H. EDGELL

AMS PRESS

NEW YORK

Reprinted from the edition of 1928, New York
First AMS EDITION published 1970
Manufactured in the United States of America

International Standard Book Number: 0-404-02245-6

Library of Congress Catalog Card Number: 79-120562

AMS PRESS, INC.
NEW YORK, N.Y. 10003

PREFACE

THIS book represents an elaboration and revision of three lectures on modern American architecture which the author was asked to give for the Henry La Barre Jayne Foundation in Philadelphia. It was understood that the lectures were to be published and they were therefore rather carefully written. When finished, however, it was found that the material was so extensive, the illustrations so numerous, that they could not be delivered as composed. The lectures were therefore abridged, delivered without manuscript, and the text, rewritten and reclassified, the three lectures changed to four chapters, was reserved for publication. Albeit the book varies in many important respects from the lectures as delivered, the flavour of the printed lecture may cling to it still. If so, the writer craves indulgence and reminds the reader that this is almost inevitable in any modern book on the fine arts, where every major statement is fortified by an illustration, and the arrangement must perforce resemble that of an illustrated talk.

In one respect the book coincides exactly with the lectures: it is addressed to laymen. Indeed, it is a layman's review for laymen. The writer is not a professional architect, but a student of the history of art. Moreover, he has no claim to special expertness in the field of modern American architecture. As a student of the history of art, a critic, and an observer of beauty, he was asked to review for laymen some of the tendencies of the fascinating architecture of America to-day. The book is the result.

The architect may find the book interesting. We hope he will. We even dare hope that parts, at least, may not only stimulate him but help him to think of his work in a new way. The last thing we should arrogate to ourselves, however, is the desire to instruct him.

To the architect, however, the writer owes many thanks and many apologies. First be it noted that when the material is so vast, it is impossible to do justice to the work of any individual, and the work of the many cannot be mentioned at all. Our review must be illustrated with a series of monuments. No one man, the writer least of all, would be capable of selecting or even being sure of knowing the best examples. For every building selected there might be another, or a dozen, or a hundred other examples that would illustrate the point as well or better. Yet weighty importance will seem to be given to those selected and correspondingly to the skill and taste of the architect of each, while the worthy designers of many other monuments as fine will go unmentioned. This is unfortunate but inevitable. The writer can only disarm criticism by confessing that he is more keenly alive to the defect than any reader, and by begging each reader to regard each monument discussed as an example of a type and not of necessity, in the majority of cases, even the best of the type.

This we must insist on the more strongly, as in every possible case the writer will name the designer of any building discussed. This he does deliberately in an attempt to combat the present vicious tendency to ignore the name of an architect while enjoying his work. Why this tendency should exist in the case of architecture and not in those of the other arts it is rather hard to explain. The first question about a painting or a piece of sculpture is usually with regard to its authorship. Indeed the modern trend in the study of painting is to emphasise the importance of connoisseurship at the expense of any serious attempt to analyse the artistic merit of a work. Yet those very *dilettanti* who are so exercised over the question as to whether or not a feeble panel really is by Niccolo di Pietro Gerini will enjoy and pass by a great building without once inquiring the name of the architect, be he ever so well known and the authorship beyond dispute. Despite the danger of false emphasis and the greater danger of an occasional error, we shall name the architects of the monuments we mention and try to give credit where credit is due.

Another point should be stressed in the Preface. The reader will soon find that the book is the work of an optimist. Consistently, the author has tried to take the appreciative and constructive point of view. Much bad architecture has been done in the United States; much is still being done. It is a temptation to write about it. Jeremiah probably enjoyed himself, though equally probably he would have denied it. The bad, however, is better ignored. This would not be true were there not so much good. To analyse, isolate, and honestly expound virtue is far harder than to do the same with vice. Moreover, it lacks a sensational appeal. None the less it is the more worth doing, and especially so in the case of American architecture. No thoughtful person will deny that the American of to-day is living in one of the most interesting architectural periods in the history of the world. We are not improbably on the threshold of a great Renaissance. It is the opportunity of the artist to bring it about, the duty of the critic to give it recognition, the privilege of the layman to observe and enjoy it.

The author has many acknowledgments to make; so many indeed that he despairs of making them properly. First his thanks go to the trustees of the Henry La Barre Jayne Foundation. Their imagination, their confidence, and their material assistance made possible both lectures and book. Among them the writer is indebted especially to Mr. Roland S. Morris. At the same time he is glad to take this occasion to recognise the courtesy and help of Mrs. David La B. Jayne. To Mr. C. C. Zantzinger especial thanks are due. His assistance in obtaining and preparing material, in suggesting ideas and filling *lacunæ* has been generous and constant. It seems ungracious, however, to mention any one architect by name. The lion's share of thanks goes to the profession as a whole. In preparing material it was necessary to approach hundreds of architects, to ply them with questions, to beg from them photographs, to ask their co-operation. The generosity and courtesy of their response was inspiring.

To his colleagues on the Faculty of Architecture at Harvard the author owes a constantly increasing debt. To Miss Sally Symonds, Secretary of the School, belongs credit for indefatigable work upon the manuscript and in proof-reading. Above all, the author owes to Miss Ruth V. Cook, Librarian of the School, a debt which it is hard to liquidate. Her assistance in classification, in collecting photographs, and especially in assembling vast amounts of bibliographical material and preparing the bibliography, was so great as to belittle the thanks which the author takes this occasion cordially to extend.

G. H. E.

CONTENTS

I

THE DEVELOPMENT OF AMERICAN ARCHITECTURE

Page 1

II

THE DOMESTIC AND ACADEMIC ARCHITECTURE

Page 85

III

ECCLESIASTIC AND MONUMENTAL ARCHITECTURE

Page 195

IV

COMMERCIAL ARCHITECTURE

Page 285

BIBLIOGRAPHY

Page 377

NOTE: A Classified List of Monuments mentioned and illustrated will be found immediately following the List of Illustrations.

LIST OF ILLUSTRATIONS

xi

64953

CLASSIFIED LIST OF MONUMENTS

The references are to pages, not figure numbers; those in
italics indicate illustrations; those in roman, text mention

BANKS

BRIDGES

CAPITOLS AND TOWN HALLS

CATHEDRALS, CHAPELS

(See "Churches")

CHURCHES

CITY HALLS
(See "Capitols and Town Halls")

CLUBS

Knollwood, N. C.: Mid-Pines Country Club, *96*, 97.

Locust Valley, N. Y.: Piping Rock Country Club, 154, *155*.

New York, N. Y.: University Club, 154.

Philadelphia, Pa.: Philadelphia Athletic Club, 338, *339*.

COURT HOUSES
(See "Capitols and Town Halls")

EXPOSITIONS

Buffalo, N. Y.: Pan-American Exposition, Electric Tower, *50*, 51; Building of Graphic Arts, Horticulture and Agriculture, 51; New York State Building, *50*, 51.

Chicago, Ill.: World's Columbian Exposition, 42, *43*; Administration Building, 38, *39*; Agricultural Building, 44, *45*; Court of Honour, 42, 44, *45*; Fine Arts Building, 44, *48*; Horticultural Building, 42; Manufactures and Liberal Arts Building, 44, *46*; Plan of Exposition, 44, *46*; Transportation Building, 42, 47, *48*, 79.

Omaha, Neb.: "Trans-Mississippi" Exposition, Government Building, 49, *50*.

Philadelphia, Pa.: Centennial Exposition, Agricultural Building, 40, *41*; Art Gallery, 40, *41*; Horticultural Hall, 40; Machinery Hall, 40, *41*; Main Exhibition Building, 40; Michigan State Building, 40, *43*.

Plans of Expositions, *52*.

San Diego, Calif.: Panama-California International Exposition, 58, 61; Bridge and California State Building, *63*, 64, *65*; Laguna de las Flores, 64; New Mexico Building, 66, *67*.

San Francisco, Calif.: Panama-Pacific Exposition, 58, *59*; Arch of the Rising Sun, *59*, *60*; Cloister of the Court of Abundance, 61, *62*; Horticultural Hall, 61, *62*; Rotunda and Palace of Fine Arts, *59*; Tower of Jewels, *59*, *60*.

Seattle, Wash.: Alaska-Yukon-Pacific Exposition, California Building, *56*, *57*; Perspective, *57*.

LIBRARIES

LOFT BUILDINGS

(See "Office Buildings")

MEMORIALS AND MONUMENTS

MUSEUMS

OFFICE BUILDINGS AND OTHER COMMERCIAL ARCHITECTURE

RAILROAD STATIONS

SCHOOLS

(See "Universities")

STADIA

STATE–HOUSES

(See "Capitols and Town Halls")

THEATRES

Boston, Mass.: Metropolitan Theatre, 332, *335*.

Chicago, Ill.: American Theatre, *327*, 328; Auditorium Building, 77, *78*; Capitol Theatre, *331*, 332.

New York, N. Y.: Capitol Theatre, 329, *331*; Century Theatre, 323, *325*; Neighbourhood Playhouse, *326*, 328; Roxy Theatre, 332.

Rochester, N. Y.: Eastman Theatre, *327*, 328, *330*.

Seattle, Wash.: Fifth Avenue Theatre, 332, *333*.

TOWN HALLS

(See "Capitols and Town Halls")

UNIVERSITIES AND SCHOOLS

Boston, Mass.: Boston College, 176, *178*.

Cambridge, Mass.: Harvard University, 160, 179, *180*; Harvard University Graduate School of Business Administration, 157, 162, *164*; Competition Drawings for same, 162, *166*, *167*, *169*; Mower Hall, 161, *163*; Memorial Hall, 33; Yard, 160, *163*; Massachusetts Institute of Technology, 179, *180*.

Chicago, Ill.: University of Chicago, *155*, 159.

Denver, Colo.: East High School, 189, *192*.

Galveston, Tex.: Goliad School, 189, *191*.

Greenfield, Ohio: Edward Lee McClain High School, 188, *190*.

Hanover, N. H.: Dartmouth College, 168, *170*.

Houston, Tex.: Rice Institute, 176, *178*.

New Haven, Conn.: Yale University, 171, *174*, *175*.

Pittsburgh, Pa.: University of Pittsburgh, 179, *182*.

Princeton, N. J.: Princeton University, 171, *172*.

West Point, N. Y.: U. S. Military Academy, 173, *177*.

I

THE DEVELOPMENT OF AMERICAN ARCHITECTURE

I

THE DEVELOPMENT OF AMERICAN ARCHITECTURE

THE bane of every contemplative or analytical work is the necessity of beginning with a definition. In our case we cannot proceed without considering the meaning of the word "modern." It may be taken in two senses. Used by one writer, it means contemporary; by another, radical. Discussing the tendencies of modern architecture with a distinguished critic of conservative bent, the writer mentioned the theories and practice of Frank Lloyd Wright. In reply he was told that this phenomenon was not a modern tendency, but a modern freak. The same day, another distinguished critic advised that it would be improper to include any mention of the Lincoln Memorial in a series of lectures on modern architecture, as there was nothing "modern" about it. By modern he meant what it might be clearer to call "modernist." At the outset, therefore, let us agree that by modern we mean contemporary. Modern American architecture includes all the architecture of America which has recently been built, or is being built to-day. It includes the conservative and the radical, the archæological and the original. To limit modern architecture to that which seems to embody what are called modernistic tendencies would be not only foolish, but arrogant. The architecture which to-day is regarded as unprogressive, a generation from now may be in the van, and no man, be he layman, critic, or designer, can pass an infallible judgment, or even make a good guess, as to what is to be the architecture of the future. Modern American architecture is the American architecture of to-day.

As architecture, however, it stands or falls on its own merits, without reference to the past. Let no designer defend his work on the ground that it is historically correct. The proud owner in a smoking-jacket, who plumes himself in his "pure Louis Quinze drawing-room," makes a fool, not only of himself, but of his architect—at least, so long as he bases his satisfaction on the stylistic "correctness" of his room. On the other

3

hand, if he bases it upon the beauty of the room, quite aside from historical reference, he has a good case, although there is no question that there is less life in an imitative work than in one that is designed originally, with imagination and a fresh eye.

Although the merit of modern architecture can never depend upon its correctness with relation to the art of the past, an understanding of it involves a familiarity with the art of the past, its character, development, problems, and successes or failures. In a book on modern architecture, work of the past should be stressed as little as possible, but some historical discussion is necessary to understand the tendencies of to-day. Behind even the most radical work there is a development which must be understood, if we are to understand what we are trying to do and whither we are going. In certain categories of modern architecture, especially domestic, constant reference to the past is inevitable.

Our first task must be, therefore, to trace as concisely as possible the development of American architecture, with its tendencies both conservative and radical, from its beginnings to the present time. We must remember as we do this, that we do it solely to understand the art of to-day, and not as an historical exercise, nor as an attempt to prophesy the architecture of the future. We are concerned with to-day, not yesterday, nor to-morrow. To-morrow, to be sure, intrigues us. We are tempted to speculate about it, but we can do so to little profit. President Lowell, of Harvard, in the introduction to one of his books on government, humorously attacked the commonplace conception of the government as a "ship of state." We can paraphrase him freely as follows. A government is not a ship, nor in any way like a ship. A government might better be likened to a coach. The coach is drawn by powerful horses who are running away. On the box a strong man is attempting to guide the team, while several other strong men try to take the reins away from him. Within are a number of passengers who display not the slightest interest in the behaviour or the progress of the coach, but in the rumble are several old gentlemen with spy-glasses who, by an intent scrutiny of the road behind, are attempting to prophesy the character of the road ahead. These old gentlemen may make some shrewd forecasts, but it is not our purpose here to join them. The historian is as well qualified as any, and is perhaps better qualified than most, to understand the present. Any man, however, lay or expert, who pretends to prognosticate the future, is a charlatan, unconscious or no.

If we cannot ignore history, no more can we ignore the theories of architecture, current and past. At every step we shall be forced to make æsthetic judgments and, if we are honest, we shall demand a basis for these. In so doing, we shall inevitably run the risk of becoming entrapped by the fallacious æsthetic theories of past and present. This very desire to have a definite basis for æsthetic judgment has caused the great philosophers of art, one by one, to erect their systems and create an infallible philosophy by which masters may be judged, yet one by one, like Theudas and his four hundred, they have gone their way.

Many of their ideas have lingered, however, and are quoted, from authority or as original, to-day. Perhaps at the start we could do nothing more constructive than to clear the garret of our minds of some of the old lumber of æsthetic theory. Four of the most insistent of the old fallacies have been brilliantly, if somewhat maliciously, exposed by Mr. Geoffrey Scott.* Since the ideas which they involve will recur constantly in our discussion, it is worth while to mention them. Of the four, the least important is what the author calls the "biological fallacy." By this he means the belief, so persistent among critics, that every phase of architecture or style runs through a biological revolution, involving birth, growth, bloom, and decay. There is a basis for the theory if it be not pushed too far, and we must realise the continuity of art history and the relation of style to style. We must, on the other hand, rid ourselves of the belief that the phase of a style which is late in its development must, *ipso facto*, be decadent. For such a reason, flamboyant (late Gothic) and baroque (late Renaissance) architecture have been bitterly and absurdly condemned. To be sure, progressive thinkers nowadays have abandoned such a belief, but many laymen and not a few architects even to-day will condemn flamboyant Gothic on the ground of the false biological analogy. When this condemnation is extended to include a modern building, like the Chicago Tribune Tower, which uses a flamboyant Gothic vocabulary, injustice and, worse still, confusion is bound to ensue. Note that this confusion arises when the attack is made not on the grounds of a too archæological treatment, which involves an entirely

* *The Architecture of Humanism*, London, 1924.

different question, but on the grounds of the historic position and expression of the archæological source.

The so-called "romantic fallacy" in modern taste and judgment is far more dangerous. "Romanticism may be said to consist in a high development of poetic sensibility towards the remote as such."* In architecture it is responsible for reversions to styles with poetic literary associations in the past. Its most obvious manifestation was the Gothic revival of the nineteenth century. In a less obvious way its spirit is responsible for much that is deliberately exotic or theatrical in our art. With the most sincere motives in the world, an artist may study, let us say, the mediæval farm and attempt to attain in modern expression a group the charm of which is got by simulating the conditions which produced the ancient building and, thus, its forms. Charm there may be, but it may be as much the charm of historic association as of actual design. If the former, it will be lost as soon as taste changes and we cease to have pleasant romantic associations with a mediæval farm. Even before then, the effect for the thoughtful is marred by an inevitable theatricality. Nevertheless, the human mind will never purge itself of all poetic and literary interests and associations. Their presence in a work of art should not condemn it. To the contrary, they are legitimate aids to æsthetic enjoyment, provided they be aids and not principals. The moment they appear as substitutes for the fundamentals of design, however, the ultimate æsthetic value of the building is doomed.

Much more dangerous in modern times is what has been called the "mechanical fallacy." This theory would have us believe that true beauty lies in the satisfactory solution of structural problems and, secondarily, in the frank revelation of the means by which these problems have been met. The ideal example which the protagonists of the theory would point out is the French Gothic cathedral of the thirteenth century.† It has been said, on the whole correctly, that the truest æsthetic expression of the French Gothic cathedral of the thirteenth century lies in the logical way it is constructed and the scrupulous honesty with which the structural system is revealed.

* Scott, *op. cit.*, p. 39.

† The theory is advanced in its most glorified and convincing form by C. H. Moore in his *Gothic Architecture*, 2d ed., New York, 1909.

Yet such a theory has grave limitations. It ignores the æsthetic values of form, balance, and harmonious relation of part to part, wherein may lie the real value of the Gothic cathedral and which may have been attained unconsciously in the pursuit of a logical structural solution. Moreover, it takes no account of the many beautiful buildings, even contemporary Gothic ones like those of England, which attain a magnificent artistic success without following the logical organic system of the French. Lastly, one cannot be sure whether the æsthetic effect of French Gothic depends upon its logical revelation of structure or its *apparent* revelation, a very different matter. Let us examine one concrete example. The French double flying buttress is supposed to be a logically revealed solution of the problem of meeting the active and concentrated thrust of a Gothic vault. Since a continuous abutment along the whole vault is impractical, the fully developed flying buttress is given the form of two slender arches, designed to take the thrusts at the two conspicuous danger points of an arch or a vault: the springing and the haunch. Now, we think of a French Gothic cathedral as an organic composition, in scientifically cut stone, with vaults, ribs, supports, and abutments scientifically and skilfully related one to another. We forget that a very important part of the building is its towering roof, steep-pitched and lead-covered, carried on walls which project above the crowns of the stone vaults which are to be covered. How strange, ungainly, and awkward a great Gothic building can look without its roof was unhappily shown at Reims, in 1914, after the first bombardment had destroyed the roof, but before the vaults were blown in. Photographs show it a paradox: a great Gothic cathedral with its accent in design upon the horizontal balustrade which crowned the wall and formerly appeared as a decorative point of springing for the great pitched roof. Yet at this stage of the monument's destruction, all the stonework, all that we could call its "organic" architecture, was preserved.

The first bombardment revealed, however, another feature most upsetting to the orthodox theory of structural honesty. A double buttress, properly placed against the walls of a roofed cathedral, looks low. The upper arch, to catch the thrusts even of the haunch, must be placed a considerable distance below the balustrade. Caused by the fact that the wall is raised high above the springing of the vaults, however, and the bulky, lofty roof which it carries, the eye imagines a mass of material much higher than actually exists in a building. Buttresses placed, therefore, low enough properly to exercise their function as perfectly as possible, *appear* to be placed dangerously low. When at Reims the burning of the roof exposed the upper surface of the vaults, it was for the first time observed that the designers had deliberately placed the upper tier of buttresses too high. They are so high that they abut the wall above the vaults, instead of the vaults themselves. Since flying buttresses have themselves an active thrust inward, there was a danger of their pushing in the wall on top of the vaults. To eliminate this danger, flat arches or beams of stone were thrown across the nave, above the vaults, from the upper buttresses on one side to those on the other. For some seven centuries all the upper buttresses at Reims have been thrusting at one another, across the nave, and playing no structural rôle in the building whatever. They were deliberately so placed, at the expense of structural logic, in order to give its appearance. In this, as in every other period of great design, the architect has resorted to deception, backed by safe engineering, to secure an effect that would satisfy the eye.

The mechanical fallacy, or, if we approve it, the mechanical theory, has loomed large in the criticism of modern American architecture. The analogies, most of them superficial, between Gothic architecture and steel construction made it inevitable. Almost as soon as the first timid attempts in the "Chicago construction" appeared, critics at home and abroad began insisting upon the desirability of the design revealing in the skyscraper the system of construction which made it possible. The criticism was provoked partly by the logic of the theory and partly by the ugliness of the first examples, when a new form of construction had been invented, but design had had no time to study the problems which it presented. Obviously, it was necessary to study the new structures in a new way from the point of view of design, and arrive at an expression pertinent to the new type and as different from anything else as was the type itself from what had gone before. This is being done by some in observance of the tenets of the mechanical theory, by others ignoring them. One thing, as we shall see, is certain: the theory of structural revelation may be applied, and successfully applied, to the problem of the skyscraper, but there is no necessity which imposes it, and perfect solutions of the problem may be found in other ways.

The fourth of the great fallacies mentioned by Scott, the ethical, will probably never be eliminated entirely from criticism. On the other hand, it will probably never again be reiterated with such savage dogmatism as appears in the writings of John Ruskin. In essence, this theory confuses with art, ideas of morality, conduct, and ethics with which it has nothing to do. Ruskin's sweeping condemnation of Renaissance architecture as "immoral" brings the matter home in its clearest light. Of course we should not belittle the work of the great critic. He was an evangelist of the fine arts, and by his art of English composition—as great and constructive an art as any he used it to defend—he converted thousands who might otherwise have gone through life with eyes shut to beauty. His work now, however, is done; his theories obsolete. In modern life they are a stumbling-block rather than an aid.

Yet they have survived in countless catchwords which are constantly used as gospel by the thoughtless and, indeed, by those who consider themselves thinkers. Take, for example, such a phrase as "Truth is beauty; beauty is truth." Approach any cultivated gentleman and ask him if it is not fundamentally sound to say that truth is beauty. There are nine hundred and ninety-nine chances in a thousand that he will assent, grave as an owl, thinking himself confirming an axiom, using his mind not at all. For truth has nothing to do, necessarily, with beauty, nor beauty with truth. If I say, "We are such stuff as dreams are made on and our little life is rounded with a sleep," I utter a truth, which is beautiful because framed by a great artist. If I say, "The Japs are a wonderful little people," I say what is equally true, but trite in form and dull by repetition. If I say, "A certain critic of my acquaintance is an unmitigated bounder," I utter a truth as sound as gospel, but nothing of beauty. The truth, beautifully expressed, is beautiful. So may a lie be. If it is possible to build an ugly thing, it is possible to do so truthfully. Truth as an abstract concept is beautiful; as a concrete fact it may be beautiful, dull, or ugly. Not until we cease to throw ourselves into a state of self-hypnosis with words shall we be able truly to comprehend and estimate the eternal verities of beauty and art.

The function of architecture is twofold and can be stated in the simplest terms. Architecture must be practical and beautiful. It is a profession and an art. In this it is distinguished chiefly from the sister arts of sculpture and painting, and it is the practical side of architecture which has made it the most precocious of the arts. It is very noticeable in any great artistic period that the various arts do not appear or culminate simultaneously, but in a sequence which is fairly constant in each revolution of civilisation. Music, for example, is a laggard art as well as a gracious one, that is apt to illuminate the end of an era. One can hardly, for example, date the beginning of the Renaissance in music before the time of Palestrina, yet the beginning of the architectural Renaissance in the same period would take us back to Brunelleschi, a century earlier.

The precocity of architecture proves its practicality. Men must house themselves before they think of delighting their eyes with sculpture or painting, and the first problem of architecture is the practical one. From its earliest beginnings, its success must be gauged in large part according to its solution of the practical needs of its clients. Nevertheless, considerations of beauty entered almost as soon as those of use, and the good designer in all ages has been occupied equally with both. Architecture which fails in either is bad, for practicality can no more excuse ugliness than can beauty of form destroy the evil impression that comes from revealed stupidity on the practical side.

The practical aspect of architecture is not, however, merely an æsthetic liability. Even from the æsthetic point of view, the sense of a satisfactory solution of practical needs has value. This leads us to consider a little more in detail the problems of architecture which the modern designer has to meet. Their enormous complexity needs especially to be stressed to a lay audience. The architect, to be sure, is only too bitterly alive to the difficulties of his problem, but the average layman is blithely unconscious of them. In making comparisons, oftentimes odious, between the great designers of the past and those of to-day, we too often forget that the problems of the past were almost childish compared to those which face the practitioner in modern times. Even giants like Michelangelo or Wren, when they built St. Peter's or St. Paul's, were confronted with problems of infantile simplicity as compared to those which were met by Warren and Wetmore in the Grand Central Station, or by Cass Gilbert in the Woolworth Building. Many elements produce this fact. Specialised function, for example, has enormously complicated the problem. In the Middle Ages men built churches, fortresses, dwellings, and town halls. These offered comparatively simple problems and satisfied practically all needs.   Moreover, within the building functionalism scarcely existed.   What was the dining-room at one time might, without alteration, be used for another function at another time.   Also, the same great hall was used for many functions.   Even in so splendid and enlightened an era as the age of Louis XIV, the functionalism of rooms at Versailles was little regarded.   It was not until the eighteenth century that problems of function, diversified communication, and the real comfort of the occupant began to be studied.   In a homely way the truth can be brought home to us rather vividly when we remember that such an obvious modern necessity as the flushable toilet was forgotten from the Minoan age to the latter part of the eighteenth century.   Yet even by the end of the eighteenth century the problems were still very simple.

Contrast this with the facts to-day.   Even the simplest architectural problem, the dwelling, has developed a complication undreamed of a few generations ago.   Any one who has built even a modest house, or commissioned one to be built for him, will know the complexity of things to be considered.   The character and arrangement of the heating plant, the plumbing, ventilating, wiring, the arrangements for electric outlets, telephones, etc., make the design, even of a moderate dwelling, a serious piece of work.   And if this unæsthetic and dull work be not well done, how quickly the wrath of the client falls upon the head of the architect!   In a work on a small scale, all this must be done in addition to making the house beautiful, both within and without.

If the moderate dwelling has become, comparatively speaking, so complicated, what, then, of the highly specialised, modern types of monumental and commercial buildings?   The modern school-building, for example, offers a special problem so distinct that certain architects have made it their field and become specialists in it, much as a physician specialises in certain diseases.   The theatre, with its immensely complicated stage machinery, lighting system, and considerations of acoustics, has no precedent in history before the time of Victor Louis.   Still more striking are the complexities of the great railroad terminal, the great department store, and the commercial skyscraper, which is in itself a combined town and vertical railway.

Moreover, other considerations than those of function enter to complicate an already amazingly complicated problem.   Modern materials, especially, are very different from those of the past.   Steel construction has unloosed possibilities of scale and altitude which have revolutionised the art.   Concrete, and especially concrete reinforced with steel, has added another entirely new element.   Engineering skill and invention, forging ahead at railroad rate, have produced such phenomena as the high-speed elevator, again revolutionising architectural design.   Similarly, rapid and easy communication within the city, with the suburbs, and with the country, have produced enormous concentrations of population diurnally within limited districts, bringing with them a host of difficulties undreamed of in the past.   Even in the use of materials familiar through centuries, the problem is a new one, for the architect may use, if taste and expediency demand it, materials from almost any source and brought from almost any distance.   The Romans used travertine partly because it was a beautiful and easily worked building stone, but largely because it was ready to hand. We can use it without hesitation, if we so choose, even though we have to send to the Campagna to get it.   The extent to which the designer should use local material is, therefore, only one of the many decisions he is called upon to make.

All this makes the position of the modern architect, and especially the American architect, entirely different from anything that it has ever been in the past.   Though he were an encyclopædic genius, with a mind like Leonardo da Vinci's, it is inconceivable that he should design all of his building, with all of its component parts, as an individual so designed it in the Middle Ages or the Renaissance.   He cannot design the bulk of a skyscraper and, at the same time, its machinery for elevators, for heating, for plumbing, and for lighting.   He must call in assistance for all of these things, and he must consider his building with relation to its neighbours.   He must employ and co-operate with the engineer in his many specialties, and even, in many cases, with the lawyer, the sociologist, the sanitary expert.   He must be the able administrator and the chairman of a board of experts.   Withal, he must be the artist, attaining these things, yet steadfastly keeping before his eye the purpose and the ideal of his profession—the ultimate beauty of the thing he creates.

The attainment of beauty is, after all, the most important of the many functions of an architect.   Were this not so, the able business man might be substituted for him.   Without beauty, there is no architecture, and it is this most intangible of qualities that we employ an architect to attain. His means to attain it are form and colour. From his earliest training, he must think in terms of three dimensions. He must reach harmonies in solids, thinking of his design simultaneously in plan and elevation. He has also at his disposal colour and texture, though these are subordinate to mass and proportion.

The importance of colour, however, has been neglected in architecture and especially in the United States. The reasons for this are manifold, but probably in the United States the chief difficulty has been the inaccessibility of great polychromatic architectural monuments. The American student of architecture, since Colonial times, has derived much of his knowledge from books and printed illustrations. With consistent respect for the achievements of the past, he has studied his reproductions conscientiously, learning proportion, refinement, delicacy, but nothing of colour. As a result, he has usually eschewed colour, satisfying himself on the grounds of simplicity and architectural chastity, as though an architecture which was colourful must necessarily be frivolous. In the rarer attempts when he used colour, he either followed a theoretical and archæological method, which led him nowhere, or, through the inexperienced use of his materials, arrived at dissonances varying from the combination of a few sooty monotones to a nerve-shattering cacophony of clashing full intensities. The history of American architecture is dotted with disasters in polychromatic design. Happily, this difficulty is being recognised and met. The great monuments of colour in the past, like Raphael's loggia or Pintoricchio's decorations for the Borgia Apartments, are being studied as such monuments should be studied—not for imitation, but as successful solutions of a problem—and a few monuments of American architecture have just appeared which can compare, in the matter of successful colour, with anything that has been done in the past.

For the layman, the most needful advice in æsthetic judgment is to urge alertness and common sense. In spite of the warring philosophies of the past, there is such a thing as sense of beauty, and most people have it. A few may be born without it, as a few are born deaf or blind, but the vast majority of people can recognise beauty and enjoy it in some form. Almost any one can enjoy the beauty of landscape, whether of the hills, the plain, or the shore. The moment this sense of beauty begins to be sophisticated, however, it becomes confused with literary and philosophic ideas.   These are useful but dangerous, especially as, in the case of the layman, they are applied with lack of true understanding.   In other words, we use the ideas of others as an easier method than analysing and applying our own.   As a result, the sense of beauty becomes partly contaminated, partly atrophied.   Like every other faculty, the sense of beauty needs exercise and the more healthy exercise it gets, the stronger it becomes.

The duty—and the pleasure—of the layman is simple.   He should constantly observe and constantly discriminate.   He need not do this in humility, for the architect is producing beauty not for himself and a select few but for all.   He should, however, remember his limitations and, to return to our physical analogy, not attempt a too massive judgment with a too little exercised critical faculty.   Above all, he should judge and discriminate with charity.   Most of us, lay and expert, are seduced by the ease and trenchancy with which we can formulate an unfavourable judgment.   It is a form of mental cheap smartness which few of us escape.   The opprobrious catchwords of criticism are quick-caught and far-flung.   The witty sneer brings a ready laugh, when thoughtful approval will only start an argument.   "Critic" comes from κριτικοσ and means capable, or apt for judgment.   It means one who should discriminate, not necessarily condemn, yet too often it is taken in the former sense.   How often do we say that a man is "critical," when we really mean that he is disagreeable!   Intelligent appreciation is far more difficult than condemnation, and it is correspondingly more worth while.   It need not interfere with a just discrimination, and it is especially worth while in America to-day, where there is as much great architecture to appreciate, to analyse, to understand, and to enjoy, as in any period of the development of the art.

Although our subject is the architecture of to-day, no possible comprehension of it could be obtained without reference to the architecture of the past.   Happily, however radical the modern may intend to be, his innovations have their roots in the past and cannot be explained without reference to it.   Sometimes these roots go down only a short way, sometimes they tap the centuries, but always they are there.   A brief sketch, therefore, of the development f American architecture, with especial reference to that side of it whic' affects modern design, is the necessary prelude to any discussion of the types of buildings, or the tendencies of architecture to-day.

The traditions of American architecture date back to the earliest Colonial period. Colonial architecture varied widely, however, period by period, and was influential more in its later phases than its earlier. Its influence on modern architecture is felt tremendously in domestic design and only occasionally in monumental architecture. American Colonial can be divided into two main classes corresponding roughly to the seventeenth and the eighteenth century work. The former can be called mediæval; the latter, Renaissance design. To the general public, the statement that there was any native American "mediæval" architecture will come as something of a shock; nevertheless, the distinction is a fair one. It is, moreover, a useful one to understand in connection with our critique of modern work. Mediæval architecture is picturesque. Renaissance architecture is formal. The reason for this is that in mediæval architecture the primary, and one might say the sole, interest is in structure. The mediæval builder, except in monumental works, was concerned only with the most direct solution of the practical needs of the occupant. He used no vocabulary of ornament derived from the classical past or other historic source, but strove to construct with an eye fixed on the exigencies of material, weather, site, and other practical considerations. The beauty he attained, often most satisfactorily, came through the structure, its frank revelation, and the harmonious forms which it frequently imposed. The expression of his building was thus frank, naïve, and picturesque.

This is particularly true of the wooden framed buildings which the Colonial settlers first erected. They were not only æsthetically but actually historically mediæval, and this despite the late date at which they were erected. We are accustomed to think of the Middle Ages as coming to an end in Italy about 1400; in northern Europe, about 1500. Because in England Inigo Jones, in the latter part of the sixteenth century, and Sir Christopher Wren, in the latter part of the seventeenth, set the style for neo-classicism by such great designs as Whitehall and St. Paul's, we are apt to think of all English architecture as suddenly having undergone a complete transformation. Nothing could be farther from the truth. For a long time, the new style was confined to the buildings of polite society, of the wealthy and the sophisticated. The peasants and the lesser burghers continued to build in full accord with the ancient mediæval tradition.   The great bulk of the seventeenth-century settlers in America came from these sturdy, but artistically reactionary, lower classes.   They gave their buildings in this country a new expression, perforce, because they used different materials.   Stone was expensive and hard to work, brick kilns were scarce and inadequate.   Wood was plentiful, cheap, and easy to use, so most of the architecture was in that material.   In artistic expression, however, it maintained strictly the mediæval point of view. The average American seventeenth-century dwelling was a wooden version of the English yeoman's cottage, a purely mediæval type.

Nothing is easier than to illustrate this.   Take, for example, such a building as the Fairbanks house at Dedham, Mass. (Fig. 1).   It dates traditionally from 1636, and cannot be more than a decade later.   It is a wooden structure, solidly framed in imported oak.   Its proportions are compact, its plan of the simplest, its chimney centrally placed and massive, its windows filled with small panes of leaded glass in casements.   It lacks the slightest display of polite ornament or formality.   To some it is mere building, not architecture, yet it has undeniable picturesqueness and real charm.   Moreover, its type has had a very real influence on much modern domestic design.   It is, however, a building mediæval not only in expression, but in fact.

Examples of the type could be multiplied almost at will.   As one other, we might glance at the old "Scotch House" or "Boardman House" at Saugus, Mass., authentically dated 1651 (Fig. 2).   It has the central chimney, the characteristic mediæval overhang of the second story, the simple two-room plan, with the hall in the centre, which has come down direct from the Middle Ages in Europe.   It is only one more of the hundreds of similar monuments, dating from the seventeenth century, which exist all along the Atlantic coast wherever the early settlers penetrated.

In ecclesiastical architecture, the effect was the same.   Such a building as the "Old Ship" church, at Hingham, Mass., built in 1681, is purely mediæval.   It is literally a "meeting-house," fulfilling perfectly the needs of its simple congregation and avoiding any suggestion of the frivolity and pretense which its congregation would have associated with a classical, or in any way a formal style.

Contrast with these such a typical building of the eighteenth century

FIG. 1.   DEDHAM, MASS.   Fairbanks House.

FIG. 2.   SAUGUS, MASS.   Scotch-Boardman House.

as Mount Airy, Richmond County, Va., built in 1758 (Fig. 3). Here, the expression is completely formal and sophisticated. Ultimately, the design is based upon the work of the Italian Renaissance, and notably that of Palladio. The rustication; the angles reinforced with quoins; above all, the exact symmetry of plan and the æsthetic expression got by simple proportion, and the easily caught relation of space to space and measurement to measurement—all this represents the movement inaugurated by the Italian Renaissance. American architecture has become sophisticated, polite; the whole point of view of the designer has changed. The "Georgian Colonial" has arrived, the style which exerts the profoundest influence of any upon American domestic architecture of to-day.

The immediate source of inspiration of such buildings as Mount Airy is not far to seek, and brings us to another point of interest in Colonial architecture, as it is of interest to-day: the use of published documents. Such documents are commonly used and often abused. In the eighteenth century, there were few, if any, real architects in America. The wealthy client, now having arrived at a dignified position in Colonial society, employed a builder of skill, taste, and a familiarity with the published works —actual or hypothetical—of fashionable architects abroad and especially in England. The influence of such books on American architecture cannot be overestimated. Some were elaborate folios, like that of James Gibbs, published in 1728 and widely used for monumental works in this country. Others, more modest and therefore even more widely used, were such publications as that of Robert Morris (from 1728), Abraham Swan (from 1745), William Pain (from 1758), and many others. Some are amusingly naïve, though none the less influential, like the *New System of Architecture* by Asher Benjamin, who describes himself as "architect and carpenter," and Daniel Raynerd, an "architect and stucco worker." This was published in Boston as late as 1806.

If we compare Mount Airy with Plate 63 (Fig. 4) in Gibbs' monumental *Book of Architecture, Designs, and Ornaments*, we see very clearly where the American got his ideas. The main mass in elevation is the same, with central block in two stories, connecting passages, and symmetrical wings in the form of pavilions and outhouses. Similarly, the plan (Fig. 5), with its U-shaped passage leading to the pavilions, is taken direct from Gibbs' book. In his elevation, to be sure, the designer

FIG. 3.   MOUNT AIRY, VA.

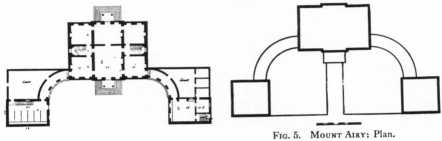

Plan of Country House in Fig. 4.

FIG. 5.   MOUNT AIRY: Plan.

From James Gibbs, "A Book of Architecture."

FIG. 4.   Scheme for a Country House by James Gibbs.

has not followed the publication so closely, but its main elements were none the less got from the book. Plate 55 of the same publication, for example, gave him his ideas for the triple-arched and heavily rusticated entrance vestibule. When to-day we admire the designs of the charming Colonial work and, in the same breath, chide the modern architect for slavish copyism, we should bear in mind the directness of the debt of Colonial to published European work. The modern is scarcely ever as direct a "cribber" as the Colonial.

Indeed, as one turns over the pages of Gibbs, one feels almost as though one were running through a treatise on Colonial architecture. Plate 3, his front elevation of St. Martins in the Fields in London, shows us one of the ideals of the Colonial designer. The same may be said of Plate 21, St. Mary-le-Strand, which was the prototype of so many Colonial and, less directly, so many modern churches. Plate 30 (Fig. 6) gives us a study of three church spires as they might appear, crowning Colonial churches anywhere from Maine to South Carolina, or reflected in a hundred attractive monuments of the Colonial movement to-day.

For details of construction or ornament the American would consult a book like William Pain's *Practical House Carpenter.** Plate 39 (Fig. 7), for example, gives us a charming Ionic Colonial doorway that was copied *verbatim* in a number of buildings, and can be used to-day as a source of inspiration, as well as information. For simpler houses and churches, where the polite and formal design was required by the taste of the time, yet where a modest purse made economy a necessity, there were many books with illustrations that gave ideas and were often directly imitated. We reproduce one, Plate 36 (Fig. 8), from Benjamin and Raynerd's *New System of Architecture,* which will illustrate the fact. Any one familiar with Colonial architecture or its charming modern offspring will find this dwelling comfortably familiar. If architects were few, books were plenty, and they made our Georgian Colonial possible.

By the end of the eighteenth century, a change came over American architecture and a new style appeared which it is of the utmost importance to recognise if we are to understand the inspiration for much of the best of our modern work. The new style we can call "Early Republican," as opposed to the "Georgian Colonial" of the earlier eighteenth

* Boston, 1796.

FIG. 6.   Elevation of Georgian Steeples by
James Gibbs.

FIG. 7.   Design for a Doorway.

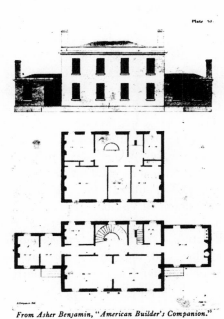

FIG. 8.   Elevation and Plan for a Country House.

century.   Because, like the Colonial, this was a classical architecture, it is constantly confused with Colonial; yet it is very different from it in that it is first, far more strictly classical, and second, far more complicated and finished in plan.   It is the architecture of what is generally called the "classical revival," but few people realise that the classical revival began earlier in the United States than it did abroad.   For the first time, with this movement, America was artistically in the van.   This came largely through the efforts of a *dilettante* of great genius, Thomas Jefferson, who designed the Virginia State Capitol in 1785, twenty-two years before Vignon's Madeleine in Paris, the first great adaptation of the temple to modern use abroad.   The whole style was actuated by the fiercest desire to conform as closely as possible to classic models.   It was the proud and perhaps youthfully pompous attempt of the first great modern republic to identify itself with the great republics of classical antiquity.

Had the early Republican style been merely neo-classic, it would not have been so admirable, nor so widely influential.   As always in any great period, the style was no mere repeat of what had gone before, but produced new effects of harmony in proportion and, above all, more interesting and more sensible arrangements of plan.   If the first great source of inspiration was classical, the second was contemporary French.   Jefferson was not only a great classicist but a great francophile.   If we examine his first design for his home, "Monticello," at Charlottesville, begun in 1796, but several times remodelled by its owner, we observe only the strictest and severest classicism in the use of the Doric order.   If we look at the elevation as it now exists (Fig. 9), however, we are struck not only by classicism but by beauty of proportion, by an elaboration which reveals a carefully studied plan (Fig. 10).   For an even earlier example, we might turn to the Hamilton House, or "Woodlands," in Philadelphia (Fig. 12), built about 1788.   The plans, both of first and second story, are absolutely typical of the early Republican style.   The staircase is removed to one side.   One enters a dignified vestibule, and behind it is a great salon. Right and left are the oval rooms so characteristic of the style.   Communications are carefully studied, so that one can ascend to the second story without entering the salon, and, once there, can enter each separate room without passing through another.   Privacy and comfort have both been studied.   The ideas which inspired this planning came from the archi-

FIG. 9. CHARLOTTESVILLE, VA. Monticello. *Thomas Jefferson, Architect.*

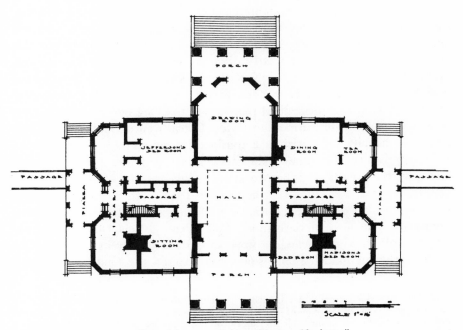

From Lambeth and Manning, "Thomas Jefferson as an Architect and Designer of Landscapes."

FIG. 10. CHARLOTTESVILLE, VA. Monticello. *Thomas Jefferson, Architect.*

23

tecture of the period of Louis XV in France. They reflect, on a more modest scale, the ideas of Aubert, Boffrand, and Héré de Corny. Outside, the appearance is harmonious and dignified (Fig. 11). It is no wonder that this style has inspired on the whole the finest and best liked of our modern domestic work. It continued in undiminished popularity until about 1835, when it began to weaken under the onslaught of Romanticism. Meanwhile, it produced real architects, imported and native, of great renown, and to it belongs the credit of beginning the first really monumental architecture of America.

Before we trace this movement farther, however, we must pause over certain other conditions which influenced the Colonial and early Republican architecture of America and through these, as well as directly, much of our modern work. The first of these is racial. American architecture varied according to the tastes of the several nationalities which settled in different regions, and the effect of these variations shows unmistakably in our modern styles. The most prominent racial influence was, of course, the English. This existed especially in New England and in Virginia and the Carolinas. On the other hand, the Dutch settlers of New York and the Hudson erected a totally different style of architecture no less properly Colonial than that of New England or the South. The Dyckman House (Fig. 13) in New York, for example, with its high basement, its covered veranda,* its gambrel roof curved to swing over the porch, represents another definite American style; Dutch-inspired and, as we shall see, most happily influential in a considerable amount of modern work. In Pennsylvania, still other influences entered with the coming of the Germans, the Swedes, and the Moravians. Cliveden, the old Chew House at Germantown, Pa. (Fig. 14), built after 1763, with its narrow central pavilion, its thin dormers, its urns at roof angles and gable peak, shows unmistakably its German derivation. This "Pennsylvania Dutch" architecture has influenced some modern work and, better yet, by its charming use of the beautiful local building stone, has inspired the modern Philadel-

---

* The wide, low veranda that is such a common feature in modern country architecture was rare even at the end of the eighteenth century. Witness the amusing correspondence between the painter, John Copley, and his builder anent the addition of a "peazer" to his house in Boston. (Fiske Kimball, *Domestic Architecture of the American Colonies*, New York, 1922, p. 98.)

FIG. 11. PHILADELPHIA, PA. Woodlands.

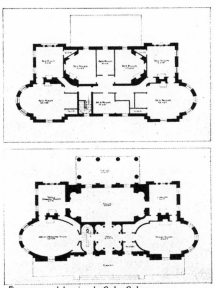

From measured drawings by Ogden Codman.

FIG. 12. PHILADELPHIA, PA. Woodlands.

25

phian architects to use this material and attain effects of beauty surpassing even those of the Colonial period.

These are all familiar types to the Easterner, but there are many other Colonial monuments which have exercised an enormous influence upon modern architecture. I refer to the buildings of the Latin invaders, French, and especially Spanish, that are just as properly "Colonial" as any Anglo-American work in Massachusetts or Virginia. Such a building is the Fort of San Marco, at St. Augustine, Fla., completed in 1756, and a purely Spanish design. Another famous example would be the "Cabildo," at New Orleans, built in 1795 (Fig. 15). Indeed, the whole city of New Orleans is full of designs, and especially ironwork, derived from Spanish and French sources, that is not only immensely interesting but perfectly suited to influence most happily modern design in these districts. Lastly there is the simple, well-adapted Spanish work of the colonists of Texas, Arizona, New Mexico, and California, which has been used as an almost inexhaustible mine to furnish ideas for modern designers in these districts. The type is, of course, admirably suited to the climate and the materials most apt. To mention one of the earliest examples, let us note the old Governor's Palace at Santa Fé, built soon after 1609 (Fig. 16), in the administration of Don Pedro de Peralta, Governor and Captain-General of the Kingdom and Provinces of New Mexico. Simple it is to bareness, yet as effective in its block-like plain surfaces, slashed with the shadows of projecting beams, as any Colonial monument in America. No wonder it has caught the eye and inspired the work of many a modern designer. In these districts, too, as along the Atlantic seaboard, instances could be multiplied. Nearly all of us are familiar, for example, with the appearance of the San Diego Missions, San Carlos Mission (1793–97), San Juan Capistrano (begun 1497), the Santa Barbara Mission (1815–20), and others. These, in spite of the late date of many, are strictly and properly speaking "Colonial." As such, they have played a vivid part in colouring the modern architecture of their districts.

Aside from racial inheritance, geographical position exercised a powerful influence upon Colonial design, as it does the design of to-day. Even when two buildings are derived from the same racial source, as in Massachusetts and Virginia, they differ on account of climatic conditions. The Northern building is compactly composed, the Southern, loosely. In the

FIG. 13. NEW YORK, N. Y. Dyckman House.

FIG. 14. GERMANTOWN, PA. Cliveden, or Chew Mansion.

27

Fig. 15.   New Orleans, La.   The Cabildo.

Fig. 16.   Santa Fé, N. M.   Old Governor's Palace.

28

North, the chimneys tend to run up through the mass of the building, radiating heat within. The kitchen is planned as part of the main bulk. This is true even of the more elaborate and aristocratic of the Northern houses like Vassall House, Cambridge, Mass., built in 1759 (Fig. 17), a pure Georgian construction, and it was invariably true of the simpler, seventeenth-century type. In the South, where warmth is more apt to be an intruder than a friend, the architectural composition, so to speak, throws open its coat. Buildings spread out, chimneys are usually built running up the exterior of the building, rather than within its mass. The composition includes outhouses, often connected with the main building by a porticoed passage, and in one of these is placed the kitchen quarters. Such a building as "Westover," Virginia (Fig. 18) (1726), is derived from exactly the same racial sources as Vassall House, yet gives one the impression of an entirely different composition, suggested, if not actually imposed, by climatic conditions. Similarly, the hot climates of the South and Southwest caused men to cling to the sensible Spanish forms, thick-walled, one-storied, with open patios, long after the Spanish, as a race, had been superseded in these districts. The heterogeneous geography of so enormous a country as the United States is bound to produce a variegated architecture in modern, as in Colonial, times, and this over and above the inevitable influence of early architecture on later. The fact we should cheerfully welcome, and not deplore, though it probably destroys the possibility of that "national American style" which so many have hoped might appear in this country. We might conceivably develop a national style in some one type of building, like the commercial office-building; we shall never develop, one trusts, a unified national style for all types. We can recognise and welcome the certainty that the dweller in northern Vermont will never be housed in a building resembling the domicile of an inhabitant of southern Texas.

It was the early Republican style, howevei, which actually brought to American architecture what we can call a modern point of view. The architect, in the modern sense, first appears in that period. At first, he was apt to be a foreigner, like Pierre Charles L'Enfant, that Frenchman with a genius for planning which seems inherent in French taste, who, in 1791, made the plan for the city of Washington (Fig. 19) and assured its being the most orderly and beautiful of American cities. When we stand to-

Fig. 17.   CAMBRIDGE, MASS.   Vassall House.

Fig. 18.   Westover, on the James River, Virginia.

day, admiring the vista from the Capitol to the Washington Monument and the Lincoln Memorial, when we discuss the pros and cons of John Russell Pope's Memorial to Roosevelt, we should realise that these effects were made possible by L'Enfant.

Other foreigners showed Americans the way, and made them accustomed to a monumental handling of architecture. Stephen Hallet came from France, to work upon the Capitol at Washington. James Hoban came from Ireland, to give us the White House. Thornton, Latrobe, and others paved the way until such men as Robert Mills (1781–1855), designer of the Washington monuments in Washington and Baltimore; Samuel McIntire, of Salem, Mass., gifted craftsman and pioneer in domestic work; John McComb, who, with Mengin, designed the Government House in New York; and, above all, Charles Bulfinch (1763–1844), at last proved that American architects were able to stand on their own feet. Monuments like the Government House (or City Hall), New York (Fig. 20), showed the combination of refinement, sense of proportion, and skill in planning that marked the early Republican style. Meanwhile, the design and construction of the Capitol at Washington taught Americans to look at architecture in a truly monumental way, while Latrobe's cathedral in Baltimore (1805–21) gave to the country a building which revealed to Americans a design comparable to, and inspired by, the Pantheon in Paris. These works awakened a conscious pride in American architecture.

Although some of the finest elements of the style of the classical revival were French, the American work was by no means purely French in character, and American architects did not continue to follow unswervingly the French tradition. A striking characteristic of American architecture, revealed in the Colonial style and emphasised in the early Republican, was refinement. Thanks to the persistent impress of the latter upon later design, refinement became a *sine qua non* of American architecture. Every thoughtful student of modern American work has been struck by the way most of the greatest modern American architects have gone to Paris for training and yet, on their return, primed with the sense of planning, construction, and unity of the French genius, have persistently rejected the florid and exuberant phase of modern French design. Trained to do a Grand Palais or a Musée Galliera, they have returned to do work like the Boston Public Library or the Temple of the Scottish Rite at Wash-

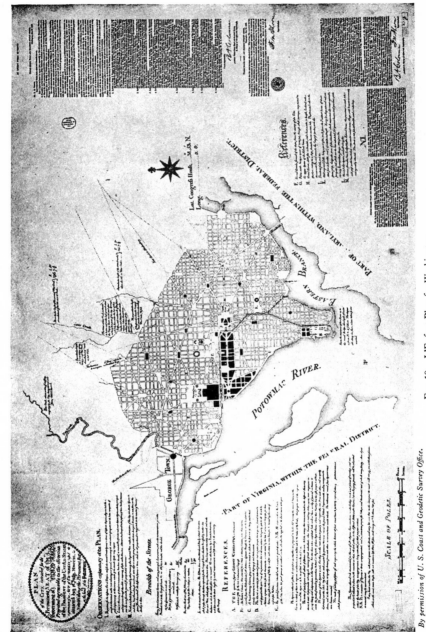

FIG. 19.   L'Enfant Plan for Washington.

By permission of U. S. Coast and Geodetic Survey Office.

ington. The sense of refinement, if it be not permitted to stiffen into a too rigid conservatism, is one of the most precious heritages of American architecture. In any case, whether we welcome it or not, it must be recognised and reckoned with in any review of the tendencies of our architecture to-day.

Strong as was the current of classicism in the early nineteenth century, it was interrupted during the fourth decade by a new movement, also to be reckoned with in its influence on modern design. Romanticism, appearing in England and France in the latter part of the eighteenth century, invaded America early in the nineteenth. Even Latrobe, the classicist, was won over to it, and Maximilian Godefroi designed a Gothic chapel for a girls' seminary in Baltimore as early as 1807. Romanticism did not emerge as a serious candidate for architectural domination, however, until the late thirties. By the time Upjohn, an Englishman, had finished Trinity Church in New York (Fig. 21) (1839–46), the battle of the styles was well joined and classicism was beginning to look rather old-fashioned. Thus, a tradition of Gothic design, especially for churches, was started and has remained an important tendency in American architecture ever since.

Probably the best-known exponent of Romanticism in this country was James Renwick, whose design for Grace Church in New York (1843–46) was followed by his commission for St. Patrick's Cathedral in that city (Fig. 22) (1850–79), the outstanding monument of Romanticism in this country. The movement took firmest root in England, and, on account of the close affiliations between America and the mother country, was enthusiastically welcomed here. America followed all the English phases, and Van Brunt's Memorial Hall, at Harvard University, Cambridge, Mass., is an attempt, by no means entirely happy, to erect in America the polychromatic Gothic that had become popular in England with the work of Street and Waterhouse.

In America, as in England, however, the early Gothic designers caught the superficial form but not the spirit of Gothic design. Our artists knew too little of the real originals which they imitated rather than adapted. They were neither correctly archæological, nor properly inspired to originality. The task for the modern architect was to study mediæval work more understandingly, design with more correctness, and, at the same time, achieve a sense of spontaneity in his work. How admirably this has been done can be illustrated in a host of modern works.

FIG. 20. NEW YORK, N. Y. City Hall. *Joseph Mengin and John McComb, Architects.*

FIG. 21. NEW YORK, N. Y. Trinity Church.
Richard Upjohn, Architect.

FIG. 22. NEW YORK, N. Y. St. Patrick's
Cathedral. *James Renwick, Architect.*

34

Despite the lifelessness of the mid-nineteenth-century Gothic, in a period when American architecture sank to its lowest ebb, the romantic point of view persisted. Partly, as we have seen, this was on account of the relations between England and the United States. Still more, it was caused by a definite taste of the people. Paradoxical as it may seem, a new country is apt to be conservative. Invariably, too, such a country sets a greater value on the past which it has not, than does a country of long history, affably accustomed to the monuments of its architectural perspective and even apt to be impatient of their domination. Energetic, busy, preoccupied in his affairs with the most up-to-date things, the American turns for relaxation to the past. Cheated of the romance of history, he demands its artificial simulacrum, much as the kings of Bavaria built "ruins" in their grounds to stimulate the classic imagination during the period when classicism was the be-all and the end-all of good taste. Uncontrolled, this retrospective attitude has produced much that is bad in American architecture. It is responsible, however, for the feeling, so prevalent among the vast majority of Americans, that it is impossible to worship God in anything but a Gothic building, or at least a mediæval one. It is to the credit of the best modern designers in a mediæval style, whose work almost entirely postdates 1900, that they have yielded to this demand and yet produced exquisite works of art quite comparable to the mediæval masterpieces that inspired them.

A phase, or rather an offshoot, of Romanticism produced another tremendously influential movement in American architecture: the Romanesque revival of H. H. Richardson. Born in Louisiana, educated at Harvard, like so many great American architects Richardson went to France for his technical training. No man ever displayed less, however, of the academic point of view of the Beaux-Arts. Early caught by Romanticism, Richardson began by doing Gothic work which to us to-day seems little inspired. His genius was too original, however, to continue in this. By an easy extension of ideas, he began to study the possibilities of Romanesque. Its greater quiet, its comparative horizontality, above all, its rugged strength, appealed to him. Without ever making a slavish copy, he began to work in the Romanesque style. In so doing, he nearly revolutionised American architecture. European writers of a generation ago assume Richardson to have been the one outstanding original genius of American architecture.

He was in truth an innovator and a leader. His ideas were his own, and were not reflections, in this country, of current European tendencies. His architecture, above all, had power. In such a group as the Allegheny County Court House and Gaol at Pittsburgh (1854), he taught Americans a most forceful lesson in the use and expression of materials. His massive compositions in quarry-faced stone were soon discussed and imitated by a host of lesser architects. His best composed, most monumental, and most famous work was Trinity Church, Boston (Fig. 23) (1872–77). As we look at such a building to-day it seems very archæological. Its historic prototypes and its affinities with definite Spanish and Provençal buildings are quickly recognised by any student of architecture. What we should remember, however, is that first, the use of these prototypes was original in Richardson's day—and second—and far more important—his works were adaptations rather than imitations. His material, for example, was new and characteristically American. He obtained the effects of the old work that inspired him in new ways. In spite of its archæological side, his work was a step towards architectural freedom. It was stamped with a mastery that won him recognition in two continents and, at the same time, opened the road to experiments and new expressions in American architecture.

Unfortunately, the successors of Richardson were, on the whole, unworthy. None could wield Ulysses' bow, and the immediate result of his movement was the sudden propagation of a host of uninspired Romanesque post-offices, town halls, and gaols throughout the breadth of the United States. These retained the harshness of the master's design with none of its real monumentality and sense of composition. The constructive effect of the Richardsonian movement was in the letting down of the bars, the proving that interesting work other than Gothic could be done, and the paving of the way for eclecticism in architectural inspiration, which, whether we like it or no, is one of the most influential tendencies in American architecture to-day.

The most famous exponent of nineteenth-century eclecticism was Richard Morris Hunt, a New Englander, born at Brattleboro, Vt., in 1828, receiving his elementary education in Boston and then going to Europe for

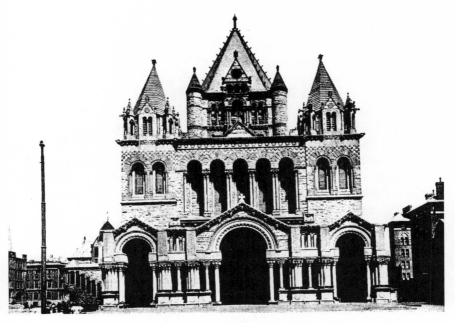

BOSTON, MASS. Trinity Church, Before Completion of Porch. *Henry H. Richardson, Architect.*

FIG. 24. ASHEVILLE, N. C. Biltmore House. *Richard Morris Hunt, Architect.*

his technical training. He studied first in Geneva, then under Lefuel in
Paris,* with whom he stayed from 1845 to 1855. He then returned to
this country, where he practised his art until his death in 1895. By the
end of his career he was America's most famous architect and one of the
most powerful in influencing our modern style. He was a whole-hearted
exponent of eclecticism, fired by enthusiasm for the masterpieces of European architecture oftentimes to a stultifying archæological imitation. Such
a building as Biltmore House (Fig. 24), with its copy of the famous staircase at Blois, would be characterised in a modern school merely as an unsuccessful historic problem. Other works, like the Tribune Building in New
York (Fig. 25), show a struggling for expression, by no means happy, in a
new problem where archæology fails as a guide. This was one of the first
"elevator buildings," and, if it looks ugly and old-fashioned, we should
remember the fifty years of experiment before the constructive solutions
of to-day were reached. It was when he turned to classicism, either enlivened by the exuberance of the Beaux-Arts, or tempered by the restraint
of the neo-Grec, that Hunt appears as a modern architect and a gifted
genius. Perhaps the most complete and satisfactory work of this later
phase was the Administration Building at the Chicago World's Fair (Fig.
26). Here, with rich ornament and imagination, he displayed a sense of
composition, monumentality, and proportion that made his work one of the
most brilliant in that brilliant gathering of the masters in 1893. Hunt
also did much monumental domestic work, especially at Newport, and set
the fashion for the elaborate country mansion, inspired by the palatial
dwellings of the nobility abroad, but in no sense copying them. In such
a building as the J. R. Busk residence, at Newport, R. I. (Fig. 27), for
example, the artist attacked the problem of a building which, using only
a modified architectural vocabulary drawn from the past, should conform
in its surface and mass to the bold and rugged landscape in which it was
set. The solution was supremely successful, and again offered suggestions
eagerly caught up by successors in the field. In such works as these one
feels that the artist has shaken off the copyism of his earlier work, has
struck out boldly in new lines, and become literally a modern architect.

Modern American architecture, in a true sense, was beginning to ap-

* See *Architectural Record*, October–December, 1895, "The Works of the late Richard Morris Hunt."

Fig. 25. New York, N. Y. Tribune Building. *Richard M. Hunt, Architect.*

Fig. 26. Chicago, Ill. World's Columbian Exposition: Administration Building. *Richard M. Hunt, Architect.*

Fig. 27. Newport, R. I. Busk Residence. *Richard M. Hunt, Architect.*

pear. One of the most powerful, progressive influences for its development came from world's fairs and expositions, which gave architects an opportunity to practise the design not only of a single building but of complicated layouts, and revealed to vast numbers of the public the last word in modern building. To Philadelphia belongs the glory of holding the first important one of these, the Centennial Exposition of 1876.* Here men saw, for the first time and on a large scale, many American buildings erected for a special purpose and planned with some reference one to another. On the other hand, the amazing progress of American architecture can be judged by comparing these buildings with those of recent expositions. Only fifty years have passed since that exposition. Plenty of people are alive who can remember its opening, yet when we look at reproductions of its architecture they seem antediluvian. Some, like the vast Machinery Hall (Fig. 28), or the Main Exhibition Building, had almost no pretence and, in a purely utilitarian way, by scale and mass, attained a not unimpressive effect. Others, like the Agricultural Building (Fig. 29), illegitimate children of Romanticism and conceived in the most inane form of Victorian Gothic, were low-water marks in American architecture. Still others, like the Horticultural Hall, and especially the Art Gallery (Fig. 30), though containing many faults, were full of promise. The latter, with its monumentality, proportion, and sense of scale, foreshadowed the great, progressive work which was to appear seventeen years later at Chicago.

The smaller buildings of the exhibition are of an interest now merely as history, or as horrible examples. As one specimen, we may look at the Michigan State Building (Fig. 31), in its day the last word in polite design. A more amusing conglomerate of Gothic jig-saw ornament and Swiss châlet mock-picturesqueness it would be hard to discover, yet it is encouraging to remember that this was done only fifty years ago. Similarly, the interiors make one shudder and be thankful. The view of the interior of the main building, with the entrance to the Spanish, Egyptian, and Danish courts, could find its counterpart to-day only in the main tent of a pretentious travelling circus. Nevertheless, though we may smile at the individual buildings, we should not belittle the exposition as a whole. It was

* McCabe, J. D., *Illustrated History of the Centennial Exhibition*, Philadelphia, 1876.

Fig. 28. PHILADELPHIA, PA. International Exposition of 1876: Machinery Hall.

Fig. 29. PHILADELPHIA, PA. International Exposition of 1876: Agricultural Building.

Fig. 30. PHILADELPHIA, PA. International Exposition of 1876: Fine Arts Building.

the nation's first ambitious attempt of its kind and made way for a series of great constructive works in our history.

The most momentous of these, and one of the most important events in American architectural history, was the World's Columbian Exposition at Chicago in 1893. The first architect to be consulted in this task was Daniel H. Burnham,* and he became the real head of the organisation which designed the exposition. His title was Chief of Construction, and associated with him, as Consulting Architect, was his partner, J. W. Root. F. L. Olmsted, who had been consulted at the outset, on the advice of Mr. Burnham, was made Consulting Landscape Architect. A. Gottlieb was Chief Engineer. Mr. Root, whose ideas about the buildings followed an older and semi-Romanesque tradition (Fig. 32), died in 1891, and in his place Mr. Burnham appointed Charles B. Atwood. Meanwhile, the original four had conferred with R. M. Hunt, McKim, Mead & White, George B. Post, Peabody & Stearns, and Van Brunt & Howe, intrusting to them the general scheme and the most important of the buildings. These gentlemen decided in favour of a Roman Classical style and a uniform cornice line of 60 feet for the Court of Honour. Other buildings were apportioned, some to the original five firms, some to others—among them Adler & Sullivan, who were given the Transportation Building; Henry Ives Cobb, later designer of the University of Chicago, who took Fisheries; and W. L. B. Jenney, of Jenney & Mundie, innovators in steel construction, who was given the Horticultural Building. Augustus Saint-Gaudens was made Consultant in matters of sculpture, doing no pieces himself, but apportioning the commissions among other sculptors best qualified for the several tasks.

The site in Jackson Park comprised 686 acres, of which 188 were to be covered with buildings. A site to the north of the city had been preferred by Mr. Burnham, but had to be abandoned on account of difficulties of transportation. To Mr. Olmsted was given the task of converting three ridges of sand-bars, separated by boggy intervals, a subsoil subject to flooding, and a site imperilled by the rising of the lake level, into an orderly scheme of terraces, roads, paths, ponds, and canals, well under control and subject to architectural treatment. His was one of the most important

* C. Moore, *Daniel H. Burnham*, New York, 1921, vol. I, pp. 31 *ff.*, for a most interesting account of the inception of the scheme.

FIG. 31.   PHILADELPHIA, PA.   International Exposition of 1876:
Michigan State Building.

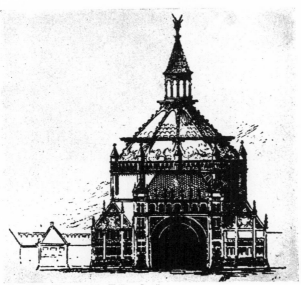

FIG. 32.   CHICAGO, ILL.   World's Columbian Exposition: H. W.
Root's Study for the Central Pavilion of the Main Building.

tasks in changing a swamp into a Dream City. William Prettyman was first put in charge of the colour scheme, but he resigned and this work was taken over by Frank D. Millet. Artistically, the work brought together the greatest gathering of giants that the nation has ever seen, and these men, coming from many different parts of the country, representing many different architectural trends, worked with an enthusiasm, a unity of purpose, a harmony that was an inspiration to the whole country. The year 1893 is the best date for the beginning of modern American architecture.

In a review of this sort there is naturally no time to go into any detailed discussion of the individual buildings of the Columbian Exposition, but some, at least, should be noted in passing. A general view of the Court of Honour (Fig. 33), with its classic buildings in gleaming white, its spacious lagoon, and its monumental fountains, will give some idea of the combined dignity and charm which so impressed the Americans of three decades ago. At the right we see the domed Agriculture Building (Fig. 34), designed by McKim, Mead & White. At the left is the tremendous building devoted to Manufactures and the Liberal Arts (Fig. 35), a work of George B. Post. Nearer views of these structures reveal a classicism which to-day seems a little archæological. The debts to definite monuments of classical antiquity are perhaps a little too outspoken, but, bearing in mind the chaotic condition of American architecture so shortly before this period, one can understand the delight with which people hailed such dignified and harmonious achievements.

A glance at the plan (Fig. 36) will show that our view is taken from the Administration Building, which we have noted as one of the happiest designs of R. M. Hunt. Indeed, the whole plan deserves careful study in its admirable combination of formality and picturesqueness. The symmetry of the Court of Honour delights the eye, while the rambling informality of the wooded island, with its lagoon, camp, and rose garden, acts as a relief from the danger of oppressiveness. Communications, both within the plot and giving access to it, are carefully studied, and the genius which America is beginning to show in city planning was forecast in the Columbian Exposition.

The building which received the greatest acclaim and the popularity of which was most permanent was the Fine Arts Building (Fig. 37), by Atwood. Of all the buildings it was the simplest. Using a delicate Ionic

Courtesy of Olmsted Brothers.

FIG. 33.   CHICAGO, ILL.   World's Columbian Exposition: Court of Honour.

Photograph by C. D. Arnold.

FIG. 34.   CHICAGO, ILL.   World's Columbian Exposition: Agricultural Building.
McKim, Mead & White, Architects.

FIG. 35. CHICAGO, ILL. World's Columbian Exposition: Manufactures and Liberal Arts Building. *George B. Post, Architect.*

THE
WORLD'S COLUMBIAN EXPOSITION
CHICAGO 1893

LAKE MICHIGAN

FIG. 36. CHICAGO, ILL. World's Columbian Exposition: Plan.

order, in two dimensions, the artist sought by refinement and proportion to attain an effect worthy of a building designed to house the Fine Arts. That he was inspired by a previous design done in the Beaux-Arts in Paris may be a just charge; that he succeeded in his purpose, none will deny. The Fine Arts Building still exists, in a dilapidated state. There is a movement now afoot—destined we trust to succeed—to repair and preserve for the nation this important landmark in its architectural history. Less showy than some of its admirable sister buildings, it struck the key-note of modern American monumental architecture. It showed that the lesson of the early Republican style had been well learned.

Of the many other important and beautiful buildings produced by the Columbian Exposition one deserves especial mention: the Transportation Building (Fig. 38), by Adler & Sullivan. The tendencies which it represented we shall discuss later. It is enough here to note its originality and its proof that, though the general classical scheme was imposed in the design of the exposition as a whole, important variations from it were not only permitted but welcomed. If the Court of Honour was the parent of classicism in modern American architecture, the Transportation Building was the father of what we can call more technically "modernism." In this work Louis Sullivan had his first opportunity on a large scale to embody his ideas in a great monument and place them before the public eye. For him, classicism was as dead as romanticism. Any "vocabulary" of architecture other than his own he considered stifling. He evolved a style from his own philosophy and the study of nature. He thought in terms of simple masses, of the play of light and shade, of colour. Avoidance of precedent became with him a creed of morals or an affectation, according to the point of view of the observer. Whether we approve or disapprove, all but the most captious will agree that the Transportation Building was a great work of art. More than that, it was an ultimatum. It was the voice of an energetic and militant Americanism calling upon the national art to throw off "the chains and bonds which architecture had laid upon herself," much as Michelangelo had voiced the same cry three and a half centuries before. It was a radical design, the embodiment of a radical theory of æsthetics, consciously attacking conservative classicism. It appealed to the young and to the younger sections of the country. The response to it was immediate, though largely confined to the Middle West,

Fig. 37.   Chicago, Ill.   World's Columbian Exposition: The Fine Arts Building.
Charles B. Atwood, Architect.

Fig. 38.   Chicago, Ill.   World's Columbian Exposition: Transportation Building.
Adler & Sullivan, Architects.

and it started a constructive movement which continued without interruption and is powerfully felt in American architecture to-day.

Of the manifold influences of the Columbian Exposition we shall have more to say later. It is enough to note here that the precept of Chicago started a brilliant series of fairs which showed not only America but Europe the energy and creative ability of American architecture. Only five years later (1898) two large expositions were staged; one, the "Cotton" Exposition at New Orleans, the other the "Trans-Mississippi" Exposition at Omaha, Neb. Chicago had led the way and the cities of the West and South were eager for emulation. Only New York held aloof, nursing a regret, we may imagine, that she had let the opportunity of holding the Columbian Exposition slip from her grasp. It was better for American architecture, however, that these expositions should be wide-spread geographically and in districts where monumental architecture was less conspicuous than in the great metropolis of the East. As in all youthful periods and communities, the architecture of the West had been primarily practical and beauty too often associated with misapplied fancy ornament than with the fundamentals of design. Nothing could have been happier for Nebraska than the erection of such a structure as the Government Building (Fig. 39) by James Knox Taylor.* Classic in design, reminiscent of Atwood's Fine Arts Building at Chicago, it might be challenged on the ground of a lack of originality, but it taught a lesson of monumentality and composition where it was sorely needed. Indeed, it was one of the propagandists of the classical movement which was inaugurated at Chicago.

The next great American exposition, the Pan-American, was held at Buffalo in 1901.† Here less was made of the ensemble. There was more variety than in previous fairs and the attempt seemed to have been to gain picturesqueness, if even at the expense of completely orderly arrangement. This was particularly true of the colour scheme. Many of the buildings of the "Rainbow City" were conceived in intense colours, sometimes very successful, but sometimes clashing in effect. Some of the individual buildings, while avoiding the vulgar, embodied a deliberate exuberance which was encouraged by the authorities behind the fair. Such a building

* Walker, C. H., "The Trans-Mississippi Exposition," *Architectural Review*, Boston, March, 1898.

† See *Architectural Review*, Boston, July, 1901, p. 83, for good, brief criticism of its architecture.

FIG. 39. OMAHA, NEB. Trans-Mississippi and International Exposition: Government Building.
James K. Taylor, Architect.

FIG. 40. BUFFALO, N. Y. Pan-American
Exposition: Electric Tower.
J. G. Howard, Architect.

FIG. 41. BUFFALO, N. Y. Pan-American
Exposition: New York State Building.
George Cary, Architect.

as J. G. Howard's Tower (Fig. 40) maintained the classic tradition of exposition architecture, but displayed a richness of ornament derived from Blondel and Boffrand in the period of transition from the reign of Louis XIV to that of Louis XV in France. None the less, of originality there was plenty, and the variegated colour, tastefully handled, enhanced the charm and freedom of the ornament. Such a building, too, as that for the Graphic Arts, Horticulture and Agriculture, by Peabody & Stearns, showed the happiest combination of big composition with gaiety of colour and detail. At the same time there were severe designs, like George Cary's New York State Building (Fig. 41), quiet, rigid, almost bare in their Doric simplicity. There were many buildings in which colour was eschewed and these, for greater order, were generally grouped at one end of the grounds. Nevertheless, the general effect of the exposition was one of variety rather than breadth. It might be regarded as something of a reaction against the thoroughgoing homogeneity of the "White City" at Chicago.

Soon after the Pan-American Exposition came one of the most extensive of all, the Louisiana Purchase Exposition, opened in St. Louis in 1904.* It was one of the most ambitious ever attempted and indeed, with all its many excellences, its scale was what gave it its greatest fame (Fig. 42). The site selected was Forest Park, an admirable choice from the point of view of the site itself, but open to criticism in that it involved the destruction of trees and developed park land. It is always a question in an exposition as to whether it is better to select the best site, or the worst and develop it. The former system makes for a better exposition but leaves the city poorer; the latter handicaps the designer but leaves the city with well-developed land which formerly it did not have. The size of many of the buildings was overpowering and, though impressive in the extreme, ran the danger of exhausting the observer. The imposing Palace of Agriculture (Fig. 43), for example, by Carrère & Hastings, measured 500 by 1,600 feet. It was, therefore, nearly a third of a mile long and, despite its awe-inspiring bulk, could hardly avoid a suggestion of monotony, while the thought of entering it to explore its collection was inhibitory to all except the most courageous and physically energetic. Other buildings, like

* For detailed account, see pamphlet published by the Louisiana Purchase Exposition Company and printed at the Government Printing Office, 1903.

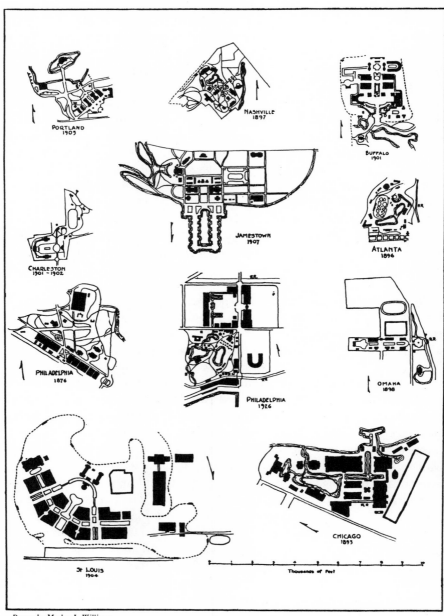

PORTLAND
1905

NASHVILLE
1897

BUFFALO
1901

JAMESTOWN
1907

CHARLESTON
1901 - 1902

ATLANTA
1896

PHILADELPHIA
1876

PHILADELPHIA
1926

OMAHA
1898

ST LOUIS
1904

CHICAGO
1893

Thousands of Feet

Drawn by Morley J. Williams.

FIG. 42.   Plans Showing Comparative Scales of American Expositions.

52

the P ... of Transportation, by E. L. Masqueray, with its frontage of 1,300 feet, the Machinery Hall, with 1,000, and the Palace of Manufactures and the Palace of Varied Industries, with 1,200 respectively, were well in scale. An intramural railway was provided to enable visitors to get about the grounds without exhaustion, but the buildings themselves were a defiance to the leg-weary.

None the less, the general effect was beautiful, even fairylike. The Festival Hall and Cascades, designed by Cass Gilbert and E. L. Masqueray (Fig. 44), were coherently planned, broadly laid out, and combined a fundamental orderliness with the richness and play of fancy which appertain properly to a fair ground, no matter how monumentally conceived. The slope of the ground was recognised as one of the assets of the site and, with the water feature, gave the design a striking individuality. There was, to be sure, a suggested note of impermanence to the work, but one might argue that this was only a propriety in the design of so evanescent a group as a world's fair.

One, however, the admirable Palace of Arts (Fig. 45), by Cass Gilbert, was destined to remain, at least in part, as a nucleus for the great St. Louis Museum of Fine Arts. Magnificently placed from the æsthetic point of view, the site has been criticised as being inaccessible from the city. The complaint has point, but it is hard to know how else to solve the problem, with the needs as to area so great and the land values in the populous centre so enormous. In the civic centres there is the additional disadvantage of heavy traffic which, unless unusual precautions are taken with the foundation, is bound to cause a certain amount of vibration in the structure. Any one who has wrestled with the problem of exhibiting delicate works of art, like the panels of mediæval Italian painting, will know that a great sacrifice is none too much for the avoidance of this danger. Nevertheless, the present placing of the St. Louis Museum renders it one more of the many unhappy examples in this country of the great building intended for all which is used only by the few. Tremendous as the present structure is, it is only a unit of what is planned and for which there is at present no need. Both designer and museum authorities have been criticised for so ambitious a plan. They should, rather, be congratulated. The rapidity with which museum collections in America outgrow their quarters is both encouraging and depressing. The designer who plans a work which can,

FIG. 43. ST. LOUIS, MO. Louisiana Purchase Exposition: The Palace of Agriculture.
Carrère & Hastings, Architects.

FIG. 44. ST. LOUIS, MO. Louisiana Purchase Exposition: Festival Hall and Cascades.
Cass Gilbert and E. L. Masqueray, Architects.

54

Fig. 45. St. Louis, Mo. Louisiana Purchase Exposition: Arts Building. *Cass Gilbert, Architect.*

according to the design, be expanded to two or three times the capacity "which will ever be needed" is only recognising the healthy and energetic tendencies of his country.

Closely following the St. Louis Exposition of 1904 came the Jamestown Exposition of 1906, in which Virginia and the South Atlantic seaboard displayed a worthy ambition not to be outshone by the great cities of the West. Although named after the famous Colonial site and in honour of the settlers who built there, for obvious reasons the exposition was placed at Norfolk, Va., where it was more easily accessible, was close to a town of considerable size, and had the asset of being upon the sea. This last was taken advantage of in the layout, and the marine feature was emphasised both in the design and in the conduct of the fair. As might have been expected, an especial point was made of the historical associations of the site and its environs. The size of Norfolk, however, and the limitation of the funds available, made the exposition more modest than the great fairs of the past. Though the charm and historic interest were great, the architectural lessons to be learned were not especially important.

Another comparatively modest exposition, the Alaska-Yukon-Pacific, was held at Seattle in 1909. Here, as at Norfolk, the tremendous pecuniary resources of Chicago and St. Louis were not available. Nevertheless, a great deal was made of a picturesque site. The exposition was placed at a point midway between Lakes Union and Washington, half an hour's trolley ride from the business section of the city (Fig. 46). Here a beautiful park, with attendant buildings, was designed, using the majestic pile of the distant Mount Ranier as a focal point for the main axis. The general layout of the grounds was intrusted to Olmsted Brothers, the architect in charge was J. G. Howard, of Howard & Galloway, architect of the University of California. As one might have expected, the Olmsteds made the most of the wooded site with its many natural advantages. The buildings were of less interest than the general design. The Government Building, with its flattened dome and huge arched base, was rather confused in composition, though the huge terraced cascade was very effective. Some of the smaller buildings—for example, the California Building (Fig. 47), by Sellen & Heming—were of greater interest. This was a reflection of the tendency, already happily manifest in California, to make the local architecture conform to the historical California type.

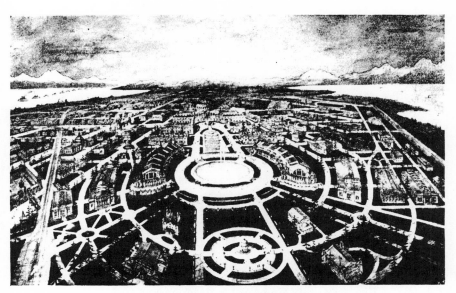

FIG. 46. SEATTLE, WASH. Alaska-Yukon-Pacific Exposition: Perspective.
Olmsted Brothers, Landscape Architects.

FIG. 47. SEATTLE, WASH. Alaska-Yukon-Pacific Exposition: California Building.
Sellen & Heming, Architects.

Though geographically out of place, of course, at Seattle, the building was justified by embodying the character of the State which it represented. Though more admirable examples have been done since then, the California Building was able to call the attention of many people to the possibilities of a typically Californian composition. The Seattle Exposition was, however, too modest in scope and in too distant a corner of the country to draw the huge crowds and exert the powerful influence on architecture of some of the earlier and more ambitious fairs. One of its happiest effects, however, was the use of its site for the present carefully planned and rapidly expanding University of Washington.

Two of the latest, most notable American expositions were held in 1915. One, the Panama-Pacific, was at San Francisco; the other, the Panama-California International, at San Diego. Both were glorifications of the State of California and celebrations of the American triumph of the Panama Canal. It was unfortunate that these occurred one year after the outbreak in Europe of the Great War. Although America was not yet a belligerent, men's minds were focussed on things more serious than fairs and, especially in the East, where the European catastrophe was realised more keenly, many people who would otherwise have made a pilgrimage to the West felt the necessity of spending their time and money on things connected with the war. On the other hand, the expositions had been planned long before any one had dreamed of war, the work had to go through, and it is to the greatest credit of the Californian cities that they made the expositions so brilliant a success in the face of obstacles which they could not have anticipated. As it was, the works were completed on time, enthusiastically received by Americans all over the country, and the attendance, though in a different year it might have been larger, was gratifyingly large.

The San Francisco Exposition was, naturally, the larger of the two. It was forcefully put through by that energetic city of optimists who wished to prove to the world that a disaster like the earthquake and fire of 1906, which might well have killed a civic community, was but an episode in the history of San Francisco. Although Eastern architects were employed, the majority of the architectural council was drawn from local talent and the attempt seemed deliberate to prove, along with broadminded co-operation and courteous hospitality to members of the profession from other States, that San Francisco *sapeva fare da se*. A most unpromising site, with distinct latent possibilities, was selected just within the Golden Gate at the entrance to San Francisco Harbour. Well over half the area was twenty-five feet deep in salt water. This artificial lake was separated from San Francisco Bay by a stout sea wall and the east lake was filled by pumping dredgers with silt from the harbour. All this was done while the architects were preparing working drawings and, as at Chicago, the city was enriched by permanently improved land. Unquestionably Golden Gate Park would have made a finer site, but its use would have involved destruction instead of permanent improvement. San Francisco followed one scheme, St. Louis, as we have seen, another.* The protagonists of both sides have strong arguments but, bearing in mind the ephemeral nature of even the greatest exposition and its enormous cost, the average man will always approve of a scheme which leaves behind it something of solid and permanent value.

The effect of the San Francisco Exposition was more splendid than refined. Colour was used lavishly, and this we may applaud, especially in a district of bright sun and vivid natural colour. The most striking architectural features were the two triumphal arches, of the Rising Sun and the Setting Sun, the Rotunda and Palace of the Fine Arts, and the Tower of the Jewels. The plan showed an orderly arrangement, with a long axis running through the Court of Abundance in the centre of the design and minor axes symmetrically developed at right angles to it. The triumphal arches, enormous in scale, marked the entrances east and west to the Court of Abundance. When we look at a photograph of the Arch of the Rising Sun (Fig. 48) (McKim, Mead & White), with its massive proportions and colossal statuary, we must visualise it as actually larger than the Arc de l'Etoile in Paris.

The Tower of the Jewels (Fig. 49), by Carrère & Hastings, was the most striking monument of all. It was 435 feet in height, built up in receding stages, angle turrets and sculpture being used to disguise the horizontal lines at succeeding levels and give the mass a soaring verticality despite its classic detail. On the top was a colossal group of herculean figures supporting a globe. By daylight the scheme was not entirely suc-

* L. C. Mullgardt, "The Panama-Pacific Exposition," in the *Architectural Record*, March, 1915, vol. 37.

Fig. 48. SAN FRANCISCO, CAL. Panama-Pacific International Exposition: Arch of the Rising Sun. *McKim, Mead & White, Architects.*

Fig. 49. SAN FRANCISCO, CAL. Panama-Pacific International Exposition: Tower of Jewels. *Carrère & Hastings, Architects.*

cessful, the horizontality of the stages being rather too pronounced, despite the efforts of the architects to break it up. On the other hand, at night, when huge search-lights were made to play upon the 125,000 cut-glass prisms set in the building, the tower was a vision of beauty.

There were, of course, many other buildings of interest and beauty. Louis C. Mullgardt's Cloister (Fig. 51) was a rich and sparkling attempt to suggest the Spanish and take advantage of the brilliance of the California sun. The same quality which makes the Spanish plateresque so fine made this piece singularly happy and appropriate in San Francisco. Behind it may be seen the saucer-shaped dome of the Pa' ᵕ of Varied Industries by Bliss & Faville, one of the most extensive, most effective, and very simplest of the great buildings at the fair. Another interesting piece, rich in ornament, was the Horticultural Hall (Fig. 50), by Bakewell & Brown. Here an enormous dome, expressed in steel and delicately buttressed, was surrounded by slender obelisks and faced by a still pool. The dome was perhaps a trifle too heavy for its base, but the whole scheme attained a desired combination of mass, grace, and ordered profusion.

Brilliant as it was, the exposition at San Francisco was partially eclipsed in the public esteem by that at San Diego. Here the problem was simpler and the work on a smaller scale. The architect in charge and designer of several of the most important buildings was the late Bertram Grosvenor Goodhue, one of the most sensitive, imaginative, and progressive artists that American architecture has produced. Studying first under Renwick, his early training was in Gothic and, as a member of the firm of Cram, Goodhue & Ferguson, he made a reputation as a modern Gothicist, able to create without imitation and bring modern Gothic as near to the level of its thirteenth-century prototype as can be done without the aid of the mediæval bands of craftsmen. Too broad in his interests, however, to use only one vocabulary, he experimented in others and sought sensibly to develop a truly modern style which might present something sanely new and yet uninfluenced by the bogey which leads many artists to avoid any suggestion of the influence of the past. At San Diego he realised the possibilities of the geographical site and decided to make the exposition an ensemble which harmonised with the historic traditions and climatic character of Southern California.

That he succeeded, every one who saw the exposition will enthusias-

FIG. 50.   SAN FRANCISCO, CALIF.   Panama-Pacific International Exposition: Horticultural Hall.
Bakewell & Brown, Architects.

FIG. 51.   SAN FRANCISCO, CALIF.   Panama-Pacific International Exposition: Cloister of the Court
of Abundance.   *Louis C. Mullgardt, Architect.*

Photograph by Herbert R. Fitch.

FIG. 52. SAN DIEGO, CALIF. Panama-California International Exposition: Bridge and California State Building. *Bertram G. Goodhue, Architect.*

63

tically attest.* His block plan was a simple one, long and narrow, with the strongest possible accent on the long axis. The approach was by a straight road over a deep gorge, to span which he designed a magnificent bridge, later simplified, but still a fine feature. Beyond the gorge rose the buildings, sparkling in sharp contrasts of light and shade and vibrant in harmonious colours boldly used in full intensity. Since the exposition was, strictly speaking, more Californian than international, Mr. Goodhue imposed a scheme of Spanish Californian architecture, recognising the value in that district and that climate of the Spanish exuberant baroque, which might have crossed the edge of vulgarity had it been exhibited in a different setting. Some of the more important buildings he designed himself, others he gave to other men, like Frank P. Allen, Carleton M. Winslow, and the Rapp brothers, who entered enthusiastically into the scheme and worked wonders in brilliant design.

It is hard to know what buildings especially to emphasise. At the outset one should consider the striking approach, with the concrete bridge (Fig. 52), its immense bare arches leading the eye across the Laguna del Puente to the California Building (Fig. 53) in the distance. This, by Goodhue himself, was perhaps the masterpiece of the exposition. It was based frankly upon the Spanish Colonial of Mexico, and recalls directly the Balvanera Chapel of the Church of San Francisco in the City of Mexico. In true Spanish fashion, the light is allowed to play over broad surfaces untouched by any suggestion of form, while the richest profusion of ornament is concentrated in other fields. Not only is there an almost dazzling glitter of light and dark within the ornamental fields, but there is the further vibration of interest between these fields and the great masses of light reflected from the planes of the juxtaposed unadorned walls. How rich the decoration was can be judged by a closer view of the façade (Fig. 54). Mr. Goodhue, a sojourner in Mexico, had assimilated the soul of Spanish Colonial as previously he caught the very spirit of Gothic art. The most was made of the luxuriant vegetation possible at San Diego, and a glance at one of the courts (Fig. 55) will show how happily the garden design was adapted to the architectural setting.

* *The Architecture and Gardens of the San Diego Exposition,* by C. M. Winslow, with an introduction by B. G. Goodhue, San Francisco, 1919. Also the "Panama-California Exposition," by Matlack Price, in the *Architectural Record,* 1915, p. 229.

Fig. 53. San Diego, Calif. Panama-California International Exposition: California State Building. *Bertram G. Goodhue, Architect.*

Fig. 54. San Diego, Calif. Panama-California International Exposition: California State Building. *Bertram G. Goodhue, Architect.*

Fig. 55. San Diego, Calif. Panama-California International Exposition: La Laguna de las Flores. *Bertram G. Goodhue, Architect.*

Though the ensemble was unusually coherent, there was no impression of monotony and within certain limits the buildings differed widely one from another. For example, in the New Mexico Building the Rapp brothers, of Trinidad, Colo., designed a structure in the "Pueblo" style. Of this we shall have more to say later. At first glance nothing would seem less promising for architectural inspiration than a pueblo village. Let us look, for example, at the pueblo village at Taos, New Mexico (Fig. 56). Rudely constructed of sun-dried adobe mud, with crude beams projecting from the walls, one would think the average architect would recoil from the idea of being inspired in any way by such an untutored and barbaric performance. Look again, however, and one notes a real harmony got by the repetition of the same simple shapes, a monumentality attained by the frank piling up of block upon block, and a sparkle reached through the deep shadows cast sharply upon the brilliantly lighted plain walls. Based upon these elements, Rapp & Rapp created a building harmoniously proportioned, monumental, practical, and vibrant in the play of light and shade (Fig. 57). In this simple way the pueblo Indians attained effects not unlike that of the Spanish baroque. A sophisticated adaptation of their style was in perfect harmony with the rest of the work at San Diego.

Modest as was the exposition in scope and scale it was an immense success. It is probably not too much to say that it made the most vivid impression upon the public mind of any exposition since the White City at Chicago. In its originality, moreover, it pointed a healthy lesson in the possibilities of variation in this type of design.

We have devoted a great deal of time in our discussion to the history of expositions, yet the emphasis is justified. They have constituted one of the most vital influences in the progress of our art. Though the general trend has been classical, hence conservative, so that the modernist often complains that the expositions, and especially that at Chicago, have acted as a drag rather than a spur to American originality, the fact remains that they have done more probably than anything else to educate the public to an appreciation of the possibilities of architecture. Indeed, since we are discussing the American architecture of to-day rather than "modern" American architecture, this very classic conservatism is one of the most important tendencies to note. As we have observed, it is exactly in line with the trend

FIG. 56.   TAOS, N. M.   Pueblo Village.

FIG. 57.   SAN DIEGO, CALIF.   Panama-California International Exposition: New Mexico Building.
Rapp & Rapp, Architects.

67

of American architecture in Colonial and Early Republican times. Though radical experiments were made even at Chicago in 1893, and are a vital force in the American architecture of to-day, classicism is still in the van. Whether it will remain so is a question for the prophet and not for the present-day observer.

Many other lessons were taught by the expositions. American architecture above all needed to learn to plan in a big way, each building designed with an eye to its relation to all the others. In our earlier municipal work and, alas, in much that is being done to-day, buildings were put up haphazard. Land values increase, cities grow at an unbelievable rate, buildings are erected swiftly in answer to sudden needs, and there seems often no time and no will to plan and to carry out a comprehensive scheme. The desirability, however, of thoughtful and co-ordinated layouts has been taught by one after another of the expositions, so that even the careless layman is beginning to see the point.

In this connection we should touch upon the work of the landscape architect. The combined skill, taste, and sense of Olmsted's plan for the Chicago Exposition won recognition not only for himself but for his profession. From that time landscape architecture began to take itself and be taken more seriously. The kind of ability which conquered the physical difficulties of the White City, while attaining the æsthetic values which were the primary object, could certainly be applied profitably to the greater problem of city planning. To be sure, city planning is a vastly more complicated thing than planning an exposition. No individual can plan a city. The architect, the landscape architect, the lawyer, sociologist, engineer, the economist, sanitary expert, and many others must confer and co-operate in city planning. Nevertheless, an individual must be the moving spirit. Though members of many professions have occupied this position, a large share—some architects would say too large a share—of the responsible work has gone to the profession of landscape architecture.* Without pushing the suggestion too far, this is no doubt due in part to the grasp of planning on a large scale which the landscape architects have shown in their co-operation in the design of our great expositions.

* The School of Landscape Architecture at Harvard has, within two years, established a special curriculum leading to the degree of Master in Landscape Architecture with special reference to city planning.

Before we can enter upon any discussion of types and individual modern buildings, there are several other points in connection with the general development of American architecture which must be discussed. The most important of these is modern steel construction. Of paramount importance in commercial architecture, no element has quite so influenced modern work as the possibilities opened by the use of steel. This, hand in hand with the development of the high-powered, rapidly moving elevator, has produced the most striking innovations in modern American design. Though Europe has had the same opportunity, the use of steel has been so much more emphasised in this country that it can almost be claimed a peculiarly American feature, as it is, in a narrower sense, a truly American invention. We shall have to discuss it in detail when we consider the category of the skyscraper, but here we must say something of its invention, its principle, its development, and the new theories of design which it involved.

Steel construction in building has been divided into two types: the "skeleton" and the "cage." The first is less important. It embodies the use of steel supports for floors and roofs, while the walls are self-supporting. The latter, however, brings us to the typical modern steel building. In it the steel construction supports not only the floors and roof but the masonry walls. The change in principle can briefly be stated. In its homeliest terms it might be put as follows: up to the invention of modern steel construction a building was conceived as a structure of walls, the walls supporting tiers of beams which carried the floors and the roof; with the invention of steel construction the process was reversed, and instead of the walls carrying the beams the beams carried the walls.

The conditions which brought about the invention are as simple to understand. Congestion, restricted areas, high land values, made it desirable to carry buildings up many stories and take full advantage of the land covered. Limiting the height of the buildings, however, were two important considerations. All walls, to be self-supporting, must have a solid base. If carried high, they must be thickened constantly at the base. Six or eight stories were practical and reasonable; raise the limit to fifteen or twenty and the enormous mass of masonry necessary to support the crushing weight of the walls themselves, and the floors which they supported, made the design impractical. Moreover, there was the difficulty of communication to the upper stories. The lower ones, cramped by the masses of masonry, were less desirable; the upper ones, difficult of access. To conquer these difficulties came steel construction and the high-speed elevator.

Moreover, the difficulties before these inventions seemed to encourage bad design. Some of the worst examples of American architecture seemed to be inspired by commercial buildings in which the emphasis was perforce on verticality. It is perhaps unfair to single out a particular example, but, as an illustration, we might consider the Fagin Building (Fig. 58) in St. Louis. It was rightly published as one of the architectural aberrations of the United States,* yet it is only one characteristic example of scores of structures which unsuccessfully attacked the problem of the vertically accented commercial building. The freedom of steel construction was needed, not only to solve the practical difficulties but to spur and stimulate the designer to a serious study of the problem and the possibility of a new æsthetic solution.

The question of the invention of steel construction has long been under dispute. As in the case of most great inventions, many contributed and there were early attempts and half solutions which gave their inventors the opportunity to claim priority in the matter. At least one structure which seemed to recognise the principle was erected in New York early in the century, but the real comprehension of the possibilities of steel construction and its first practical use was in a work by Jenney & Mundie, of Chicago, in 1889.† Though A. L. Buffington, of Minneapolis, had patented a system for a metallic skeleton in building which embodied many of the features of the new construction, it seems to have been an unscientific affair, and the suits which he sought to bring for infringement never got to the courts. By 1891 the new invention was accepted as more than an experiment and from then on American architecture was armed with a new weapon, the power of which is the most striking thing in its aspect to-day. Indeed, one great writer on the history of architecture called it the fourth of the great structural advances which have given architecture new resources, the other three being the Roman vault, the Gothic ribbed

* The *Architectural Record,* April–June, 1893, p. 471.

† A. D. F. Hamlin, "Twenty-five Years of American Architecture," The *Architectural Record,* July, 1916.

FIG. 58. ST. LOUIS, MO. Fagin Building.

FIG. 59. NEW YORK, N. Y. The "Flatiron"
Building Under Construction.
D. H. Burnham & Co., Architects.

FIG. 60. NEW YORK, N. Y. A Modern Steel
Building Nearly Finished.

Photograph by Wurts Brothers.

FIG. 61. NEW YORK, N. Y. Metropolitan Life
Insurance Company.
N. LeBrun & Sons, Architects.

71

vault and masonry skeleton, and the metallic truss, which added a wholly new spaciousness and lightness to modern construction.*

As always when a new form of construction comes into being, at first the designers fumbled, the public misunderstood, and the critics attacked. Indeed, the true conception of a steel building is understood by few laymen, even to-day. It is hard for the laymen to think of a building properly constructed with the masonry walls hung to the frame. If we look at an early work in process of construction of the type of the Flatiron Building (Fig. 59) in New York, built in 1902 by D. H. Burnham & Co.,† our eyes are shocked to observe that the walls are completed in the middle but not at the bottom. A great expanse of heavy masonry seems suspended above a yawning void and looks as though it should crash down at any moment. Yet regularly skyscrapers are so constructed, the better to allow for the admission of material at the lower stories. If the walls are carried by a cage of steel it is as easy to begin at the top and build the wall down as *vice versa*, or to begin at the middle and build both ways (Fig. 60). The writer has sometimes shocked his friends when walking down Park Avenue, New York, by calling their attention to the immense buildings which flank the street and bidding them observe that where the walls touch the pavement there is a horizontal crack of a quarter to a half of an inch in breadth. If the eye is to be believed, twenty stories of wall are carried on an open crack! The wall, in other words, has ceased entirely to be a supporting member. It is merely an envelope to keep out the weather. It is built of stone or terra-cotta, partly because these materials are non-corrosive, partly because they are permanent, partly because they are beautiful, never because they are strong or are intended to take any active part in the structural scheme of the building.

As might have been supposed, it took design some time to grasp the problems of the new construction and even to attempt to solve them. At first steel construction was only an engineering convenience, and designers merely piled up the box-like stories to the new heights which this type of construction and the rapidly developing elevator facilities allowed. It was still felt that the walls should have a classic repose, the roof a classic cornice, built at a breathless scale, usually of metal, and blatantly advertis-

* *Ibid.*   † The contractors were the Geo. A. Fuller Co.

ing its uselessness from the street. As the buildings pushed higher and higher, critics, especially foreign critics, marvelled at the engineering skill displayed, but to a man regretted that American design had not risen to the opportunity of a new æsthetic expression based upon the new structural system. At the same time there were raised the obvious objections to the possible impermanence of the medium and dark forebodings as to the probable collapse of some of the more ambitious structures when the chemical character of the steel should have been changed by the slight but steady sway which the building must undergo on account of wind pressure and the occasional tremors of the earth.

Design soon attacked the problem. At first the solutions tended to be archæological, attempts being made to find lofty buildings in past history which might be adapted to the modern needs and possess, ready-made, the æsthetic emphasis on verticality. Such works as the North Italian campanile were magnified into commercial skyscrapers, like the Metropolitan Life Building in New York by LeBrun (Fig. 61). A more constructive phase came when not monuments but styles in the past were scrutinised from the point of view of satisfactory solutions in verticality, and for obvious reasons the Gothic was hit upon as the style which solved the problem. There is, indeed, a close analogy between Gothic and steel. The Gothic system is a skeleton of masonry, the modern designer attains much the same expression in steel. The constant ideal of the Gothic designer was to push his building higher and higher to the limit of financial resources and structural safety. The designer of the modern skyscraper does much the same. In short, the Gothic ideal and even the Gothic vocabulary is well adapted to steel construction and has been so proved in a number of great monuments.

The use of no particular style, however, can ever attain a completely satisfactory solution. Soon the philosophy of æsthetics demanded a logical expression in the building of its peculiar structure. If the steel cage were the real building, the walls only an envelope, what more satisfactory than to announce this fact in the design? Indeed, could honest design do less? Thus argued the critics and many of the architects. Interesting experiments began along this line. The vertical lines were further emphasised and the main verticals of the great structural piers were indicated on the exterior of the building. Great vertical slits were opened from base

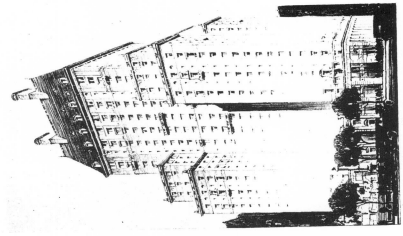

Fig. 63. New York, N. Y. Savoy-Plaza Hotel.
McKim, Mead & White, Architects.

Fig. 62. Second-Prize Design for the Chicago Tribune
Tower. *Eliel Saarinen, Designer.*

to top, as in Saarinen's drawing for the Chicago Tribune Building (Fig. 62), which indicated the structure, showed the steel lines, and revealed the cage-like framework of the whole. At the same time an attempt was made, concurrent with the expression of structure but independent from it, to shake off all classic and even historic reminiscence and design an ornament as original as the structure.

Ten years ago probably any one would have admitted the propriety of revealed structure as an axiom of design in steel. The theory was so completely logical, seemed so satisfactory, and the experiments in this direction were so full of promise, that it would have seemed presumptuous to combat the theory. Nevertheless, a number of architects ignored it and composed lofty buildings in steel, new in form and in many respects in design, but marked by no special attempt to reveal or emphasise the construction. Such a structure as the magnificent new hotel (Fig. 63), by McKim, Mead & White, at Fifth Avenue and Fifty-eighth Street, New York, has no such emphasis. The walls are plain. The rows of fine and simple windows accent the horizontal quite as much as the vertical. The envelope really conceals the structure. To be sure, the design is impressed by the structure, or rather is made possible by the structure, but it certainly is not based upon the structure, nor does it make any audible attempt to explain or, still less, to glorify it.

It will thus be condemned by many critics: as deception if they be moral ones, as old-fashioned and unprogressive if they be modernists. On the other hand, it represents a very marked tendency in the design of buildings of this construction. Indeed, if we were to render a decision in 1927, without considering the future, we should be inclined to assert that the classic and conservative point of view had won the battle against the theory of revealed structure. The defence of the conservative side would be easy to anticipate. Greater familiarity with steel construction means less necessity for expressing it in the design. At first, when the system was new, men clamoured for honesty of expression in design. If a wall were only an envelope, incapable even of supporting its weight, such a fact should be advertised on the exterior of the building. As we become more accustomed to the construction, however, we realise that the very mass and height of the building proclaims its construction. Little thought is required to convince us that a masonry wall thirty-five to fifty stories high is not self-supporting. Familiar with the fact, we become less insistent in design upon a proclamation of the obvious.

In other words, expression of the steel structure may be the solution of the problem, but need not of necessity be. The problem is much broader than that of a mere expression of structure. More classic formulæ may be applied to it without producing reactionary work.

One thing is certain, we shall never go back to the first type of sky-scrapers, box-like structures, built like expansible bookcases on end, unit placed upon unit, until the desired height is reached. And we may expect, as well as devoutly trust, that the enormous and illogical cornices which were felt necessary as crowning features to our early tall buildings have disappeared for all time.

Another element, closely related to steel construction and vastly influential, was the development of reinforced or ferro-concrete. The possibilities of concrete had long been recognised. Its resistance to crushing weight was admirable, but it afforded little resistance to shearing pressure and its tensile strength was negligible. It was found that by embedding iron, or later steel, in the concrete, these defects could be remedied. The earliest experiments in this line go back as far as 1868 in France, but the use of reinforced concrete was not seriously introduced into the United States until the late eighties, when it began to be used in California.* Its possibilities were recognised almost immediately and its use rapidly spread. It was especially adapted for great factories and industrial plants, but it was soon found that it could be treated architecturally, afforded beautiful effects, and could be applied happily to any building the functions of which required enormous scale. Perhaps the most conspicuous monuments have been the great amphitheatres and stadia that abound in our cities and universities. The possibilities of the medium are, however, well-nigh inexhaustible.

Finally there is one more general tendency to be noted in the history of architecture upon which we must dwell before we discuss any individual buildings or categories of building in detail. We have already touched upon it in connection with the Columbian Exposition, when we mentioned the Transportation Building of the late Louis Sullivan. It is the modern-

---

* Ransome, E. L., and Saurbrey, A., *Reinforced Concrete Buildings*, New York, 1912, p. 4.

istic movement which has made great strides, especially in the West. Its roots are found in the work of Adler & Sullivan, in Chicago. Of the two, Adler was primarily the business man and engineer, Sullivan the architectural designer.* The team-work was perfect, and the buildings of the firm soon attracted a wide attention. In the beginning, the æsthetic expression was probably largely determined by considerations of structure. Adler & Sullivan were about the earliest designers on a large scale of steel construction. Such a building as the Auditorium in Chicago (Fig. 64), combining a huge theatre with an hotel, offered extraordinary engineering difficulties and challenged extraordinary treatment in design. Its rugged exterior, suggesting Richardsonian Romanesque, looks old-fashioned now but was revolutionary in 1891. In the exterior ornament, however, and especially in the interior, Sullivan deliberately attempted new forms. His philosophy formed the *credo* of the new school, and its principal tenet was the avoidance of imitation of the past. With this, perforce, went the necessity of inventing new forms which were not only different, but beautiful. These were to be sought in nature, in rock forms, in crystals, in anything that could supply inspiration to the eye unspoiled by a devotion to precedent. The broad vaults of the auditorium proper (Fig. 65) were covered with a new and very interesting ornament. Colour was used, intermingling with foliate forms of a type untaught in earlier styles. Similarly, the great dining-hall received decoration of a deliberately original sort. The decorations for the bar (Fig. 66) are characteristic. Great rectangular blocks took the place of the capitals with echini and abaci of classical architecture. Ornament was devised which seemed to the designer apt for the expression of the stones and the metals involved. Imagination, invention, independence, a new structure and its new expression, were the deliberate aims of the designers.

In the beginning, as in the beginning of all philosophy, the issues were not entirely clear. Sullivan's ideas developed, however, and about him he gathered a group of young enthusiasts who helped him, who understood his aims, who carried his work further, and gave his artistic philosophy a more definite form. Among these was Frank Lloyd Wright. He not only designed in the new manner, but wrote to explain his aims as well. Through

* The *Architectural Record*, December, 1895, for interesting early account of the work of these men.

FIG. 64. CHICAGO, ILL. Auditorium Building. *Adler & Sullivan, Architects.*

FIG. 65. CHICAGO, ILL. Auditorium Building.
Adler & Sullivan, Architects.

FIG. 66. CHICAGO, ILL. Auditorium Building:
Bar. *Adler & Sullivan, Architects.*

his writing we can study not only his point of view but that of his master, to whom he pays every tribute and whose philosophy he expounds.* At the end of his career Sullivan, too, published his *Autobiography of an Idea*,† an intensely personal document which tells us much, not only of the man but of his artistic ideals.

The Sullivan movement affected the West especially, but received wide recognition abroad. The French particularly, with their modernistic tendencies, applauded it. As we have seen, Sullivan was given an opportunity to show his work juxtaposed to that of the other greatest architects in the country when he built the Transportation Building at the Chicago Exposition (Fig. 38). In an ensemble aggressively classical, he put up a building of no classic reminiscence. Superficially, it was more Romanesque than anything; actually, it followed no known style, was thought out in an entirely new way, and adorned with an entirely new decorative system. To many its force was brutality, and its lack of congruity with the other buildings was acridly discussed. On the other hand, the Société Centrale des Arts Decoratifs awarded a medal to Sullivan, the only French testimonial elicited by the display at the fair.

Adler & Sullivan carried their new style whole-heartedly into all types of buildings. Some, like the St. Nicholas Hotel, St. Louis (Fig. 67), the designers probably thought wholly original, while, as a matter of fact, they are very reminiscent of the past and notably the Queen Anne style. Others, like Mr. Sullivan's residence, Lake Avenue, Chicago (Fig. 68), were entirely original and wholly charming. The style, with its rectangularities, its sharp corners, its crushing masses, is usually forceful rather than delicate. In his own house Mr. Sullivan proved that the same style could embody delicate charm. Even tombs he designed, like the Getty Tomb in Graceland Cemetery (Fig. 69), using the new forms for the expression both of force and repose. His success in domestic architecture inspired Wright especially, whose earlier work was in this particular field.

Wright is probably the best known living exponent of the style. Such domestic monuments as the Coonley House at Riverside, Ill. (Figs. 71, 72), or, for monumental work, his famous Imperial Hotel at Tokio (Figs. 335, 336, 337), are the embodiments of modernism or even secessionism

* *Frank Lloyd Wright.* Published by C. A. Mees, Santpoort, Holland, 1925.
† Press of the American Institute of Architects, New York, 1924.

FIG. 68.   CHICAGO, ILL.   Residence of Louis Sullivan, Architect.

FIG. 67.   ST. LOUIS, MO.   St. Nicholas Hotel.
Adler & Sullivan, Architects.

FIG. 69. CHICAGO, ILL. Graceland Cemetery: Getty Tomb.
Adler & Sullivan, Architects.

FIG. 70. EL PASO, TEXAS. Mills Building. *Trost & Trost, Architects.*

FIG. 71. RIVERSIDE, ILL. Coonley House. *Frank Lloyd Wright, Architect.*

FIG. 72. RIVERSIDE, ILL. Coonley House: Playhouse Interior. *Frank Lloyd Wright, Architect.*

in American architecture. Many other architects have followed the lead, however. Such a work as the Mills Building (Fig. 70) at El Paso, Texas (Trost & Trost), is designed in the spirit, and really in the letter, of Louis Sullivan's ideas. Disciples were not lacking, though the movement has received far less attention in the East than in the West; a rather odd fact when we consider the generally greater conservatism of the West as compared to the East. The modernistic movement has its affinities with those abroad which are producing such interesting—and oftentimes, it must be confessed, such bizarre—buildings in Germany and the Netherlands. It is related to the modernism of Scandinavia and the movement which produced the Paris Exposition of 1925. It is odd that it should appear in mid-Western America, skipping almost completely the Atlantic seaboard, but such is the fact.

The whole question of modernism in American architecture is under dispute. On no point do opinions vary more widely, nor partisanships run more hot. To the modernist the conservative is an unimaginative beast in a treadmill, monotonously turning over lifeless repetitions of the masterpieces of the past. To the classicist, the designer in a modernistic manner is but a charlatan bent upon being new for the advertising that newness brings and ruining architecture by his obliviousness to all the lessons which the past can teach. We of to-day are too close to the events to decide on the merits of the question. Posterity must judge what is permanently good and what is a momentary aberration. Of one thing we can be sure, however, that any movement as wide-spread and as ardently supported must have good in it and, though its early experiments may prove to be clumsy and later be disavowed, the good eventually will appear.

The danger which the modernist runs is an excessive fear of the past and its precedent. There is no artistic merit of necessity in originality. In so far as precedent is stifling to expression it is bad, but a thing may be as new as this morning's sunrise and still be ugly and architecturally bad. Practitioners of all the arts to-day have made a fetich of originality. Straining every nerve to be new, they often lose sight completely of what should be their steadfast aim: the expression of the beautiful. Striving merely to be different is as stupid as making direct copies of an ancient masterpiece. Whatever the final verdict, it will be based not upon newness, not upon originality, but upon beauty. If the protagonists of modernism keep this in mind, they will succeed. If they lose sight of it, their work will disappear.

One good, however, they have already accomplished. They have broken down the barriers of historic precedent and familiarised our civilisation with new forms. They have encouraged us to shake off ideas of the necessity of stylistic correctness. Though we may not follow them over the whole road, we can benefit by their fresh view-point. Our architectural problems are new and demand new solutions. We may well use the past and the vocabularies of the past, in so far as they assist us in the solution of these problems. We should never retain from force of habit the imitation of work from the past that cannot so assist us. We have seen how long an absurdity like the classic cornice on a skyscraper was retained. The new point of view helps us to slough off these anachronisms and design according to the new needs. Never should we lose sight of the past and its benefits, but never should we let it tyrannise us. American architecture is meeting new conditions, adapting itself to new structural systems, attacking new and complicated difficulties of every sort and on every side. In so doing, it must arm itself with every resource. It must look back to learn, to adapt, but not to imitate. It must look about intelligently to face the problems of to-day. It must look ahead to anticipate the needs and conditions of the future and avoid those very mistakes which, in many cases, a scrutiny of the past can teach. What varied, what interesting, what successful attempts are being made we can see when we review, building by building, and type by type, the stimulating phenomena of the American architecture of to-day.

II

THE DOMESTIC AND ACADEMIC ARCHITECTURE

II

THE DOMESTIC AND ACADEMIC ARCHITECTURE

No matter what the type reviewed or district observed, the encouraging fact which must strike every student of American architecture today is the vast improvement which has occurred in the last twenty-five to thirty-five years. In no work is this fact more conspicuous than in domestic architecture, and it is the more gratifying in this field since domestic architecture leans towards the conservative.

As we have seen, during the seventies, eighties, and even nineties of the previous century, domestic architecture ran a riot of Queen Anne designs, of pseudo-Gothic, of jig-saw ornament that, except in a few examples, represented the most depressing depth to which American work has ever sunk. Towards the end of the century, however, a change set in. Picturesqueness ceased to be the chief aim of the designer and sobriety became the vogue. Romanticism in architecture began to disappear, or rather, the romantic emotions which previously had encouraged the erection of mediæval chateaux, of Swiss chalets, and of Shakesperian half-timber, came to be associated with our own Colonial style. The result was a purification of the work and an increase of simplicity and chastity in American taste. The early twentieth century saw an enthusiastic Colonial revival in all parts of the country.

That this Colonial revival was an excellent thing for American architecture few will deny. It concentrated attention on attractive models, well proportioned and with detail marked by a truly American refinement. It also permitted, in rural architecture especially, a reversion to what architect and client felt was a truly national style. Patriotic and historic interest in this case coincided with the best interests of architecture. Especially in modest rural dwellings wholesome and charming examples began to multiply in every district. Even houses on an impressive scale were built in the Colonial manner. When the houses were too large truly to imitate Colonial prototypes the desired effect was got by using a Colonial unit and multiplying it for the building of larger scale.

As might be expected, the movement pushed too far. It became too archæological. The proud client came to boast of his dwelling in terms of its being "true Colonial" instead of objectively beautiful. Effects themselves desirable were often condemned on the ground that they were not "truly Colonial," and the cult of Colonial furniture stimulated the purchase, often at absurd prices, of pieces of dubious beauty merely because of their genuineness as Colonial work. These were imitated by modern designers, while antique dealers extended the term "Colonial" to include anything up to the arrival of American Gothic. The wave of Colonial enthusiasm, like all such waves, caused a good deal of absurdity and still displays its dangers, but its tremendously beneficial effects should not be minimised.

The most modern point of view is still more encouraging. While the average client still is inclined to appreciate in archæological terms, the modern architect has learned the lessons and virtues of Colonial work, but has passed beyond its imitation. He has come to the more fruitful and sounder phase of adaptation. He has realised that the fundamental virtue of Colonial architecture is its fitness to the locality in which it appeared, and he seeks to get this feeling in his work. Much modern Colonial is still very archæological, but this is no vice provided the archæologising appears not as an aim in itself but as a means to obtain an æsthetic result.

Inevitably, at the same time, a domestic architecture appeared which was native, as fine in expression as true Colonial, but drawing its inspiration from many sources and obtaining its effects by an understanding of the proper use of local material quite as much as by the study of any work of the past. A brilliant example of this tendency one can see in the suburban work near Philadelphia. A nice conservatism, tempered by catholic taste, and a real insistence on the fundamentals of good design now marks the best of our domestic work.

In a review of the field, it is well to begin with the more modest rural houses, leaving the great estates and city dwellings for later analysis. In studying the country dwellings, too, we shall note first those which have a more marked archæological tendency and discuss next those of freer design. In both cases we must remember that for each building we note there may be a thousand others of its class that are as worth observing, and that each example we cite is to be regarded, strictly speaking, as an example and is not an unique specimen nor even necessarily the best of its class.   On such a point opinion would differ and a far more exhaustive student than the writer would never arrogate to himself the position of arbiter nor even familiar of all that is being done in modern domestic architecture to-day.

Starting with the work in New England, the Colonial style is subdivided into those buildings which reflect the mediæval point of view of the seventeenth century and those which are inspired by the more classic Georgian of the eighteenth.   To this might be added a third class, not Colonial at all, but based upon the classic architecture of the Early Republic which, as we have seen, was more sophisticated than earlier styles, generally more monumental in scale, but which had rooted affinities with the Colonial style.   The materials were varied, brick, wood, and stone being used, but the favourite material was brick, generally with detail of doorways, windows, and cornices in painted wood.   Much fine work, however, especially of the seventeenth-century type, is being done entirely in wood. Indeed, the material is apt to be based upon the Colonial material that was popular in the district.   Stone was the rarest material in Colonial times and is consequently rare in the buildings which we have under consideration.

Interesting works of all types are appearing all over New England. The perfection of the motor-car, the attendant improvement in roads, and the ease of communication between the city and the country has encouraged people, even of fairly modest means, to go long distances into the country, drawn thither either by sentimental ties of ancestry or by individual predilection for the scenic charm of a given district, and there to erect homes which are in harmony with the older architecture to be found in the region.

As a most charming example of the seventeenth-century type, we might select a house at Exeter, R. I. (Fig. 73), designed by William T. Aldrich.   Modest in effect, solid and old-fashioned in appearance, it is based upon the gambrel-roofed type so common in seventeenth-century New England.   We have already seen its prototype in the Fairbanks house at Dedham (Fig. 1).   In this case, the problem was to adapt an old design to modern needs, and especially a small house to a building on a considerable scale, since the Exeter house, for all its modest ap-

FIG. 73. EXETER, R. I. House. *William T. Aldrich, Architect.*

FIG. 74. FALMOUTH, MASS. House. *Coolidge, Shepley, Bulfinch & Abbott, Architects.*

pearance, is by no means an humble dwelling. The architect has used the device, common enough, of multiplying the single unit of an older building, but has done it so skilfully that he has kept entirely the flavour and character of a building of the seventeenth century. The wooden surface, the stout proportions, the fat, comfortable chimneys, all are drawn from the earlier style and a twentieth-century building rests in perfect harmony among the quaint and stoutly built Colonial buildings of southern New England. All this has been obtained, and can always be obtained, by a talented architect, without sacrificing one whit of the conveniences of communication, functionalism of rooms, and the like, which the modern inmate demands.

A building of a somewhat different type, but of the same general category, is the house which we reproduce, at Falmouth, Mass. (Fig. 74), by Coolidge, Shepley, Bulfinch & Abbott. Here the dwelling was a truly modest one. The designer's problem was to simulate the proportions, character, and rough-shingled texture of the characteristic buildings of Cape Cod and, at the same time, create a comfortable, convenient house, at moderate cost, for a modern inmate. How well he has solved the problem one can guess even from a glance at the elevation. Examination of the detail shows how the architect has avoided all parade of classic ornament, attaining the character of the prototype which we are justified in calling mediæval, and relying upon straightforward revelation of structure and upon sound proportion to obtain the undeniable charm which the building possesses.

For one more example of the seventeenth-century type at its simplest and most modest we may examine the Emery house at Jaffrey, N. H. (Fig. 75), by H. A. Frost and C. W. Killam. This building, with its thin clapboards, its overhanging second story, its heavy proportions two stories and a half in height, its two-storied slope of the roof in the rear, and its heavy central chimney, is seventeenth-century Colonial, derived from a purely English source. It fits its setting perfectly.* As one enters the interior (Fig. 76) one is struck by simple walls, beamed ceilings with the timbers revealed, and the emphasis on structure rather than on decoration

---

* An amusing fact is that the designers tried to produce a building in harmony with the architecture of the district and, not realising the comparatively late settlement of the central portions of New Hampshire, erected one really a hundred years too early for its site.

Photograph by Thomas Ellison.

FIG. 75.   JAFFREY, N. H.   Emery House.
Frost & Killam, Architects; Bremer W. Pond, Landscape Architect.

Photograph by Thomas Ellison.

FIG. 76.   JAFFREY, N. H.   Emery House.
Frost & Killam, Architects; Bremer W. Pond, Landscape Architect.

which marks the style. The Colonial furniture adds the last touch necessary, although a comfortable veranda at the rear saves the building from
the discomfort of a too strict archæology.

As we turn from the seventeenth-century type to the eighteenth-century Georgian, such a wealth of material exists that we are overwhelmed
by an *embarras de richesse*. The northern Georgian, brick and limestone,
or brick with wooden trim, blinds and portal painted white, is familiar to
every eye and is one of the most charming products of American domestic architecture. Almost at random we reproduce one, the residence of
Henry N. Furnald, Esq., at Fieldston, N. Y. (Fig. 77), by Dwight James
Baum. It has the gambrel roof, the squared end with chimneys sunk in the
wall, the restrained classic detail of Northern eighteenth-century work. It
is, however, by no means archæological and in details, like the veranda and
the portico (Fig. 78), asserts itself as a building which has assimilated a
style rather than imitated it. As one approaches it one feels oneself in a
late Colonial atmosphere without being able to accuse the designer of copying a given Colonial detail. It is characteristic of modern architecture that
the charming and entirely congruous-appearing terrace is over the garage.

Although by no means Colonial, it may be pertinent to mention here
the twentieth-century phase of that continuation of Colonial, the Early Republican style, and the success with which architects have adapted it to modern needs. This style, as we have seen, paid more attention to comfort than
the Colonial architecture, was generally on a more monumental scale, and is
really better adapted to inspire modern work than is Colonial. Of the two,
true Colonial is the more influential and this is rather difficult to understand. The most recent tendencies, however, are directing more and more
attention to the lessons to be learned from Early Republican architecture.

As a single example of this style in modern work, we might look at
the house done for Mrs. R. M. Bissell, at Farmington, Conn. (Fig. 79),
by Edwin S. Dodge. The plan, except for its lack of curves, has all the
quality of the Early Republican style. Communications are well studied,
living-rooms comfortably arranged, the hall is monumental yet chaste in
ornament, and everything is calculated to produce a feeling of privacy,
ease, dignity, and restraint. In elevation, the severe Doric portico recalls
the early nineteenth-century work. Above it a sunken panel with a *motif
Palladio* might have been designed by Bulfinch and adds the one ornate

Fig. 78. Fieldston, N. Y. Residence of Henry N. Furnald Esq.

Dwight James Baum, Architect.

Fig. 77. Fieldston, N. Y. Residence of Henry N. Furnald, Esq.

Dwight James Baum, Architect.

FIG. 79. FARMINGTON, CONN. Bissell House. *E. S. Dodge, Architect.*

FIG. 80. FARMINGTON, CONN. Bissell House.
E. S. Dodge, Architect.

FIG. 81. FARMINGTON, CONN. Bissell House.
E. S. Dodge, Architect.

Photograph by Kenneth Clark.

Fig. 82. Knollwood, N. C. Mid-Pines Country Club.
Aymar Embury II, Architect.

Fig. 83. Atlanta, Ga. Residence. *Pringle & Smith, Architects.*

note to relieve the severity of the three tiers of simple windows. Proportions are nicely adjusted and the whole flavour of the building is one of severity without coldness. The interiors (Figs. 80, 81), with their broad arches, simple panelling, and fine membering of the wall surfaces, ably second the impression made by the house as a whole.

Turning to the Colonial-inspired buildings in the South, we find the style as well adapted to one locality as to the other. Indeed, the same architects often work in both districts, with little change of style, and produce work that—geographically speaking—is entirely harmonious. In modern work, as in ancient, there is a tendency in the South to use less wood, but this merely follows tradition, and good architecture in wood, as well as more monumental materials, exists in both districts.

As usual, examples of the type are legion, and we must limit ourselves to very few, with no implication that they are unique, nor even necessarily the best. Fine ones may be found in the Sand Hills of North Carolina, where Aymar Embury II * had the opportunity to create a new settlement and chose sensibly an adaptation of Georgian Colonial and Early Republican architecture as his medium. The detail we show of the Mid-Pines Country Club at Knollwood, N. C. (Fig. 82), is typical of this work, frankly admitting its debt to the past, yet adapting an older style to modern conditions and needs. The affinity between this and the Northern work we have just reviewed is obvious, yet the tendency to ramble, the use of a two-storied portico, and the general airiness of the design give it a truly Southern character. Variety is got by the use of brick, stone, and wood in the same monument.

Not to confine ourselves to the work of a single man or firm, we might glance at a house at Atlanta, Ga., by Pringle & Smith (Fig. 83), that preserves the ancient tradition of Southern architecture, gives the feeling of antiquity and, at the same time, is well adapted to modern needs. Especially the great central two-storied portico, developing in the South in the late eighteenth century, is well handled, though the details of its slender supports are not repeats of any definite stylistic antecedent.

In New York and the Hudson Valley, the many remains of Dutch Colonial building tempted the modern architect to interesting experiments,

* The *Architectural Record*, June, 1924, R. F. Whitehead, "Some Work of Aymar Embury II."

and from New York the types have spread occasionally into New England and other districts. Dutch Colonial, whether seventeenth or eighteenth century, is more picturesque and less formal than English. For the rural dwelling, it had the advantage of a veranda, which was commonly covered by the same roof which protected the rest of the building, this roof taking an upward turn as it projected over the porch.

Such an informal, cosey effect is got, again by Mr. Embury, in the house for Mrs. W. H. Fallon, at Sparkill, N. Y. (Fig. 84). Here the low proportions, the slim dormers, and above all, the eccentric tilt of the roof as it projects over the veranda, betray immediately a Dutch origin. Placed among the Dutch eighteenth-century buildings in such a town as Hurley, this modern building could never be out of place.

A freer version of Dutch Colonial is the house done by Calvin Kiessling, for Mr. Benjamin P. Vanderhoof, at New Canaan, Conn. (Fig. 85). Here a two-storied portico, for which there is no precedent in Dutch Colonial and which is more reminiscent of English work, is used to give dignity and shelter to the façade. The tilted roof which covers it, however, the broad clapboarding, the shape of the chimneys and the general proportions, are characteristic of the Hudson Valley type.

Æsthetically related to these, though of a different historic origin, are the houses of Pennsylvania which betray the influences of the German and Scandinavian builders who first settled in that district. The analysis of these is not easy, however, as many houses which are based upon English or French models still retain one characteristic feature that we associate with "Pennsylvania Dutch": the happy use of purely local material. Of these we shall speak later. Some, however, show not only the use of local material, as cheap and sensible as it is æsthetically pleasing, but also forms which are more Teutonic than Anglican or French. This is true, for example, of the charming little house which we reproduce, by Carl A. Ziegler, on Cliveden Avenue, Germantown, Pa. (Fig. 86). Unlike "Cliveden," this house makes no pretense to formality, but its dormers and the slope of the roof give it a truly Pennsylvania Dutch air. Another example, still freer, and combining suggestions both of English and "Pennsylvania Dutch" prototypes, is Mrs. Meigs' house at Ithan, Pa. (Fig. 87), naturally a product of the firm of Mellor, Meigs & Howe. The "Pennsylvania Dutch" style has not been as influential as the English Georgian,

FIG. 84.   SPARKILL, N. Y.   Residence of Mrs. W. H. Fallon.   *Aymar Embury II, Architect*

Photograph by Kenneth Clark.

FIG. 85.   NEW CANAAN, CONN.   Residence of B. P. Vanderhoof, Esq.   *Calvin Kiessling, Architect.*

FIG. 86.   GERMANTOWN, PA.   House on Cliveden Avenue.   *Carl A. Ziegler, Architect.*

FIG. 87.   ITHAN, PA.   Residence of Mrs. J. F. Meigs.   *Mellor, Meigs & Howe, Architects.*

nor even the true New York Dutch, but its effects have been felt, and happily, in Pennsylvania.

Indeed, Americans in general have been too apt to associate the word "Colonial" only with the Anglo-Georgian work. Grudgingly they extend it to the Dutch and German styles of the Atlantic seaboard, reluctantly they are just beginning to realise that it applies as well to such work as the buildings of Louisiana, derived from a French Colonial type, and those of the Southwest which are as characteristically Colonial Spanish. Any one who has been in New Orleans, for example, has been impressed with the Gallic quality of the architecture there, as well as with its propriety as a Southern style. Most visitors are struck particularly with the detail, the grilles, the balconies of exquisite ironwork, wrought or cast, and overlook the French proportions, the long French windows, protected by awnings, the widely overhanging eaves, and other features which were partly imported by the French settlers and partly invented by them in the prosperous days of the eighteenth century. No local architect, nor even client, could neglect the appropriate suggestions of the local style, and its influence appears refreshingly in many a modern building of New Orleans. As an example, we reproduce the residence of Mr. J. C. Lyons, at New Orleans (Fig. 88), done by Armstrong & Koch. It would be hard to find a building that fits more perfectly into its environment. It is dignified, sheltered, yet airy. One realises at once that it smacks of France and that it is adapted to the needs of the warm, moist climate of Louisiana.

If we turn from this to the modern adaptations of Spanish Colonial, we shall find again an embarrassing wealth of material. As one would expect, the style grew up especially in Southern California, but it is found in New Mexico, Arizona, Texas, Florida, and elsewhere in regions historically and climatically appropriate. By historic chance, the Spaniards settled portions of the country with a climate not unlike their own. Their architecture, which they would of course have used anyway, happened to be entirely appropriate. It had, however, to be simplified. Means were not so lavish here as at home, and, above all, skilled craftsmen were almost non-existent. For labour, the Spanish depended largely upon Indians, and these could be taught only the simpler things of architecture. Construction became, therefore, heavier, ornament reduced, mouldings sim-

Fig. 88. New Orleans, La. Residence of J. C. Lyons, Esq. *Armstrong & Koch, Architects.*

Fig. 89. Pasadena, Calif. Residence of Herbert Coppell, Esq. *Bertram G. Goodhue, Architect.*

plified, and the effect of the local adobe material often made itself felt. The result was a picturesque superficial crudity that has often been criticised when imitated in modern work, but which ill deserves the charge of affectation. As a source of inspiration for modest dwellings it is wholly admirable and even monumental works of large scale and power can be built up of units suggested by the Spanish Colonial. Nor must we forget that, when occasion warranted it, the Spaniards did construct buildings, especially churches, comparable to those that were designed at home, so material for a more sophisticated derivation from Spanish lies to hand in the Southwest.

A perfect example of this is the house done for Herbert Coppell, Esq., at Pasadena, Calif. (Fig. 89), by the late Bertram Grosvenor Goodhue, as we have seen one of the first to realise the possibilities of American Spanish. The same ideas which he embodied in the San Diego Exposition he applied to the domestic house. In the Coppell residence he has caught perfectly the Spanish tradition of simple masses contrasting with smaller fields of concentrated ornament. Scrupulously avoiding all parade of classicism, he designed in broad walls, windows rectangular or arched, in square sections without enframement, and overhangs which cast broad shadows on the otherwise brilliantly illuminated walls. Upon the doorway, however (Fig. 90), with its portal and superposed balcony and window, he lavished a wealth of brilliant Spanish ornament. As a result, his central motif has the jewel-like sparkle which is the most striking feature of the Spanish style.

For a simpler, we might almost say a more conventional, type, and yet one that is larger in scale and as characteristically Spanish, we reproduce "Dias Dorados," done for Mr. Thomas H. Ince, by Roy S. Price, at Beverly Hills, Calif. (Fig. 91). Here, too, the walls are plain and brilliantly lighted, while deep eaves and occasional projecting timbers, similar to those which we have seen in the seventeenth-century Governor's Palace at Santa Fé (Fig. 16), cast interesting shadows. These eaves announce the protection of the dwelling against the hot sun and, indeed, the thickness of the walls, which the most casual observer must sense at a glance, proclaims a cool and sheltered interior.

Some of the smaller buildings are quite as interesting. The house of W. T. Jefferson, Esq., by Marston & Van Pelt, at Pasadena (Fig. 92),

FIG. 90. PASADENA, CALIF. Residence of Herbert Coppell, Esq. *Bertram G. Goodhue, Architect.*

FIG. 91. BEVERLY HILLS, CALIF. Dias Dorados. *Roy Seldon Price, Architect.*

FIG. 92. PASADENA, CALIF. Residence of W. T. Jefferson, Esq. *Marston & Van Pelt, Architects.*

shows in a quieter way the conventions used by Goodhue. The doorway is typical baroque, though less elaborate than the other we have noted. The walls are plain, the windows few and simple, the cornice replaced by wooden eaves with a deep overhang, and the whole effect made as quiet, yet as typically Spanish, as possible. Again one feels that the house fits its environment perfectly. One more example must suffice, the little house done for Craig Heberton, Esq., at Santa Barbara (Fig. 93), by George Washington Smith. This architect has made quite a specialty of the simplest type of Spanish house. Far from deploring the broad methods of construction imposed by lack of technical skill upon the Spanish Colonial builders, he has recognised its value in giving interest, power, and simplicity to the work. Especially, he has studied and caught the agreeable texture and play of light which such a method of building brought. Leaving out all sophisticated baroque ornament, he has simplified everything to the nth degree, and got his effects by masses, by walls as unbroken as comfort would permit, and by the play of shadows which the planting could afford. As we look at a photograph of the Heberton house we cannot but be charmed by the play of light over its surfaces, by its honesty, straightforwardness, and the delightful way in which it fits its landscape setting.

When we examine the architecture of Florida we find much of the same type of work. Here, for obvious reasons, the Spanish style has had a tremendous vogue. The modern buildings run through all phases of Spanish, from baroque to comparative academic correctness, from elaboration and great scale to the simplest and most picturesque informal tiny dwellings. As an example of the more academic and monumental work, we may examine the great residence done for J. S. Phipps, Esq., at Palm Beach (Fig. 94), by Addison Mizner. Here we find no florid baroque ornament, yet a perfect Spanish flavour is maintained. The plan is U-shaped, with arcades on the ground floor and a loggia across the centre in the second story, making an effect at once airy and dignified. The living quarters, including library and swimming-pool, are on the ground floor. Above are the master's and guests' rooms, with communication got by the loggia in the centre and corridors in the wings. The arcaded court is truly Spanish and almost monastic in expression. The essentials of good Spanish architecture of the most refined type are here combined with the comfort and logic of plan which the modern client demands.

FIG. 93. SANTA BARBARA, CALIF. Residence of Craig Heberton, Esq.
George Washington Smith, Architect.

FIG. 94. PALM BEACH, FLA. Residence of J. S. Phipps, Esq. *Addison Mizner, Architect.*

Photograph by W. A. Fishbaugh.

FIG. 95. CORAL GABLES, FLA. Venetian Casino. *Denman Fink, Designer.*

The informal type is to be found throughout the peninsula, though especially on the east coast. One need not go beyond the well-known development at Coral Gables to find plenty of excellent examples. Coral Gables brings up the whole question of rural community planning which we cannot discuss here beyond merely applauding the attempt to plan many houses with relation one to another, and attain a real homogeneity without losing variety and picturesqueness.* The criticism of Coral Gables is that it is too exotic, yet there is something in the air of Florida which challenges exotic treatment. Here we need not discuss the propriety of creating artificially the effect of Venice or the Riviera; we need merely note the fact and admire the amazing skill with which it is done. The view of the Venetian Casino (Fig. 95), for example, with its Venetian gondola posts, its Italo-Spanish architecture, its tropical planting, and its picturesque lagoon, is a triumph in exotic design, and as long as people flock to Florida to escape the drab winters of the North they are bound to revel in the exotic and the picturesque.

Turning to the modest type of domestic Spanish which here concerns us, we might select the residence of J. H. Humphrey, Esq. (Fig. 96), as typical. Here the workmanship is purposely made as crude as possible and all classic ornament is omitted. The thickness of the walls is emphasised and the expression attained is very like that of the Indian-built Spanish of the Southwest. Indeed, one can trace the influence, if remote, of what has come to be called in the Southwest the pueblo style of architecture. Above all, the designers have made the most of the planting, so that a riot of foliate form and colour envelops the dwelling. One might find the effect of such work cloying, if one lived with it year in and year out. To the jaded eye of the northerner, however, surfeited with gazing upon bare country landscapes, or slushy streets, the dwellings of Coral Gables seem like a fairy-land.

Thus far, we have discussed domestic architecture solely under the head of historic derivation. It is very hard, however, to do this consistently and some of the finest work cannot fit into any such classification at all. At times, as in the case of the house at Jaffrey, by Frost and Killam, the archæological effect is so frank and outspoken that an historic classifi-

* The author is deeply indebted to Mr. Frank M. Button, landscape architect at Coral Gables, for information and photographs.

FIG. 96.   CORAL GABLES, FLA.   House of J. H. Humphrey.

Photograph by P. B. Wallace.

FIG. 97.   ST. MARTINS, PHILADELPHIA, PA.   House of N. M. Seabreeze, Esq.
Duhring, Okie & Ziegler, Architects.

110

cation works admirably. In other cases, as we have seen, the historic influences are mixed, and the designer has learned from the solutions of the
past without imitating any one. This is particularly true of the work of
Georgian flavour. We reproduce a small house, done for Mr. N. M. Seabreeze, at Philadelphia (Fig. 97), by H. L. Duhring. Compactly composed, built in brick, classic in detail which is sparingly used, it is more
English Colonial than anything else, yet one hardly can call it Colonial.
It is truly and at the same time unobtrusively modern. It represents careful study in proportion, in planning, and in surface textures, revolutionary in nothing, satisfactory in everything, and, though we may congratulate the designer on the excellence of this particular performance, the
encouraging thing to note is that this example is by no means unique. We
could probably find hundreds of similar ones in America by scores of
architects which could illustrate our point as well. It must be confessed,
however, that, as a group, the architects of Philadelphia have been particularly successful in this problem of the carefully studied small house.
Simplicity can be very dull, as well as admirable, and successful simplicity
can be attained only by the most careful study. In the best examples, as
here, the study disappears in the completed monument, leaving only its
effect, and we have the pleasantest of all monuments, a seemingly unstudied one.

Aside from the pseudo-Georgian type, we find thousands of examples
of good domestic work in America, large or small, historic or no, which
have little geographical reference in their styles. Gothic, for example,
and especially Tudor Gothic, has been used with great success in American country houses, though it can have no reference to any historic period
in this country. Such work oftentimes annoys the foreign critic of American architecture. The Englishman is apt to resent the incongruity of a
Tudor house in a country which has had no Tudor history. On the other
hand, if the house be well designed and well placed, if the architecture
be suited, as in the North, to the climate, there is no reason why the designer should not express himself in this vocabulary if he chooses. The
fact that America was discovered in 1492 instead of a century or so earlier
is a poor reason for allowing to America one style of architecture derived
from England and not another. The obvious fallacy appears when we
realise that once more the dispute narrows to a question of historic pro-

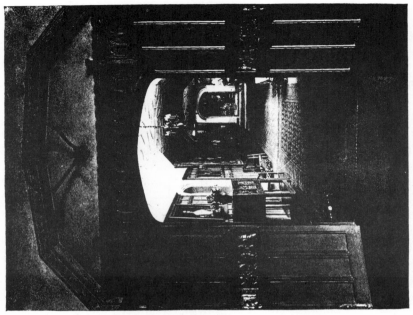

Fig. 99. Newport, R. I. Residence of Stuart Duncan, Esq.
John Russell Pope, Architect.

Fig. 98. Newport, R. I. Residence of Stuart Duncan, Esq.
John Russell Pope, Architect.

priety, and modern architecture, though it may be swayed by such considerations, will not and should not be dominated by them.   The real question in many cases is whether or not the treatment be too deliberately
archæological, but this must be determined by individual opinion in individual instances.

As an excellent example of the Tudor type, we may select the residence of Stuart Duncan, Esq., at Newport, R. I. (Fig. 98), by John Russell Pope.   Here we get a straightforward acceptance of Tudor forms,
frankly archæological, but repeating no known historic monument.   The
designer, feeling the exquisite charm of the original in England, has set
himself to get the same effect in modern America, and has succeeded.
His building is monumental as well as picturesque, his textures a delight
to the eye.   The interiors are frankly inspired by such buildings as Knole,
Haddon, Lynhydroc, and a score of other English prototypes which we
could mention, but they are beautiful and well suited to their purpose.   If
the long galleries of the Tudor houses were beautiful, there is no reason
why a modern architect should not take them over, as in the view we show
of Mr. Duncan's house (Fig. 99), and adapt them to modern needs and
conditions.   The worst that can be said of such archæological treatment
is that it is unprogressive and does not lead to the development of something new.   On the other hand, the price is not too great to pay occasionally for a monument of great beauty, especially in a country where historic examples are not available.   An archæological reliance on the past
need not worry us if it be not universal in our architecture and if it be done
with an understanding of the spirit of the ancient example.   The latter
is what we are getting in present-day American work as completely as we
missed it a couple of generations ago.

In the dwellings which make no pretense to following a local style
geographically, the influence of local material is often most happily apparent.   In New England, where good building stone is scarce, where the
field stone is ill adapted to any but heavy effects and the abundant granite is better suited for massive structures than modest ones, brick has come
to be the favoured medium.   The suggestions of brick Colonial are eagerly
accepted and, as we have seen, brick is becoming almost the recognised
local material.   On the other hand, the prevalence of abundant good white
pine encouraged the use of wood in Colonial times, and modern domestic

work has often followed in this. The comparative impermanence of wood is often urged against it, but the vast numbers of seventeenth and eighteenth century wooden buildings that exist in New England attest the fact that wood, properly cared for, is as permanent a medium as need be. Only the constant menace of fire makes it inferior in this respect to brick.

Perhaps the most charming and successful examples we have of the tasteful use of local material occur in or near Philadelphia, where a group of brilliant designers have made a study of the use of the attractive local limestone. In most of these buildings they have made no attempt to express a local style historically, and the character of the buildings is more often English or French than "Pennsylvania Dutch." It muddies our conception of the work, however, to try and associate it with any historic style. It is straightforward building and honest design, with an eye to fine proportion, picturesque composition, and the use of the full possibilities of the material. That this is so abundant locally may be luck,* but the recognition of its possibilities is to the credit of the designers. Though some of the houses are on a monumental scale and some are very small, the vast majority are of moderate size, running in cost from twenty to forty or fifty thousand dollars.

When it comes to illustrating this work, it is embarrassing to have to choose among so many brilliant examples by such a number of able men. Almost at random, let us look at a typical example by Robert R. McGoodwin (Fig. 100). It has all the charm of an old-world cottage, without the slightest pretense to being anything but what it is. It is quaint, delicious in the expression of the texture of its masonry, picturesque in silhouette, and yet one grasps immediately that it is well planned, up to date in its appointments, and entirely suited to the needs of a modern owner. Even on the exterior, one senses the light and roominess of the wing nearest the observer, while one admires the relation of this wing to the rest of the building. Indeed, here the designer has caught the charm of Compton Wynyates, without imitating any of its details.

A view of another building by this architect (Fig. 101) will fortify this impression. Here the masonry is rougher, more binding is used, and

---

* Mr. C. C. Zantzinger, of Zantzinger, Borie & Medary, recently built a parish house in Chestnut Hill, using only the stone which he obtained in excavating the site of the building.

Fig. 100.   Chestnut Hill, Pa.   House for Staunton B. Peck, Esq.   *Robert R. McGoodwin, Architect.*

Fig. 101.   Chestnut Hill, Pa.   Residence of Persifor Frazier, 3d, Esq.
Robert R. McGoodwin, Architect.

the architects vary their methods in this respect.   At times they attain the maximum of cheapness in the handling of the stone without abating one whit the charm of texture.   Here again we have picturesqueness, charming composition, and the suggestion of solid modern comfort.   The glimpse of the motor beyond the doorway, at the end of the drive, is in no sense incongruous.   The designers have attacked the problem in the most praiseworthy way and, by making the most of local stone and modern demands, have attained the success that such an attack can always make in any age or style.   Similarly in the house for Mr. J. M. Reynolds, at St. Martins, Philadelphia (Fig. 102), by H. L. Duhring, one senses the domesticity, the privacy, the aristocratic economy of means that proudly avoids self-advertisement and as discreetly glorifies the taste of designer and tenant.

In these cases, the effects are generally English.   The same general effect is obtained in the "French Village," as it has come to be called, designed by Robert R. McGoodwin (Fig. 103), and forming a part of the attractive development that is making Chestnut Hill, Philadelphia, one of the most distinguished districts architecturally in the United States. These buildings, however, with their exaggeratedly pitched roofs, their turrets and their lofty chimneys, are just a trifle theatrical and perhaps not quite so admirable as the simpler type.   All have, however, the same taste in material and are interesting variants of the local design.   The same may be said of the delightful set of farm buildings, designed for Mr. Arthur E. Newbold, Jr. (Figs. 104, 105), by Mellor, Meigs & Howe.*   Here the designers worked with a deliberate theory in mind. They believed that the charm of the European farm group came from the presence of the animals as well as the human occupants, and the expression of functions of the buildings as a farm unconsciously expressed, but none the less felt.   Mr. Newbold's house was designed to attain this expression.   The effort had to be conscious, however, and partly on that account, partly on account of the use of sagging roof lines and similar details to give an impression of age, it borders on the theatrical.   The group is, none the less, one of the most interesting and attractive in modern American rural work.

The temptation to multiply examples of this work is almost irresistible.   We reproduce, for example, a house by Gilchrist (Fig. 106).   Pur-

* A. J. Meigs, *An American Country House*, New York, 1925.

FIG. 102. ST. MARTINS, PHILADELPHIA, PA.

House for J. M. Reynolds, Esq. *H. Louis Duhring, Architect.*

FIG. 103. CHESTNUT HILL, PA. The "French Village." *Robert R. McGoodwin, Architect.*

117

FIG. 104. LAVEROCK, PA. Newbold Farm from the Pasture. *Mellor, Meigs & Howe, Architects.*

118

posely we have selected one built of the cheapest possible masonry construction, yet as straightforward and as full of charm as any in the group. Looking at a number of these houses juxtaposed, as in the group we reproduce by H. Louis Duhring (Fig. 107), we see what an admirable harmony the consistent and tasteful use of this material gives to an ensemble. When we realise that a large area of Chestnut Hill is covered with buildings of this type we see that the Philadelphia designers have solved one of the most important problems of American architecture. One can hardly give them too much credit for their work in this line. Given a thirty-thousand-dollar commission, they have expended on it the study that would normally go with a structure costing three times that amount. Best of all, this study is sensed rather than advertised. The result is a considerable number of buildings, of the utmost variety, yet telling as entirely homogeneous in the district, as fine as can be found in the modern architecture of America, and one is tempted to say of Europe as well. In this particular line the architecture of Philadelphia is unique.

This does not imply, however, that good, original domestic work is not being done elsewhere. We have seen the use of stucco and of native adobe in the South and Southwest. In the Rocky Mountain States most interesting work is being done, using local stone and bringing the buildings into harmony with the landscape in which they are placed. It is fair to say, however, that in the small suburban home, most carefully studied in a pleasing local material, Philadelphia has led the way.

There is yet another type of rural and suburban dwelling that is interesting and has attracted especial attention abroad. A review of it leads us anew to a consideration of the æsthetic ideas of Louis Sullivan and Frank Lloyd Wright. As we have seen, these men and their followers have stood for an architectural revolution. The philosophy of this group is, for the layman at least, somewhat obscure. It is a new movement and would probably be willing to admit itself still in an early evolutionary stage. In such a stage, however, it is doubly hard to define and its adherents would as probably resent the attempt to define it. One thing is certain: it stands for something new. It is the spokesman of "modernism" in the United States. Its practitioners have a horror of the use of archæological or, as they would put it, "stolen" forms. They feel that modern problems, modern materials, American conditions, demand a mod-

Photograph by P. B. Wallace.

FIG. 106.   CHESTNUT HILL, PA.   House.
Edmund B. Gilchrist, Architect.

Photograph by P. B. Wallace.

FIG. 105.   LAVEROCK, PA.   Newbold Farm.   Tower from Forecourt.
Mellor, Meigs & Howe, Architects.

FIG. 107. ST. MARTINS, PHILADELPHIA, PA. Group for Doctor George Woodward.
H. Louis-Duhring, Architect.

FIG. 108. SPRINGGREEN, WIS.
House of Frank Lloyd Wright, Architect.

ern and an American architecture, and that the designer who attempts to use classic or Gothic forms, or even the suggestions of these, is playing false to the art of architecture. At best, he can be but a clever plagiarist; at worst, his work is but meaningless muttering in a dead tongue.

The credo of the group is to meet modern conditions as they exist in an honest and a modern way. Its members do not quarrel with modern conditions, nor materials. They accept steel and concrete, or the lavish use of the machine in the production of ornament. The machine to them is a tool, like any other tool, but a modern one and therefore presumably a legitimate and an admirable one, which must be made to serve in the creation of a great modern architecture. The forms which it is made to create, however, must be "clean," and not mechanical repetitions of something that was done long ago for a different purpose. To evolve these forms, the honest designer must study nature and, at the same time, use his imagination. Given a clean form, virile pattern will creep in and the designer will attain a harmonious expression of the third dimension, the most important verity in architecture.

So much for the philosophy, as well as one can understand it. We, however, are interested primarily in its results. It has created an architecture undoubtedly new, certainly interesting, intriguing in its possibilities, and beautiful or no, according to the opinion of the observer. It is an architecture of large masses, of rectangularity, of generally horizontal emphasis. Its forms are kept as simple as possible, apparently to drive home upon the observer the character of the forms themselves. It is an architecture which of course scrupulously avoids any similarity with past styles and we venture to suggest may be hampered by a morbid fear of the dangers of being identified in any way with the art of the past. It is a style of undeniable virility, bought at the price, some will maintain, of brutality. It is a colourful style, though here again, many observers would consider the colour harsh. It makes a point of the original and functional use of materials, and keeps an eye to the colour possibilities of each material as used.

Later we shall have something to say of it, as applied to buildings on a monumental scale. At present we are concerned only with its expression in the rural and suburban dwelling. It can be very well illustrated here, however, as its greatest living protagonist, Frank Lloyd

Wright, has done a great deal of work in this field. As a younger member of the firm of the late Louis Sullivan, the design of a number of domestic works was placed upon him, while Mr. Sullivan was concerned primarily with buildings upon a larger scale. Though Mr. Wright has, of course, done many monumental buildings, it is only reasonable to expect his style to be revealed clearly in the domestic house.

For the first example, let us look again at Mrs. Coonley's House, at Riverside, Ill. (Fig. 71). It is entirely different from anything we have hitherto examined. Built up in great block-like forms, it tells as a series of masses, horizontals, and rectangular openings harmoniously and skilfully adjusted to the design. The eaves project widely, as in the Hispano-American work in the Southwest, and indeed the two styles have much in common, although they arrived at a certain affinity of expression along entirely different paths. The philosophy of the designer shows clearly in the work, and yet it looks anything but revolutionary.

The interior probably will not appeal as quickly. When we examine the little playhouse (Fig. 72) at Mrs. Coonley's, we shall be interested surely, but not so charmed. We feel the same conscientious adherence to the tenets of the style, but the result is harsh. The lighting is interesting, the relation of rectangles—vertical and horizontal—immediately felt, but the ruggedness of the brick, the angularity of the furniture, and the heavy projection of sharp-cornered masses of masonry, all have a tendency to repel. Many of us, at least, might like to look at a room of this sort, but dislike to live in it.

A really extreme example of the style is Mr. Wright's own house at Springgreen, Wis. (Fig. 108). Here he has designed with the most deliberate severity and used masonry cut and joined in the ruggedest possible way. As usual, the masses are kept low and the projections, especially of the roof, wide-flung. Not a curve is allowed to break the impression of angle and rectangle in the main mass. Force there certainly is in this design, grace not at all. Whether it be beautiful or ugly, we leave to the individual observer and to posterity. Interesting it certainly is.

The style is spreading rapidly. Its home is in Illinois and Wisconsin, where so many progressive ideas arise to plague us. Its adherents, however, are carrying it afield and, in some cases, sugaring it down in a way which probably ill pleases its founders and sincere protagonists. That it deserves watching, none will deny, and of all phases of modern American architecture, it has probably attracted the most attention abroad.

Returning to a more conservative type of design, although the purpose of our study is architecture and not landscape architecture, no discussion of the American architecture of to-day could be balanced without some mention of the formal estate and the combination of architecture and landscape architecture in an harmonious whole. Sometimes the architects have done their own landscape work. More often, an architect and a landscape architect have collaborated. The work runs from the most magniloquent and overpowering formal designs to the modest and seemingly unstudied arrangement of a simple garden. In such work, two distinct and in general opposing tendencies appear. One is the attempt to make something typically American, with direct reference to the character of American landscape. The other involves the study of classic examples and the attempt to reproduce similar designs in this country. As usual, however, these tendencies are by no means clearly marked. Oftentimes a classic prototype will be studied and then adapted to American conditions. At other times, the honest attempt to make a truly American garden design will unconsciously arrive at an expression very like that of an Old World one.

Here, again, we must not let theory run away with appreciation, but must approach the matter in a common-sense spirit. Nearly any one would agree that it is absurd to remove, let us say, an entirely formal Italian design from its setting and place it in an incongruous setting in a new country. Expressed in those terms, the absurdity is manifest, but often those terms do not honestly express the facts. Let us, for example, consider the setting of a formal Italian landscape composition. Unless one is familiar with the originals, one thinks of these as placed in a well-kept, trim landscape with the formality of the design only refining the general expression of the ancient country in which it occurs. The truth of the matter is that so famous an example as the Villa Lante at Bagnaia is placed in a rocky, uncultivated, almost forbidding landscape. Though the vegetation is different, the contours and lines of the landscape of central Italy are often surprisingly like those of northern New England. The Villa Lante is an artificial, cultivated oasis, its boundaries sharply defined and dividing it deliberately from the rugged landscape about. We hold no brief for the importation of Villa Lantes into New England. We may even sympathise with the theory that the best design is that which brings the house and garden into relation with the more distant landscape about it. We should be able to take the point of view of the designer, however, who, seeing the classic example and admiring it, tries to do something of the same sort in his own land. At any rate, we are wholly inconsistent if we admire the one thing in Italy and object to the same thing in America. The man who admires our formal Colonial and Early Republican architecture, with its derivation from Georgian England, from Inigo Jones, and thence back to purest Palladian work and, at the same time, objects to Italian villa architecture on the ground that it is Italian, fine at home, but unsuited to America, is blowing hot and cold with the same breath. If Palladio is fine and suited to America, surely Vignola is. In this, as in all things, we should not deal in universals but use our eyes, our taste, and our judgment in individual cases.

In general, American garden design falls into three classes, based respectively on the English, the French, and the Italian types. The English is least formal and best suited to residences of small scale, though it can, of course, be used with large. The French is best suited for the enormous and rigidly formal estates of those whose means permit an almost unlimited outlay. The Italian expression lies somewhere between the two, though nearer the French than the English. All, however, are subject to local modification and comparatively few are pure English, pure French, or pure Italian.

For the most informal type, we might select the house and garden of Mr. and Mrs. Louis E. Shipman, at Plainfield, N. H. (Fig. 109). Mrs. Shipman, a landscape architect of national reputation, has designed, for a modified but still rural wooden New Hampshire house, a garden that in its charm, seclusion, and informality, harmonises entirely with the dwelling. Whether one looks at the house from the garden, the service wing from the garden (Fig. 110), or the garden from the house, everything has the air of privacy and of almost haphazard informality which conceals the exquisite artistry that produced it. If we were forced to classify this according to the types we have outlined, we should call it English, but we should prefer to coin a name and call it "New English." It is the perfect expression of the New England country garden and only one, though an

Fig. 109. Plainfield, N. H. Breed Farm. *Ellen Shipman, Architect and Landscape Architect.*

Fig. 110. Plainfield, N. H. Breed Farm. *Ellen Shipman, Architect and Landscape Architect.*

FIG. 111. GLEN COVE, L. I. Estate of J. E. Aldred, Esq. Air View.
Bertram G. Goodhue, Architect; Olmsted Brothers, Landscape Architects.

FIG. 112. LOCUST VALLEY, L. I. Estate of Byrford Ryan, Esq. Air View.

127

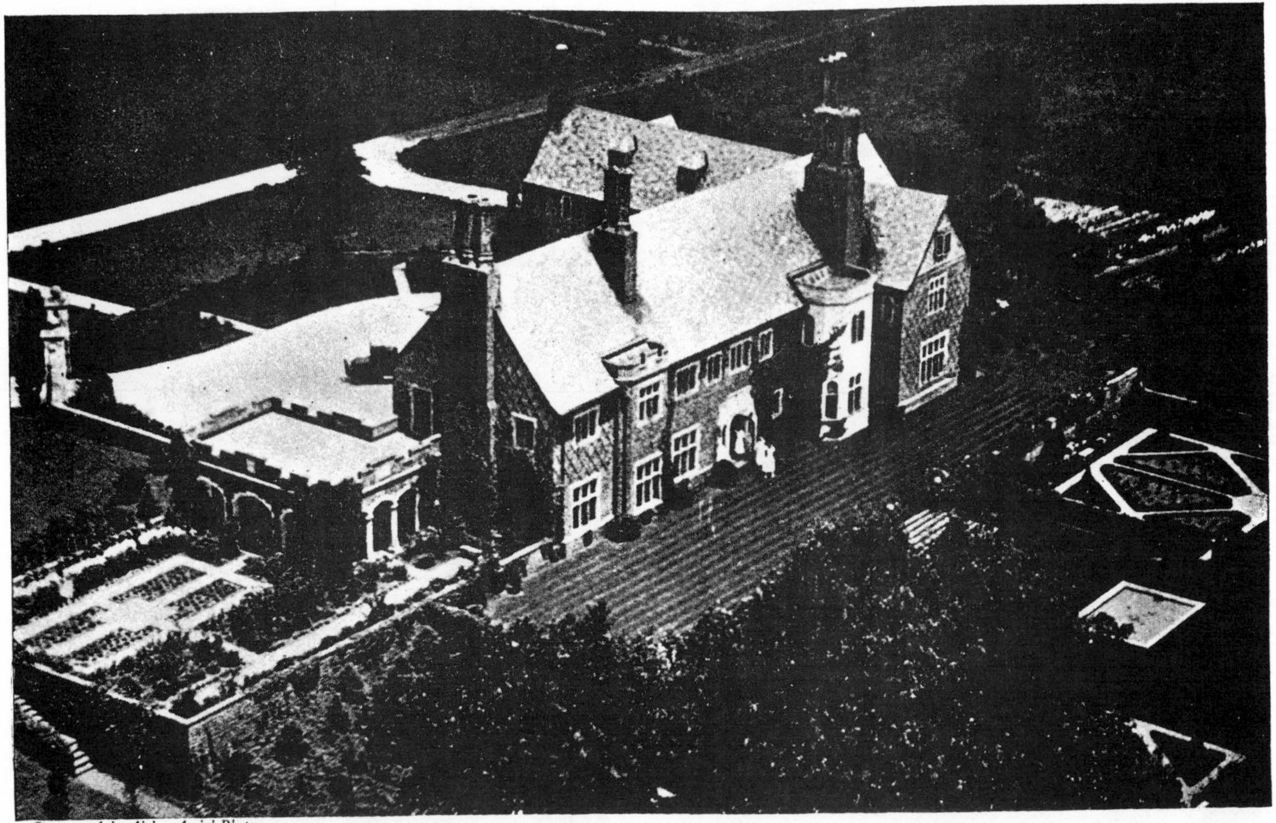

Courtesy of the Aiglon Aerial Photos.

FIG. 113. LAKEVILLE, N. Y. Estate of L. F. Sherman, Esq. Air View. *James W. O'Connor, Architect; Paul Smith, Landscape Architect.*

unusually brilliant, example of thousands that occur in New England and elsewhere in the United States. The principles here involved can be applied all over the country, in the South, in the West, in the Southwest, producing different effects according to the vegetation and climate, but retaining the same charm, simplicity, and honesty. Such work is truly American.

It can be, of necessity, applied only to the small, informal dwelling. The principles of English garden design can, however, be applied to most monumental works. Let us look, for example, at an aeroplane photograph of the estate of J. E. Aldred, Esq. (Fig. 111), the architecture by the late B. G. Goodhue, the landscape design by the Olmsted Brothers. Here the scale is large, but the general effect informal. Not that all is not carefully planned, but a careful asymmetry is preserved. In this the gardens reflect the plan of the house. They are shut off one from another, hemmed by heavy planting, and are arranged to give unexpected vistas and allow the rambler frequently to come upon unexpected cosey nooks.

Somewhere between the complete informality of Breed Farm and the large scale, but typically English, work of the Aldred estate, is the residence and garden of Mr. Byrford Ryan, at Locust Valley, L. I. (Fig. 112). This shows a modest but roomy country dwelling, with one symmetrical garden attached, quietly done and generally English in character, though truly more American than English. For the complete English plan, with all its asymmetry, privacy, and yet bigness of conception, we might look at the estate of L. F. Sherman, Esq., at Lakeville, L. I., the architecture being done by James W. O'Connor, the landscape work by Paul Smith (Fig. 113). Here there are walls, sunny and vine-grown, enclosing delightful flower-gardens. A broad lawn leads to steps and a terrace with a water-table. Right and left are more walled gardens, some concealed by hedges. Such a design fulfils the best English ideal in eliminating the sharp division between house and garden. One feels that the owner lives as much in the garden as in the house and has almost as much privacy there. The garden is not a mere setting for the house, to be enjoyed by the public and passers-by while the owner conceals himself within. The garden, like the house, is for the owner. The effect is happily undemocratic.

For the French type, at its most formal and monumental, we could find no finer example than the estate of E. T. Stotesbury, Esq., at Chestnut Hill (Figs. 114, 115). The architect was Horace Trumbauer, the landscape architect a Frenchman, Grèber. The mansion is in the style of Louis XV and the landscape design is in perfect harmony with it. From the lodge gates the main axis sweeps away, down a decline and up again, for a mile and more, past formal terrace, fountain, and lawn until it leads to the centre of the façade of the house. The view from a distance is stunning in its scale; from above one feels a sense of the severest order. As one nears the house, the spaciousness and sunniness of the open parterres seem even more accented, along with the perfectly appointed formality of every detail. Such a palatial scheme, and we are speaking now of a palace, not a dwelling nor even a mansion, is comparable to the greatest feats of landscape architecture in the Old World. Smaller in scale than Versailles, it is at least comfortably comparable to Vaux-le-Vicomte. It requires, of course, practically unlimited means to support. It may be challenged as un-American and archæological in its reliance on a pure French type. It is, however, one, and by no means the only one, of the many such great estates that have been constructed in America. Whether they are ephemeral need not concern us, though it is interesting to note that fewer are being designed than were done ten or twenty years ago. The responsibilities of such an establishment and especially the difficulty in America of recruiting the necessary army of competent servants to run it, make even the very wealthy hesitate to build on such a scale.

The photographic material which best illustrates such work brings up another interesting point in modern American architecture. We reproduce an aeroplane photograph of the estate of Walter E. Maynard, Esq., at Jericho, L. I. (Fig. 116). We seem almost to be looking at the architect's and landscape architect's final sketch for the work. All is laid out beneath our eyes in map-like form. We immediately grasp every axis, major and minor, every relation of part to part. It is a commonplace to say that the architect thinks in terms of a plan, the layman in terms of an elevation. In general, this is true. In a series of sketches, let us say for an architectural competition, a good architect will spend most of his time studying the plan to see if it be orderly and sensible. The layman will spend his time looking at the elevation to decide if it be pretty. The photograph

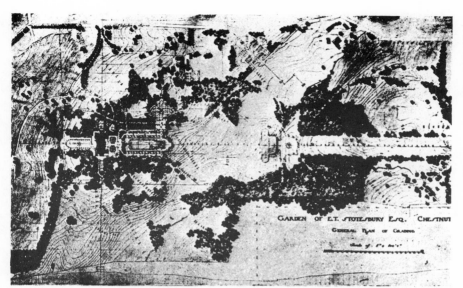

FIG. 114. CHESTNUT HILL, PA. Estate of E. T. Stotesbury, Esq. *Plan by J. Grèber.*

FIG. 115. CHESTNUT HILL, PA. Estate of E. T. Stotesbury, Esq.
Horace Trumbauer, Architect; J. Grèber, Landscape Architect.

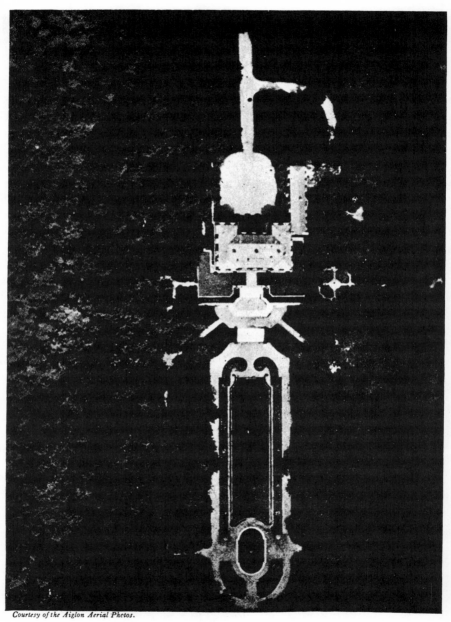

FIG. 116. JERICHO, L. I., N. Y. Estate of Walter E. Maynard, Esq. Air View.
J. Gréber, Landscape Architect.

from the air, however, forces the layman to see the plan. Without conscious effort, he takes the architect's point of view; indeed, he would have to make a conscious effort not to.

It is fascinating to toy with the possibilities of this idea. The architect's design should look well from the air. Otherwise it is ill-planned. The layman should be able to enjoy the view from above, otherwise the design is not reasonably legible. Even the architect, however, accustomed as he is to planning and the third dimension, probably was not wholly prepared for the impertinent peeping from above which the aeroplane allows. He probably did not design every detail of the roof, as seen from directly above, with the care which he would have devoted to the elevation and the surrounding garden. On the other hand, the aeroplane view is already usual and in a very short time will be a commonplace. Already the aeroplane has given the student of architecture his very best instrument for studying an architectural ensemble. Certainly before long traffic by air will be general. In other words, the alert architect must now begin to think of paying as much attention to the beauty of his design from *above* as from any side. This places something of an added burden upon him, but he gets as his reward a magnificent opportunity to reveal his plan in a completed work, a phase of his design which to date is always lost, partially at least, when the completed building is viewed by a layman.

How beautifully the aerial camera reveals an elaborate estate may be judged by a view of the estate of Otto Kahn, Esq., at Syosset, L. I. (Fig. 117), by Delano & Aldrich, with landscape architecture by Olmsted Brothers. Here, again, we are dealing with an absolutely formal French design. The architecture, reminiscent of the style of Jean Bullant, is echoed in the typically French setting of the garden. The camera reveals the design as though we saw the plan, yet by taking the photograph at an angle, upon approaching the estate, the eye grasps something of the beauty of the vista as well.

A photograph of another work by the same architects and landscape architects, the estate of Harry Payne Whitney, Esq., at Wheatley Hills, L. I. (Fig. 118), reveals the indiscretions of the aerial camera. The type here is Italian, rather than French. The garden from above, however, appears confused, despite its symmetrical layout. The horseshoe curves, concentrically repeated, are monotonous from above, and the rustic water-chain and fall seems crowded by planting. Still worse, the house, with

FIG. 117. SYOSSET, L. I. Estate of Otto Kahn, Esq. Air View.
Delano & Aldrich, Architects; Olmsted Brothers, Landscape Architects.

FIG. 118. WHEATLEY HILLS, L. I. Estate of Harry Payne Whitney, Esq. Air View.
Delano & Aldrich, Architects; Leavitt and Olmsted, Landscape Architects.

its delicate detail and wholly delightful *motif Palladio* as seen from the approach on the ground, from above appears as an ugly and haphazard roof. We are not blaming the architects. They were designing for men, not birds, but we merely note that the architect of to-day should, and the architect of to-morrow must, design for both.

Whether or not we approve of the Italian formal garden in America, like the French, we find many beautiful and successful examples of it. Oftentimes, too, the American garden is inspired by the Italian prototype rather than seeking to imitate it. If we look, for example, at the formal garden done by Charles A. Platt, at Maxwell Court (Fig. 119), we cannot but be delighted by its beauty and we should be captious indeed if we criticised it as archæological or in any way out of place in America. The same is true of another characteristic "Italian Garden" done for the estate of Mr. Walker, at Great Barrington, Mass. (Fig. 120), by Feruccio Vitale. Such order, such colour, such a play of light and shadow would be gracious and grateful in any land or period.

A rather special type of formal estate has been evolved by the conditions of Florida and California. As we have seen, the prevailing architectural styles in these districts has properly been Spanish. Both the climate and the inspiration of a florid style have inspired designers to work along baroque lines, until designs have been created that, on account of exuberance, would be condemned as vulgar in any other clime, yet which in their setting seem reasonable and apt. As a single instance, we may look at some of the views of Vizcaya, done by Chalfin and Hoffman for the late Mr. Deering, of Chicago. Here the architects, supplied with lavish means, have taken full advantage of a picturesque shore and a hot Southern sun (Fig. 121). Working in a combination of Spanish and Italian baroque, thinking in terms of such a monument as the Villa at Isola Bella in Lake Como, they have created a fairy-land of free fancy and a monumental design. The house, or Villa Palace—for it is no less—shows considerable restraint of ornament, while it towers up in a monumental way. In the garden and the lagoons, however, fancy has been given free rein. We see a baroque water-chain (Fig. 122), not unlike that of the Villa Lante at Bagnaia, but doubled, which carries water in a series of pools and plashes from one level to another. The lagoon, almost hemmed in by piers, is picturesque with statuary, bridges, rough masonry, and mooring-piles in

FIG. 119. ROCKVILLE, CONN. Maxwell Court. *Charles A. Platt, Architect.*

FIG. 120. GREAT BARRINGTON, MASS. Estate of Mr. Walker. *Ferruccio Vitale, Landscape Architect.*

Fig. 121. Miami, Fla. "Vizcaya," Villa of the late James Deering. East Façade.
F. Burrall Hoffman and Paul Chalfin, Architects.

Fig. 122. Miami, Fla. "Vizcaya," Villa of the late James Deering. South Cascade and Obelisk.
F. Burrall Hoffman and Paul Chalfin, Architects.

137

the Venetian manner. An island is transformed into a baroque ship (Figs. 123, 124), with squirming dolphins, winged genie, and beasts' heads sprawling in picturesque abandon. On its prow it bears a latticed tea-house. A gesture more florid, a design more theatrical, could hardly be imagined, and there have not lacked tongues to attack it on the ground of ostentatious vulgarity. Each has a right to his own opinion, and one can see the reasons for criticism here. On the other hand, let him who criti-cised Vizcaya be very careful to extend his attacks to the Villa d'Este at Tivoli. That famous work, with its hundred fountains, its water-tables, its water-organ blaring one continuous chord, its miniature city of Rome, its balustrade with water running along the surface that guests might dabble their hands as they descended the stairs, even its concealed jets which played their streams up under the skirts of lady guests, when a waggish host set the mechanism and they stepped on a certain flag, was a nightmare of crass vulgarity compared to anything which modern Amer-ica has produced. If we condemn one, we must condemn the other. On the other hand, if we admire the Italian parent, we should not withhold admiration for its more refined child in Florida.

In all this discussion, we have been dealing with country or suburban houses, or, at least, with those that had enough ground around them to make them in some fair measure independent of their neighbours. Even in such a case, however, it is better to have some unity of design and ma-terial in architecture of a given district. We have seen how the architects of Chestnut Hill have attained a most praiseworthy unity in their design, so that each house is not only a thing of beauty in itself, but assists in the appreciation of the beauty of its neighbours. Note, too, that this has been attained by a number of men, working independently, and uncoerced by any zoning restriction or ukase from a single authority to force them to do as they did.

If such an eye to the ensemble is desirable in the isolated suburban houses, how much more desirable should it be in city houses juxtaposed so that façade touches façade and we see only the fronts of the dwellings. This is the case whenever land values are exaggeratedly high and certain restricted areas have an exaggerated social desirability. The phenomenon can be observed in any large city, but for examples in a brief review we may confine ourselves to the city of New York, where more of this type of building is found than in any other city of the Union.

Photograph by Mattie E. Hewitt.

FIG. 123. MIAMI, FLA. "Vizcaya," Villa of the late James Deering. The Island.
F. Burrall Hoffman and Paul Chalfin, Architects.

Photograph by Mattie E. Hewitt.

FIG. 124. MIAMI, FLA. "Vizcaya," Villa of the late James Deering. Boat-House and Island Tea-House.
Figure Sculpture by A. Stirling Calder; F. Burrall Hoffman and Paul Chalfin, Architects.

Two tendencies immediately reveal themselves; a vast improvement in the design of the houses as individuals, and a positive retrogression as far as attention to the ensemble is concerned. Many of the houses are palatial. Indeed, the majority of the houses of upper Fifth Avenue are, properly speaking, *palazzi*. Had they been done in the Renaissance, they would have been so called, and many are far more elaborate, larger in scale, and more costly than the Palazzo Riccardi or the Palazzo Rucellai. Only the lingering democratic terminology of America continues to call them houses.

Be it noted at the outset that the owners of these houses are generally people not only of wealth but of taste and refinement. Magnificence they may desire, but never vulgarity or the extremes of ostentation. They employ the best talent, and all possible care and taste is used in the design of the structure. Radicalism, however, is repellent to them, so that the designs are conservative and often archæological. As individuals, the buildings, or their fronts—for we see nothing else—are often of exquisite beauty. Thanks to the rapid growth of cities and the changing fashions in sites, such buildings are apt to be ephemeral, and when one sees, as at the moment of writing, a house like R. M. Hunt's residence for Mr. Vanderbilt, on Fifth Avenue, being torn down to make way for a commercial building, one's heart is apt to bleed at the demolishment of exquisite mouldings, refined and beautiful carving, and the destruction of the child of an exquisite brain and hand. The beauty of the individual is undeniable.

The ensemble of a single block of houses, however, is apt to be atrocious. In the old New York of the author's childhood we were afflicted with the brown-stone front. Block after block of houses, built of that least happy and most friable of materials—brown sandstone—assaulted the eye with its cheerless monotony. Nevertheless, there was real unity and dignity in the ensemble. Then taste changed. Persons of a cheerier and more optimistic temperament began to modify their houses or rebuild, using the more convenient basement entrance and for materials brick or Bedford stone, or a combination of the two. Such houses appeared as slices of meat in the brown bread of the older type. They became popular and multiplied, but the daring which caused the first break encouraged individualism. Each built for himself what pleased him best, with no desire for harmony with his neighbours. This tendency has increased almost without a break till to-day, and the result is chaos.

When the building is large enough to cover the narrow end of a city block the disaster is largely avoided. Sometimes one architect has been employed to do a number of houses with reference one to another, and here again unity is preserved. A conspicuous example of this is the Villard group (Fig. 125), on Madison Avenue and 50th to 51st Streets, built many years ago by McKim, Mead & White. For an example of the self-sufficient single type, large enough in scale to avoid the chief difficulty, we might cite the palatial, yet exquisitely refined, building on upper Fifth Avenue, done by Thomas Hastings for the late Henry Clay Frick, Esq. Even here, however, without blaming artist or client, one deplores the lack of relation between this fine work and the houses on either side of the narrow streets which bound it.

It is when we come to the important and costly house which still does not occupy the whole of the narrow side of a city block that the defect becomes glaring. We reproduce a view of the beautiful residence, done by Delano & Aldrich, for Harold I. Pratt, Esq. (Fig. 126), on Park Avenue and 68th Street. Chaste in detail, pleasant in proportion, magnificent yet unostentatious, it is a delight in itself, but one cannot look at it without being conscious of the buildings at right and left. Concerning these, we have nothing to criticise but their lack of relation one to another and to the Pratt house. At the immediate right is a gap which quite probably will be filled by a well-designed structure which will have nothing in common with its large neighbour, nor with its small.

Let us look at a kodak snap-shot taken of Fifth Avenue opposite the Metropolitan Museum (Fig. 127). The eye immediately notes several beautifully and restrainedly designed buildings, juxtaposed and reflecting the styles of Louis XVI, Louis XIII, François I, and the flamboyant Gothic of the end of the Middle Ages. At least, the sources are French, but this is hardly enough to give unity. As far as an harmonious ensemble is concerned, and despite the tremendous amount of wealth, taste, and skill involved, we might as well be in a mining-camp.

It is pleasant to observe that people, lay and professional, are beginning to awaken to these absurdities. They are the more difficult to correct, since to do so involves a restraint on the personal liberty of client and architect—a thing becoming abhorrent to Americans. Legislation would be impossible and probably undesirable, as well. Anything that is done

FIG. 125. NEW YORK, N. Y. Villard Houses. *McKim, Mead & White, Architects.*

Photograph by Tebbs Architectural Photo Co.

FIG. 126. NEW YORK, N. Y. Residence of H. I. Pratt, Esq. *Delano & Aldrich, Architects.*

FIG. 127. NEW YORK, N. Y. Upper Fifth Avenue.

FIG. 128. NEW YORK, N. Y. Houses on Park Avenue.

143

must be done by agreement and common consent, each owner being brought to realise that his own house would be finer if it had some relation to its surroundings.   What New York needs is a magnate like Ralph Allen, of Bath, and an architect like John Wood to educate, bully, and wheedle its citizens into some conception of the idea of architectural harmony.

That this result is sometimes attained on a modest scale can easily be proved.   We reproduce a photograph of a block of buildings on upper Park Avenue between 67th and 68th Streets, by McKim, Mead & White, Delano & Aldrich, and Trowbridge & Livingston (Fig. 128), where the architects have sought and reached an architectural harmony.   Though the buildings differ one from another, the group is brought into some sort of unity by means of a uniform material, brick with a limestone trim, a uniform cornice line and belt course for the third story.   Only the third house, with its break in the cornice and belt course, jars the harmony of the ensemble.

It seems ungracious to dwell on one questionable point, however, when so much fine work is being done.   To analyse would require a separate book.   We have the fine "period" house, such as we have just noted on Fifth Avenue.   We have friendly and pleasant adaptations of brick Georgian, such as the house we reproduce, by John Cross, on upper Park Avenue at 64th Street (Fig. 129), a most interesting adaptation of the American Colonial to a long, thin site, all of which for reasons of economy had to be covered and which might well have been the despair of the architect. We have houses of a true originality, such as the exquisite study in textures which we reproduce and which was done by Frederick Sterner for Maurice Brill, Esq. (Fig. 130).   We have the transformation of old buildings in Greenwich Village into sober designs, reflecting the architectural history of old New York, and here again oftentimes we have studies in unity. Indeed, it gives an unfair *réclame* to mention any specific examples, so many good ones are being done.   We can congratulate ourselves heartily on the improvement in city house design, while we forecast and have faith in a movement towards greater unity.

Although we are reserving until later our discussion, under commercial buildings, of hotels, the problem of the apartment-house is so closely related to that of the home that it is best to say a word about it here.   One of the most striking phenomena of the American architecture of to-day is

FIG. 129.   NEW YORK, N. Y.   House on Park Avenue.   *John Cross, Architect.*

FIG. 130.   NEW YORK, N. Y.   Residence of Maurice Brill, Esq.   *Frederick J. Sterner, Architect.*

the extraordinary growth of the apartment-house and, if we may use the term, the apartment-house idea. A generation or two ago the idea of the apartment was generally rather abhorrent. It had a faint association with the tenement. A few families lived in genteel apartments, but generally they were regarded as the homes of bachelors or of the more flighty and impermanent families. A solid citizen demanded a home, which he spelled with a capital "H" and which he always associated with a separate house of his own.

Nowadays, however, this prejudice against the apartment has almost entirely disappeared. Its conveniences have overcome its ancient associations of a lack of privacy and a too marked gregariousness. The servant problem has largely been responsible for the change. The apartment can be run with far fewer servants and offers so many labour-saving devices to these that they submit more readily, or rather less unwillingly, to the service which an American seems always to regard as a degradation. Moreover, the responsibilities of heat and light are thrown upon the superintendent. If there is a coal strike, the lord of the apartment does not have to rush upon a mad search for coal or its substitutes. He has nothing to do but grumble at the superintendent if there is not heat enough. He is relieved, too, of all the problems of caretaking. In the summer, he turns his key on his apartment, confident that it will be well looked after during his absence and be in good condition on his return. For these and many other reasons, he has come to reconcile himself to living in a warren and to making the first stage of his eventual transportation to the cemetery a trip in the high-speed elevator of a modern skyscraper. With the propriety and taste of this point of view we have no concern. Personally, the writer finds it deplorable, but he realises that he is old-fashioned and has no intention of bidding the tide turn back. For good or ill, apartment-house life is growing apace and may very well supersede in a short time the life of the single home.

To understand the phenomenon, we must rid ourselves for all time of the idea that the dweller in an apartment lives there because it is cheap. He lives there because it is convenient and often pays more for the apartment than he would pay for a house with double the cubage of actual space in as good a locality. This being the case, the apartment is in a position to invade the district that ordinarily would be reserved for the private house and this is precisely what it has done. No matter how exclusive the neighbourhood, nor how costly the homes it contains, unless there is a zoning law to prevent, a house-owner has no earnest that his home will not be overshadowed at any time by a fifteen or twenty story apartment-house. We reproduce a snap-shot taken on upper Fifth Avenue (Fig. 131). There is no site in New York, save Riverside Drive, finer in natural advantages than this, nor one that bade more fairly to develop into an exclusively residential district. Many beautiful and *de luxe* houses were built there, but now there is an apartment for every few houses. Our photograph shows three great apartments and the skeleton of another in the building. The apartments are as carefully designed and as beautifully made as the houses. Generally they are conservative in expression, retaining the classic point of view, with plain walls rhythmically broken by windows, a band projection and balustrade which takes the place of the obsolete cornice at the top, and no hint of the steel construction beyond the obvious fact that buildings of this scale and form could be built in no other way. They are intruders in the residential district, but self-respecting ones, and they assume that they will be taken as the social and artistic equals of the private residences which they supersede.

The scale of some of these buildings is literally enormous. We reproduce a view of the apartment at 277 Park Avenue, by McKim, Mead & White (Fig. 132). It seems not so much a building as a town. Indeed, it is a town. Many walled towns in France and Italy, which call themselves such, have fewer inhabitants than 277 Park Avenue. The interior court, secluded as it is vast, with its driveways which are real city streets and its gardens, suggests again a unified city design. It is a most impressive building, yet nothing in the development of modern American architecture causes us to doubt that in a generation it will look like a very modest work.

Though the old-fashioned will deplore the development of the apartment-house, they had better reconcile themselves to it. Some of its conveniences we have already sketched, and others may be divined. It has many advantages over the ordinary house. Air becomes purer as we go up, breezes blow more steadily in warm weather, dust is less, and the noises of the street recede to a soothing mumble. Exquisite views are often afforded, and, now that the New York Zoning Law is in operation,

Fig. 131. New York, N. Y. Upper Fifth Avenue.

Fig. 132. New York, N. Y. 277 Park Avenue.
McKim, Mead & White, Architects.

these views, though becoming more restricted as buildings multiply, will probably never become dull. In short, the cliff-dwellers have much to say in favour of their mode of living. For us it is enough to understand their point of view.

One interesting effect of the new development is a tendency for the modern apartment-house dweller actually to own and have clear legal title to his apartment. Apartments are now bought and sold like houses. Often they are co-operatively built, a number of citizens combining to form a corporation, employ an architect, and build an apartment to suit themselves. This means considerable freedom in the design of the apartments and the possibility of the owner's expressing, to some slight degree, his personality in his own. Often these are of the duplex variety, when an owner purchases two floors and has a dwelling of two stories, reverting in some degree to the point of view of the house, with different general functions for different stories. There is nothing but expense to prevent an individual from purchasing as many floors or portions of them as he chooses, and making his own design within them, provided, of course, that his plans are formulated and accepted before or during the erection of the building.

It must be confessed that to date apartment-house owners have by no means taken advantage of the freedom offered to the owner as the apartment-house goes up. One would have expected rooms of two stories arranged, say with a library and gallery, and the generous proportions and lofty ceilings that are possible in a private house. Such are rare, however. The rooms of apartments are still generally low as compared to their length and, despite the exquisiteness of furniture and finish, proclaim their apartmental origin. Nothing stands in the way, however, of attaining much the same proportions and effects in an apartment as are obtainable in an ordinary dwelling and, when the apartment idea is a little older, this may very well come and remove some of the most unpleasant connotations of apartment-house life.

Thus far, we have dwelt rather snobbishly with the dwellings of the well-to-do. The same comfort which they demand as a right is also in generous part the portion of people of humbler means. This suggests another type of dwelling most interesting and most characteristic of a tendency in modern American architecture: the community settlement. Such settlements are not entirely modern; they have appeared occasionally since the industrial revolution became an accomplished fact. In modern times, however, they have become more numerous, far better planned and more complete in detail. Sometimes these have been the result of a philanthropist's ideal, as at Mariemont, in Ohio, where a public-spirited and wealthy woman supplied the necessary capital for a complete community unit. The purpose here was purely philanthropic, but it has been found frequently that such communities can be financed and run at a profit, the increment in land values far overbalancing the cost of the project. A number of such community settlements have been created by the government in war time, or by great corporations which felt the necessity of comfortable and sanitary housing for large bodies of workmen employed on some specific and reasonably permanent task. The designers employed on such work naturally tried to make the buildings and the ensemble attractive as well as comfortable and sanitary. In justice to the clients, we must add that they also bore this in mind. They realised both the ethical satisfaction and the commercial value of a contented community, comfortably and pleasantly housed. It is hard to say whether such projects are philanthropic or commercial. They are both, and teach a valuable lesson that the two are not only compatible but mutually encouraging.

Such projects offer an ideal opportunity to the architect and city-planner, for the sites are usually undeveloped and unencumbered with buildings which confuse the problem. As a typical example, we might select the settlement known as Atlantic Heights, built for the Atlantic Corporation on the Piscataqua River, above Portsmouth, N. H., by Kilham & Hopkins. The site was some sixty acres of ledgy, undulating ground, unprepossessing at first glance, but fraught with possibilities to an artist or firm with æsthetic imagination and practical common sense. The plan (Fig. 133) shows a compact village, designed to meet the complete needs of a community. Buildings of every function are arranged to suit the maximum convenience of the dwellers. Communications are carefully studied, and houses are arranged and designed with an eye to convenience, economy, and beauty withal. If we look at the architect's sketch of some of the houses on the Raleigh Way (Fig. 134), we are struck not only by their homey comfort, their practicability and economy of material and construction, but by their picturesqueness and real beauty

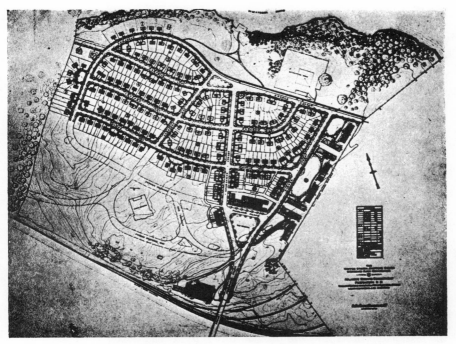

FIG. 133.   ATLANTIC HEIGHTS, Portsmouth, N. H.   A War Emergency Industrial Village.
Kilham & Hopkins, Architects.

FIG. 134.   ATLANTIC HEIGHTS, Portsmouth, N. H.   Industrial Village.   Raleigh Way.
Kilham & Hopkins, Architects.

151

as well.   Contrasting such a settlement with the squalid and hideously ugly surroundings in which our labouring classes often have to dwell, one can gauge the tremendous advance that modern American architecture has made in this particular field.   The cynic often observes that the labouring man cares little for sanitation and nothing for beauty, and will cite the bathtubs filled with coal in some tenements in which a civic spirit has attempted to better the condition of the working classes.   The observation is superficial.   Accustom the labourer to the blessings of decent living conditions and he will not readily revert to squalor.   Correspondingly, accustom him to beauty and he soon develops not only a pleasure, but a pride in it.   The æsthetic sense is a universal one, manifest in the scrawniest geranium placed in a tomato-can on the window-sill.   All that the sense needs is stimulation and guidance to become one of our great national assets.   We should remember what history teaches us, that no great artistic period ever occurred in which the masses did not share.   The creative artists and the educated elect must always lead, but they will struggle in darkness if their efforts are not at least partially understood and enjoyed by the majority of the population.   Impatience with the professional "uplifter" should not blind us to the fact.

Instances could be multiplied to a surprising extent.   We reproduce, for example, the interesting plan of Hilton Village, in Newport News, Va. (Fig. 135), done for the Newport News Shipbuilding and Dry Dock Corporation.   Here, Henry V. Hubbard, as landscape architect; Francis Y. Joannes, as architect; and Francis H. Bulot, as sanitary engineer, collaborated to create a self-sufficient, coherent, and agreeable community.   When we look at the School Group, or the group of shops and theatres (Fig. 136), we see how well convenience, utility, and beauty are combined.   A similar scheme was put through in Lake Forest, Ill., by Howard Shaw.   Although the majority of these communities have appeared along the Atlantic seaboard, the problem is being attacked in many parts of the country and the numbers of such communities is steadily on the increase.   At the same time the scale increases.   Electus D. Litchfield's scheme for Yorkship Village, Camden, N. J., involves the planning of a town nearly a mile long by half a mile wide.   The architects are fully alive to the dangers of mechanical feeling and "stock" design, and are honestly striving for charm as well as economy and effi-

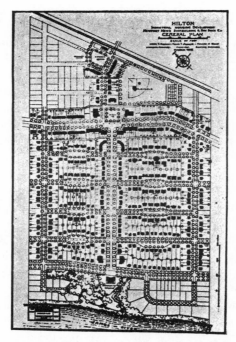

Fig. 135. Hilton Village, Va. Industrial Village. *Francis Y. Joannes, Architect;
Henry V. Hubbard, Landscape Architect.*

Fig. 136. Hilton Village, Va. Industrial Village. *Francis Y. Joannes, Architect;
Henry V. Hubbard, Landscape Architect.*

ciency. The result is one of the most interesting phenomena of modern American architecture.

In discussing domestic architecture, it is hard to know where to draw the line. Great apartment-houses come under the heading, yet they are commercial buildings as well. Similarly, clubs might be so classified, though they offer very special problems. The great country clubs might well have been discussed in connection with the formal country estate. Generally they conform to the architectural character of the district and are laid out with greater lavishness, though less formality, than even the most opulent private estates. In Florida there are many examples, usually conforming architecturally to the prevailing Spanish type. As a foil to these, we might glance at such a work, so modest as to conceal its real luxury, as the late Guy Lowell designed for Piping Rock, L. I. (Fig. 137). Using wood, and detail and composition which conforms to the Dutch traditions of Long Island, the architect produced a work that in its appointments fulfils all the requirements of the luxurious country club, yet in appearance looks as though it might have existed on the spot for two centuries.

In like manner, the city clubs have produced buildings which are great works of art and, at the same time, embody every aspect of up-to-date convenience and luxury. Such a building as the University Club in New York, by McKim, Mead & White, produces a special architectural problem of its own. The designer has to allow for dining-rooms, grill-rooms, squash-courts, a library, a great lounge, a swimming-pool, the bedroom facilities of an up-to-date hotel, as well as all the kitchens and other services which accompany one. All this he must attain, with a constant eye for beauty as well. His clients will be among the most cultivated and exacting, quick to criticise an ugly or an ill-planned feature, proud of the æsthetic success of the ensemble or of any given room.

Before we leave the subject of domestic architecture, however, there is one phase of it so obvious that it might well be overlooked if we do not emphasise it: the extraordinary regard for the comfort of the inmate, rich or poor, which modern American architecture is showing. This is a tendency of all modern architecture, but especially so of American, since the standard of living in this country is so high and means are so abundant. When we compare modern architecture with that of the past, this

FIG. 137. LOCUST VALLEY, N. Y. Piping Rock Country Club. *Guy Lowell, Architect.*

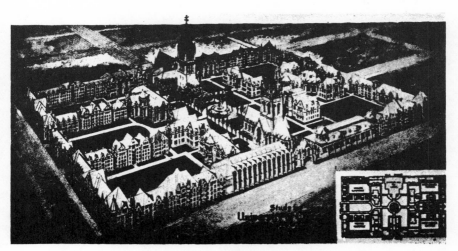

FIG. 138. CHICAGO, ILL. University of Chicago. *Henry Ives Cobb, Architect.*

is one of the things that strikes us most forcibly.   Indeed, the comforts which surround even an humble American house-owner of to-day make the private life of Le Roi Soleil seem like that of a savage.   Bent as he may be upon beauty of elevation, the architect spends by far the majority of his time on the plan.   Even a modest house must have its carefully functionalised rooms.   Bathrooms, with hot and cold running water, must be aplenty, and the guest must not be asked to share his with the host.   Electric lighting is assumed even in the tenement.   Heating-plants of hot air, steam, or water must keep the house comfortable in the iciest weather and, as the weather-strips exclude the intrusion of cold drafts, provision must be made for the circulation of air and the expulsion of vitiated atmosphere.   The odour of cooking—a genial welcome to the guest of Colonial times—must not offend the nostrils of the modern until the moment that his food is placed under his nose.   Lest the heating-plant be too efficient and overheat the house, electric thermostats control the temperature and close the dampers, disconnect the electricity, or check the flow of oil when the mercury rises to a given point.   Mechanical devices for washing, drying, carpet-cleaning, and a dozen other occupations lighten the burden of the servant, or of the housewife, if the menage be of an humble sort.   The age of machinery has invaded the home.   Though we grumble at the loss of picturesqueness and sigh for the charm of the "good old days," we can console ourselves with the thought that the commonplace American of to-day is living a life of luxury which would have made the magnate of a few generations ago gasp with amazement. What the future will be, with the further developments of electric power, the radio, and a thousand other inventions that are crowding us apace, we leave, as usual, to the seer.   However we are tempted to arraign it, it will certainly be interesting.

Distinctly related to the category of domestic architecture is what we may call academic, or institutional, architecture.   This includes particularly collegiate building and the collegiate ensemble.   Bearing in mind the large percentage of Americans who go to college, the impressionability of youth, and the enormous influence which the American college has upon the taste and thought of the class from which leaders are most commonly drawn, it is hard to overestimate the importance of this category of architecture.

The special problems which it involves are manifold. The first is that of function. Most American colleges are housed in more than one building. Many include a hundred, or more. These buildings have many functions. One is a library. Another is a laboratory for physical science. Another is an astronomical laboratory. There are buildings for administration, for classroom instruction, for worship, for student board, and for a score of other purposes, and of course there are the many dormitories bulking large in the scheme. In the larger institutions there are graduate schools of law, medicine, divinity, architecture, engineering, business administration, and the like. Sometimes a single building will house one of these schools; more often several are required. The Harvard Graduate School of Business Administration, just erected, is an independent collegiate unit, larger than the whole university was fifty years ago. The natural and desirable tendency is to group these buildings according to function, or academic relation. The buildings for the physical sciences should be together. The school of architecture should be close to the museum of fine arts. For social reasons, the dormitories should be kept together, and the college recitation buildings should be near them. The administration building and, above all, the library should be centrally located; the largest lecture hall and the theatre should be where they are easily accessible, both to the students and to the public, which will often come to them from afar. Room must be found, not too far away, for the athletic-field, and if the university be a large one, a stadium seating thousands has come to be regarded as a necessity. In this case, communications and traffic conditions must be studied carefully. Any one who has attended a great football game, like the Harvard-Yale, or Yale-Princeton games, or one of the major games in the Middle West or on the Pacific coast, will realise the difficulty not only in assembling and dismissing a crowd of fifty to a hundred thousand in the stadium itself, but of arranging traffic so that these immense crowds can be brought to and sent away from the field. Indeed, the whole problem of the athletic quarters, with stadium, baseball diamond, cage, locker building, courts, track, etc., is a special one. These are a few of the problems which confront the designer of an academic group. So complicated are the considerations involved, that the laymen can hardly list them, let alone grasp their real significance. The architect intrusted with the design of a collegiate group is faced with one of the gravest responsibilities and glowing opportunities which the profession affords. The same may be said of the architect responsible for the expansion of a university already in existence.

The latter involves, if anything, more serious problems. Sometimes a great university may become so cramped that it has to move bodily to a new site, as in the case of Columbia or, more recently, the University of Rochester. More often, however, a university has to remain on its old site and provide there for its expansion. It would be absurd, for example, to think of moving Harvard University. The invested capital in the present plant would make a move impossible, even if there were not a thousand sentimental reasons which would prevent it. As a result, it must take care of its expansion in its present site, despite the fact that it is in the centre of a large city, with land values steadily rising and apartments and business buildings crowding it on every side. It must provide for new buildings, remodel old ones, and replace others, all with an eye both to efficiency and beauty, and with the minimum sacrifice of any which have those sentimental or historic associations so dear to any university. The problem as it exists at Harvard is acute, but it exists in a hundred other American institutions.

A further difficulty is presented by old buildings: the difficulty of style. When a great institution like Columbia, or the Massachusetts Institute of Technology, moves to a new site, it can determine arbitrarily the style of the new buildings. A growing university on an old site cannot disregard the older buildings. Too often these are the worst aberrations of the mid-Victorian period. Some institutions are venerable enough to run back beyond this work, and have Colonial buildings on the site with which the new buildings can be made to harmonise. If this is not the case, however, no architect for the sake of unity will try to bring his new work into a close harmony with the architectural atrocities of the seventies and eighties. Some sort of a compromise must be arranged and its success will depend upon the skill and imagination of the architect.

At the outset, we must note that the tendency of academic architecture is conservative. In America, far more than in Continental Europe, the university atmosphere tends to be conservative. Paradoxically, a new country tends to place an exaggerated value on the historic traditions which it possesses, and this is a marked feature in university life. A well-known epigram at Harvard states that one can establish a "tradition" there in four years—a college generation—and this is hardly an exaggeration. Ask any Harvard or Yale man how long the official colours of Harvard have been crimson and Yale blue and he will almost surely reply "always," despite the fact that the writer has recently talked with a member of the Harvard crew which, by wearing red bandannas on the day of the Yale race, started the "official" use of crimson as a Harvard colour. We shall find, therefore, only rare instances of radicalism in collegiate architecture.

Generally American universities have been and are being built in one of two styles: Georgian Colonial, or Gothic. Both represent the conservative tendency. The one asserts our connection with the Colonial past and revives a style which, in spite of its English and eventually Italian origin, we have come to consider nationally American. The other is inspired by American respect and admiration for the English universities of Oxford and Cambridge, so rich in examples of academic Gothic. From the enormous mass of material which confronts us we must select a few examples which will exhibit the problems and their solutions in both styles.

Gothic has never died in the United States since the romantic revival, but it fell somewhat into disfavour in the nineties, after the Chicago Exposition, when America reverted to classicism as her national style and Gothic survived chiefly in churches. Its unpopularity was on the whole justified by the stupidity of many of the monuments done in the style during the Victorian period. Nevertheless, an occasional house was built in the style, most Americans continued their belief that one can worship God properly only in a Gothic building and, for the cloistered atmosphere of the university, Gothic was considered eminently apt. An ultimatum of this came in 1891 when, thanks largely to the munificence of John D. Rockefeller, Esq., work was begun on the new buildings for the University of Chicago. Henry Ives Cobb was the architect, and he worked out a consistent Gothic scheme, with the maximum of unity both in plan and elevation (Fig. 138). On the main axis were the university library and the chapel; one the building which is most important in any university, the other that which many people think ought to be. Right and left were four great quadrangles, surrounded with buildings. Two were for undergraduates, one was for women, and one for graduate students. In this case, the architect was practically unhampered by old buildings or difficulties of site. He could plan from a clear start and his Gothic design was the parent of many in American colleges. Though his buildings look a little old-fashioned now and cannot compare, either in beauty or an understanding of Gothic, with the modern work, for example, at Princeton or Yale, his scheme was a profound one and he deserves the great reputation which his design won him.

As an example of the other type of building, in which a Georgian style is followed and in which many older buildings of heterogeneous style had to be considered, we could find none better than Harvard. Harvard rejoices in the possession of some beautiful structures and some of the ugliest in the United States. Her buildings run in date all the way from 1720 to 1927. As a general thing, the eighteenth-century buildings are nicely proportioned and quaint, constructed in a warm brick, with a pleasant texture. Her early nineteenth-century buildings are in the dignified classic style which Bulfinch, a graduate of the university, and the designer of at least one of its buildings, had helped to evolve. Then, soon after the Civil War, came a wave of pseudo-Gothic; responsible for some fine things with many faults, like Memorial Hall, and some things which were wholly ugly, like Weld. Fortunately, the Victorian Gothic was built in brick, except the library, which was a poor imitation in granite of King's Chapel, Cambridge, and which has been destroyed in order to make way for a much larger building on the site. There was at least, therefore, harmony of material. The modern buildings, with few exceptions, have happily followed the Georgian tradition.

If we look at a map of the Harvard Yard (Fig. 139), however, we see what a nightmare confronts the future planner of Harvard. Our admirable forebears had little idea of planning an architectural ensemble. As they acquired means, they added buildings, putting each where they happened to find room for it. There is not a building really on axis with anything else. Almost no coherent arrangement can be found for new buildings, or for the modification of old. To make matters worse, a peaceful village has turned into a bustling city and the Yard itself, the heart of the university, has been hemmed about by business blocks and roaring traffic. The problem becomes one of cloistering the Yard from the noisy streets and at the same time connecting it with the groups of new buildings which are built outside of it. Several sites have been developed for several functions. The freshman dormitories have been built on the left bank of the Charles. On the right are the playing-fields, and recently a large lot has been taken for the Graduate School of Business Administration. This must be connected with the left river-bank by a bridge, both for handier communication and for architectural unity. Northeast of the Yard the lots are devoted to the laboratories of the physical sciences and northwest are the buildings of the Law School.

The problem is to bring all these into harmony and to plan for future expansion and new needs. This, too, should involve the minimum of destruction of old buildings, partly because such destruction is uneconomical, partly because our taste—though seldom we admit it—is not infallible. We can never be sure that a building execrated in our day will not be admired to-morrow. Man tends to dislike the styles of his immediate forebears and admire those of several generations ago. The very Colonial buildings at Harvard which now inspire our modern designers were, by that cultivated gentleman, James Russell Lowell, described as "factories of the muses," to which nothing could lend even dignity, let alone beauty.

The task at Harvard has been, therefore, to erect barriers against the noise of the surrounding streets, to attain as much order as possible without destroying the older buildings placed haphazard in the Yard, to develop a brick architecture as nearly in harmony as possible with the previous work, and to mask, as far as possible, the older buildings which are generally conceded to be ugly. As an example of the work, we might study a view of one of the new small dormitories, Mower Hall (Fig. 140), designed by Coolidge, Shepley, Bulfinch & Abbot, to complete a small quadrangle and shut off the Yard at that point from Massachusetts Avenue. The building is frankly designed in the style of Massachusetts Hall, the earliest eighteenth-century building in the university. It is quiet, of the severest economy of material, but well proportioned and full of the picturesque charm of its Georgian prototype. It adjoins buildings of the eighteenth and early nineteenth centuries and yet is perfectly in harmony with them.

It brings out one great advantage of the Georgian style: its economy. Dignified and beautiful work may be done in brick and limestone, or even brick and wood, in the Georgian style at infinitely less cost than Gothic. Gothic must be in stone. Modern architecture has yet to learn to do good Gothic in brick. There are plenty of original examples in brick, but attempts to imitate them have as yet been pitifully unsuccessful. Gothic is easy to do; good Gothic, extremely difficult. Bad Gothic can be built cheaply; good Gothic, in study, detail, and material, is a costly medium.

To bring home more vividly the problem of designing a unified group in a style conformable to the other buildings of a university, we might cite the Harvard Graduate School of Business Administration. Thanks to the generosity of Mr. George F. Baker, means were made available in 1924 to build a complete group to house the school. A competition was arranged. Six architects were invited to compete and six more were selected from a preliminary competition. When the designs were submitted, all had conformed to the Georgian traditions of Harvard architecture, yet there was the widest divergence in plan, and even elevation. The winner, McKim, Mead & White, arranged a formal group (Figs. 141, 142), almost in a French manner, with radial lines from the river, a vista on the main axis leading to the library,—the largest building,—and the dormitories and professors' houses relegated to the rear. This gave the latter the disadvantage of exclusion from the river front, but the advantage of a southern exposure.* The individual buildings, such as the library (Fig. 143), were designed in the simplest Georgian brick, beautifully proportioned and daintily refined in detail.

As a foil to that, we may examine the design submitted by Professor J. J. Haffner, of the Harvard School of Architecture, associated with Perry, Shaw & Hepburn. Although Professor Haffner is a graduate of the Ecole des Beaux-Arts and a winner of the Grand Prix de Rome, he scrupulously avoided the symmetry and formality which we associate with French design, feeling it out of harmony with the traditions of Harvard architecture and the semidomestic character of a school of learning. His

---

* After winning the competition the architects changed this scheme and placed the dormitories on the river front, an arrangement which had been submitted by some of the other competitors.

Fig. 139. Cambridge, Mass. Harvard University.
Plan by Coolidge, Shepley, Bulfinch & Abbott, Architects.

Photograph by Fay S. Lincoln.

Fig. 140. Cambridge, Mass. Harvard University: Mower Hall.
Coolidge, Shepley, Bulfinch & Abbott, Architects.

FIG. 142. Perspective.

FIG. 143. Elevation of Library.

FIG. 141. Plan.

CAMBRIDGE, MASS. Harvard University: School of Business Administration. Winning Design in the Competition for the Building Group. *McKim, Mead & White, Architects.*

164

perspective (Fig. 144) shows us order, to be sure, but an unself-conscious order. Exact symmetry is avoided and a corner of the lot is used for an irregular group of professors' houses. His group plan (Fig. 145) shows no vista to the river, he apparently being unwilling to orient the design to face north in a group that was to be used largely in winter. There are neither formal axes, nor entirely enclosed courts, the designer trying in an orderly way to attain the complete informality of grouping of the older university buildings. The dormitory plans show the same tendency, a carefully studied geometric scheme giving the appearance almost of a rambling design with informal quadrangles and unexpected vistas through the communicating lanes from building to building and group to group. The chief building is the library (Fig. 146), carefully planned from the point of view of library efficiency and exhibiting a monumental but simple façade. Here, too, the detail harmonises perfectly with Georgian work.

A different solution was reached by Shepley, Rutan & Coolidge (now Coolidge, Shepley, Bulfinch & Abbott). This firm had done many buildings for the university; among them, the freshman dormitories, two of which we reproduce (Figs. 147, 148). These are supremely successful adaptations of Georgian Colonial to modern academic design. The freshman dormitories are placed on the north bank of the river, two of them facing it and oriented south. It naturally occurred to the architects to echo this group across the stream (Fig. 149). Changing the main axis to east and west, with the chief entrance on the street instead of on the river, they brought the dormitories to the river edge and gave them an appearance definitely re-echoing that of the buildings on the other side of the Charles. It was a satisfactory and entirely logical solution.

Still others were to be found. Aymar Embury II reverted to the north and south axis (Fig. 150), but, like Haffner, avoided absolute symmetry and blocked the vista from the river front. He also set his buildings back farther from the river. His designs for the library and the dining-halls were exquisitely appropriate, and proportioned so perfectly that one feels that the jury must have been strong-minded not to award the competition to him on these elevations alone. Still another interesting solution was found by Guy Lowell (Fig. 151), who avoided both the north and the east axes and oriented his group northwest and

FRONT ELEVATION OF LIBRARY

FIG. 146. Elevation of Library.

FIG. 145. Plan.

CAMBRIDGE, MASS. Harvard University. One of Competitive Designs for the School of Business Administration, Group Plan.
J. J. Hafner and Perry, Shaw & Hepburn, Associated Architects.

166

FIG. 147. CAMBRIDGE, MASS. Harvard University: Gore Hall. *Shepley, Rutan & Coolidge, Architects.*

FIG. 148. CAMBRIDGE, MASS. Harvard University: Standish Hall.
Shepley, Rutan & Coolidge, Architects.

FIG. 149. CAMBRIDGE, MASS. Harvard University.
One of Competitive Designs for the School of Business Administration.
Coolidge, Shepley, Bulfinch & Abbott, Architects.

167

southeast, with the main entrance at the corner nearest the Anderson bridge, which crosses the Charles at this point. Again, it was an entirely logical and sensible scheme.

We have examined the Harvard Business School in some detail, not because, as a group, it is more important than many others we might select, but because it is such an illuminating example. It shows clearly the variety of schemes, all of them sensible, which can be used to solve a problem. It shows how much variety will be got by a number of brilliant architects, working independently, yet all restricted to a given style. It reflects credit on all the firms that took part in the final competition and brings out vividly the tremendous amount of talent which a single competition of this sort will call forth. Indeed, it might almost be used as an argument against such competitions, since only one firm can win, and the effort, the skill and the talent of the others are thrown away. The jury did not publish its deliberations, but we know that it had a very difficult task in selecting the winner.

In our survey of other academic work, we cannot, of course, go into the detail that we have in reviewing that at Harvard, else we should leave no space for the other types of architecture which we must study. On the other hand, there is so much of this work and so much of it is good, that it is difficult not to overemphasise it. The same problem which we have exhibited at Harvard we might have illustrated at many other sites. One closely related to that at Harvard was worked out by John Russell Pope for the expansion of Dartmouth College, Hanover, N. H. Here, as at Harvard, in a Colonial college, the tradition was Georgian and the architect cheerfully accepted it. His library court (Fig. 152) is a charming ensemble of Georgian brick buildings with a white trim, so perfectly in keeping with the traditions of the college that we feel that they might have been built a century and a half ago. The perspective view of two dormitories (Fig. 153) shows a work which might have been born of a union of Massachusetts and Harvard Halls at Cambridge, repeating neither, original, yet so convincingly Colonial that we can hardly believe that it is not a charming sketch of an eighteenth-century work. Whether these buildings will actually be constructed is dubious. That they would be a credit to the college, if built, is beyond dispute.

This classic Georgian or Republican work is indigenous to the Atlan-

FIG. 150. CAMBRIDGE, MASS. Harvard University.
One of Competitive Designs for the School of Business Administration. *Aymar Embury II, Architect.*

FIG. 151.. CAMBRIDGE, MASS. Harvard University.
One of Competitive Designs for the School of Business Administration. *Guy Lowell, Architect.*

169

FIG. 152. HANOVER, N. H. Dartmouth College. Sketch for Library. *John Russell Pope, Architect.*

FIG. 153. HANOVER, N. H. Dartmouth College. Sketch for Dormitories.
John Russell Pope, Architect.

tic seaboard and especially New England and northern New York. Its dignity, its economy, and its practicability, however, have commended it to other localities where it can be used without clashing with older work.

We must not linger too long over classic work, however, when so much fine Gothic clamours for our notice and admiration. Cobb's lesson at Chicago bore fruit and "academic Gothic" became the word at many a great institution. One of its happiest examples is at Princeton, where a bold decision was made to sweep away as much as possible of the earlier, ugly work and expand and rebuild in a Gothic style. The charm, picturesqueness, and Old World flavour of Gothic art seemed appropriate to academic halls, and however we may criticise the propriety of Gothic in modern times, we cannot gainsay the charm of the work at Princeton. A number of architects contributed to make it one of the most beautiful universities in the United States. We reproduce one of the great halls done for Princeton by Day & Klauder (Fig. 154), a Philadelphia firm, skilled in the use of native stone. Not only is the work fine Gothic, but it shows textures as agreeable as in an ancient building. The modern architect is confronted with the difficulty of producing modern Gothic and, without artificial ageing, attaining the beauty of surface texture and colour of old work. By a careful selection of materials and the harmonious and careful use of stones of different tones, Day & Klauder have attained just this effect. A view of the east wing and court of Pyne Hall, with its terrace, its broken sky-line, and its studied irregularity, forms a composition as charming as one could hope to find in the Old World. That it is an inspiration to students to live in such beautiful surroundings is enthusiastically attested by many a Princeton man. This work was ably furthered by Cram, Goodhue & Ferguson, when they built the Princeton Graduate School. They did a massive pile (Fig. 155), dominated by a great stone lantern, which is a landmark for miles, as one approaches the town. Solidity, seriousness, age are symbolised in their work, modern as it is, and even the classicist, when he visits Princeton, becomes a convert to the Gothic point of view.

Yale has followed Princeton. Both are universities of Colonial foundation, but both seem definitely to have abandoned Colonial architecture for academic Gothic. James Gamble Rogers has been the chief spirit at Yale. His Harkness Memorial (Fig. 156) is justly regarded as one of

Fig. 154. PRINCETON, N. J. Princeton University: Pyne Hall. *Day & Klauder, Architects.*

Fig. 155. PRINCETON, N. J. Princeton University: Graduate School.
Cram, Goodhue & Ferguson, Architects.

the gems of modern American architecture. He seems happily to have been untroubled by expense, but given *carte blanche* and requested to spare nothing which would make the building more beautiful. He has gone farther than the architects at Princeton to get a true Gothic effect, even resorting to such expedients as hollowing the thresholds to give the appearance of stone worn for centuries by plodding feet. A view of one court (Fig. 157) shows even early Renaissance design included with the Gothic, as work of a later date so often obtrudes itself upon Gothic in England and the Continent. The designer has made an especial effort in the sculpture, encouraging good sculptors to carve the ornament and express their own personality in the work. Individuality, even humour, are everywhere, and the general impression is startlingly like that of a true Gothic building of the thirteenth century, upon which a hundred independent artist craftsmen worked under the loose supervision of a *magister operarii*. The tiny scale of some of the dormitory openings contrasts deliberately with the massiveness of some of the large gateways. The whole is dominated by a slender and graceful flamboyant tower, one of the masterpieces of Gothic, ancient or modern.

The Harkness Memorial is an undoubted gem. It was got, however, at a price. One cannot build in this way if one has to consider expense. In so building, too, one sets a standard which it is very hard to live up to in later work, when abundant funds are less available. Moreover, such work is hardly as practical as is classic. The charge is often brought that, in order to gain the necessary picturesqueness, the windows are made too small and not as well placed as they might be from the practical point of view. Although this charge is probably exaggerated, there is some truth in it, and it is very open to question whether Gothic can ever be as satisfactory from the practical point of view as the broad-walled, horizontally accented, classical styles. Whatever the truth may be, however, we shall always be glad that the Harkness Memorial was done.

Another great Gothic work, properly of a less delicate character, is the pile of buildings designed by Cram, Goodhue & Ferguson for the United States Military Academy at West Point (Fig. 159). Here the style lent itself to the character of the building. Not only had it academic associations, but it was also one of the great military styles. Of necessity it was given a sterner character at West Point than in a purely academic work. The

FIG. 156. NEW HAVEN, CONN. Yale University: Harkness Memorial. *James Gamble Rogers, Architect.*

174

Fig. 158. NEW HAVEN, CONN. Yale University:
Harkness Memorial. Wrexham Tower.
James Gamble Rogers, Architect.

Fig. 157. NEW HAVEN, CONN. Yale University:
Harkness Memorial. Court, Showing Renaissance Details.
James Gamble Rogers, Architect.

Post Headquarters has a most fortresslike solidity. Even the Chapel (Fig. 160), with its beautiful proportions, has a severity got by the rugged masonry, the rectangular sections with the maximum elimination of mouldings, the turreted buttresses, and the battlemented sky-line, which re-echoes the military ensemble. The site, towering above a picturesque and mighty river, is to the highest degree impressive and the architect has taken full advantage of it.

We must not linger too long over Gothic academic architecture, but its charm makes it difficult to leave it. Nothing reflects more credit on the modern designer than the way he has learned to handle this style. Such buildings as those designed by Maginnis & Walsh, for Boston College (Fig. 161), have charm and modernity. They adapt Gothic to modern needs, with none of the dryness and lifelessness which marked the style as it was used in this country a generation ago.

We must not get the impression, however, that all academic work is necessarily Georgian or Gothic. Many other styles have been applied successfully to the problem, especially when geographical locality suggested it. One of the most interesting examples is the Rice Institute, at Houston, Texas, by Ralph Adams Cram. Here a broad plain, semitropical vegetation, and a brilliant sun suggested a special treatment and especially one that involved polychromy. Using forms derived from Byzantium and Venice, but in no way copying anything that had gone before, the architect created an impressive ensemble (Fig. 162). To see it in the black and white, however, is to lose its greatest beauty. American architecture is very timid in the use of colour. Our Victorian designers did such hideous work in colour that the moderns have leaned to classic monotone and the safe chastity of white, or white and brick. We forget that classic architecture was colourful. We forget the great colour designs of Pintoricchio and Raphael in the Renaissance. Our students see photographs of great masterpieces and acquire a superb sense of form and proportion, but they have little idea of colour in architecture. Too often we associate colour with vulgarity and display, feeling it somehow undignified, and forgetting that only bad colour is vulgar. American architecture needs nothing more than a knowledge of the possibilities of rich colour handled with taste. The Rice Institute proves that an American architect can, if he have courage, originality, and taste, compose in colour as successfully as any of the great designers in the past.

FIG. 159.   WEST POINT, N. Y.   U. S. Military Academy: Post Headquarters.
Cram, Goodhue & Ferguson, Architects.

FIG. 160.   WEST POINT, N. Y.   U. S. Military Academy: Chapel.
Cram, Goodhue & Ferguson, Architects.

FIG. 161. NEWTON, MASS. Boston College: Recitation Building.
Maginnis & Walsh, Architects.

FIG. 162. HOUSTON, TEXAS. Rice Institute: Administration Building.
Cram, Goodhue & Ferguson, Architects.

It is not impossible to design an academic architecture entirely from the modern point of view. A good example of this is the enormous building done by W. W. Bosworth for the Massachusetts Institute of Technology (Fig. 163). In designing a great technical school, the architect felt the desirability of expressing a truly modern feeling. Gothic, in such a work, would have been absurd. An engineering building, above all, should express its engineering structure. In the Technology Building, we feel the steel with its envelope of stone. We rejoice in the practicality of the great glass openings, slashed from attic to pavement, and revealing the steel floors of the various stories frankly and honestly. Another unusual feature is the enclosing of all the various schools of Technology under one building, instead of trying to group many buildings together. This gives a striking sense of scale and spaciousness. At the same time, plenty of opportunity is left for expansion according to the original design. Of course the building has points one can criticise. The great entrance court looks too much for show and too little for use and, indeed, it is seldom used. Most of the students have found more convenient openings for ingress and egress, unobtrusively placed in other parts of the building. None can deny, however, that the Technology buildings are beautiful and even inspiring. They are a good example, incidentally, of the advantage of moving a great institution to an entirely new site, when it has outgrown its old one, and giving the architect an opportunity to work unhampered by the consideration of old buildings. If we compare an aeroplane photograph of Technology with one of Harvard (Figs. 163, 164), only two miles away, this fact appears in almost comic relief.

The last word in modernism in academic architecture is the proposed "Cathedral of Learning" at Pittsburgh (Fig. 165). Here the university authorities have proposed a tremendous skyscraper, towering thirty or forty stories skyward and housing the chief departments of the institution. The building has actually been designed by Charles Z. Klauder, of Philadelphia, and his scheme is one of great interest and beauty. In form, he has been painstakingly careful to avoid any archæological tendency, and the beauty of his building depends upon its mass, its soaring grace, its terrific suggestion of verticality, and its interesting silhouette. As a skyscraper, none will deny its effectiveness and beauty.

FIG. 163.   CAMBRIDGE, MASS.   An Aerial View of the Massachusetts Institute of Technology, Looking Eastward from Charles River.   *William Welles Bosworth, Architect.*

FIG. 164.   CAMBRIDGE, MASS.   Harvard University and Surroundings.

On the other hand, the authorities of the University of Pittsburgh must have realised that what they proposed was revolutionary and would be attacked. Indeed, they probably took satisfaction in their originality and gloried in the attack. The question remains whether a steel skyscraper is an appropriate or a practical house for a university. That it has not thus far been used for the purpose we can discount. This should not be urged against its use in the future and, if it were proper and apt, we should rejoice in the adaptation of one of the most ingenious and beautiful forms of American architecture to academic needs.

There are, however, serious objections to the use of such a building for this function. In theory, the high-speed elevator has made vertical communication as easy as horizontal. In fact, this is not entirely true. The university day is regulated by a bell. At the stroke of ten, let us say, it is necessary for a class of several hundred to leave a hall and another class of several hundred to enter it. Supposing there were fifteen hundred students involved, it would be difficult to see how elevator service could take care of the circulation in less than twenty minutes or a half an hour.* This brings up merely one practical difficulty. Related to it is the feeling that student life in such a building would be disjointed. The congregating in corridors or crowding into elevators would be a poor substitute for the mass movements from building to building and the genial grouping before a building of a class awaiting its time to enter. Even the question of economy comes in, for students in an ordinary collegiate building can be trusted to transport themselves, while those of a Cathedral of Learning would have to be transported at every move.

Other considerations, more abstract and less easy to answer dogmatically, are bound to enter. A steel building is not merely modern, it suggests impermanence. Steel, we know, is subject to change. To be sure, the life of steel is uncertain and no one seems to worry about the impermanence of our great steel bridges; nevertheless, we know that steel, unlike stone, is not everlasting. At a guess, we might give the Cathedral of Learning a life of two or three hundred years, or even more; one could hardly imagine such a building existing for a thousand. The modernist will retort that this makes no difference; that *any* building will be

---

* It is fair to say that no one is more alive to this difficulty than the designer, and he promises to solve it.

FIG. 165.   PITTSBURGH, PA.   University of Pittsburgh: Proposed "Cathedral of Learning."
Charles Z. Klauder, Architect.

obsolete in a thousand years and ought to be pulled down.   Practically, this may be so; æsthetically, it is certainly wrong.   Granted that the Cathedral of Learning will not be needed a thousand years from now, it ought not to remind us of the fact.   Age and association have not only a sentimental value, but a practical one, as well.

The question resolves itself into whether the beauty and the suggestion of American dynamic vitality embodied in Mr. Klauder's building compensate for the impermanence, restlessness, and bustling modernity of his design for an academic building.   It is a question whether there is any value in old association, in a feeling of solidity, in at least the partial cloistering of the student during the period of his education, when concentration is so necessary and distraction such a stumbling-block.   Perhaps the student has the world too little with him.   Perhaps he is too little in touch with modern life.   On the other hand, we could hardly expect him to read his book in the officer's cage of the traffic control on Fifth Avenue and 42d Street.   Whether or not the Cathedral of Learning is apt and suitable, each must answer for himself.   One doubts, however, if it will set a type of any far-reaching influence in modern American architecture.

Our brief review of academic architecture has, of course, been superficial and general.   We have left out many important individual features which demand special study, are immensely interesting, but which must be excluded from a review of this sort.   Laboratories, college libraries, medical schools, and a dozen other types thrust forward special problems which we have no time to analyse.   One type has grown up, however, not necessarily of academic origin, but almost always appended to an academic group and so important in modern American architecture that some mention of it must be included.   This is the great stadium, seating anywhere from fifty to a hundred thousand people, in which the university athletic contests are staged.   There are, to be sure, similar amphitheatres and arenas constructed for commercial sport and some of these now surpass the academic athletic structures, but the great stadium in this country was developed in connection with the universities and can be considered under that head.

A few examples will suffice.   All amaze one by the skill of the engineering design.   Some are given a truly architectural character.   One of the earliest great stadia was that at Harvard, built by McKim, Mead & White, and Professor Hollis, Professor Johnson, and J. R. Worcester as engineers (Fig. 166). The construction was, of course, reinforced concrete. The stadium is U-shaped, its long sides straight, and one end open to permit a 220-yard straightaway for the running-track. Round the top is an open, Doric colonnade of concrete. The sides are very steep, affording good views for the spectators and making the building more picturesque. The Harvard stadium, in spite of its severity and practical utility in material and construction, is a very splendid work of art.

Another very impressive American stadium is Franklin Field, at Philadelphia (Fig. 167), built of brick and concrete. Its architects were Day & Klauder, its engineers Gavin Hadden and H. T. Campion. It is even severer than the stadium at Harvard and is effective chiefly through the sense of power and scale given by its simple masses.

Still another type is the Yale Bowl, by Donn Barber (Fig. 168). Here the ingenious idea occurred by which half the depth of the stadium was reached through excavation and the elevation attained with the material excavated. The spectators enter by tunnels on a level with the ground and find themselves, when they reach the interior, half-way between the playing-field and the top of the stadium. Such a system requires the most careful drainage, but this was perfectly handled at New Haven, so that the field is entirely satisfactory from this point of view. The slope of the Yale Bowl is gentler than that of the Harvard Stadium and the shape is rounder. This means that many seats are disagreeably far from the players so that one can see them well only with glasses. This is the more inevitable, since the Yale structure seats half again as many people as that at Harvard (approximately 75,000 at Yale). Indeed, the Yale Bowl brings home squarely the impossibility of expanding indefinitely these great structures. Only one way exists of increasing the seating capacity without putting the spectators absurdly far from the play, and that is by double-decking the arena and having tiers of seats superposed.

This has actually been done in the case of the Yankee Stadium * (Fig. 169), a commercial structure for professional baseball, built by the Os-

* The upper galleries at Franklin Field were recently added. They not only greatly increased the seating capacity but actually improved the design.

FIG. 166. CAMBRIDGE, MASS. Harvard University: Stadium.
McKim, Mead & White, Architects; Hollis, Johnson, J. R. Worcester, Engineers.

FIG. 167. PHILADELPHIA, PA. University of Pennsylvania: Franklin Field.
Day & Klauder, Architects.

FIG. 168. NEW HAVEN, CONN. Yale University: Yale Bowl. *Donn Barber, Architect.*

born Engineering Company. The field is entirely enclosed by building in reinforced concrete. Within, the steel construction allows for three tiers of seats, the lowest gently sloping, the highest steeply pitched, so that every seat has a good view. The whole is covered with a roof. The effect is ingenious and practical, but not beautiful. We cannot get away from the impression that we are looking at the skeleton of an exaggerated theatre, unhappily exposed to the air, and we miss the spaciousness of the true amphitheatre.

Space lacks for any further discussion of this interesting subject and it is a pity, for very fine structures of this sort are going up in many parts of the country. One is tempted at least to mention the magnificent Coliseum at Los Angeles (Fig. 170), by John and Donald Parkinson, one of the most magnificent in scale and impressive in appearance of the type. Like the Yale Bowl, it is partly excavated and, like the Yale Bowl, its tiers of seats are gently sloping, removing many of the spectators to a disagreeable distance from the play. There is a physical limit to the size of these structures, not from the point of view of the designer or engineer but from that of the human being, whose ocular power cannot increase with the ambitious expansion of the building, and this limit seems about reached. Space lacks, too, to discuss the open-air theatres, such as that at Virginia, or the beautiful one at the University of California. We can simply note that our colleges and universities, however conservative in other design, have been progressives in the study of the stadium and the open-air theatre.

Any discussion of academic architecture, however brief, must include some mention of the extraordinary development in the design of schools. A generation ago there was practically no scientific study of the school problem. The chief aim of school-builders seemed to be economy. Hideousness was generally not dreaded, with the result that the youth of the country spent a large proportion of their hours in their most impressionable years amid surroundings that did all that they could to stimulate the depression caused by compulsory tasks, themselves none too congenial. It would be interesting to discover how much of the hatred which many a man cherishes for algebra or the Latin declensions came from the subjects themselves and how much from the grisly interiors in which these subjects were taught. Even when beauty was considered and in some

Fig. 169. NEW YORK, N. Y. Yankee Stadium. *Osborn Engineering Company, Engineers.*

Fig. 170. LOS ANGELES, CALIF. Coliseum. *John and Donald B. Parkinson, Architects.*

measure attained, little attention was paid to the practical side other than to have rooms large enough to accommodate the estimated number of pupils.

Nowadays all this is changed. Designers are alive to the threefold necessity of beauty, practicality, and economy. Perforce the last has usually imposed simplicity in design and material, but simplicity and beauty may go perfectly hand in hand, though they have not always done so. The modern American school, and especially the high school, is thus a new creation. Questions of communication have been studied as never before. The fire hazard has been nearly eliminated by means of wide corridors and safe and adequate exits. Modern heating and ventilating plants now provide a constant temperature and pure air in place of the old conditions of dusty, germ-laden atmosphere and variations of twenty degrees' temperature between rooms or even in a single room. Lighting has been carefully studied and light is brought in from one side to desks, so arranged that it falls over the left shoulder of the pupil. Furniture has been made more attractive, as well as more practical, and interiors are treated in simple materials, but with agreeable textures and colours.

The most difficult problems of school design involve the gymnasium and auditorium, large units in any modern school. The question is whether these units should be isolated from the rest of the building or centrally placed. There is an advantage in isolating them, as by putting them in separate wings in a plan and thus eliminating from the common schoolrooms the noise of the gymnasium and from the auditorium the noises of both. On the other hand, there is an advantage in having these units centrally placed so that classes may enter them from several sides and with the minimum loss of time and confusion. There is, of course, an obvious economical gain in combining the gymnasium and the auditorium and, if necessary, separating the auditorium stage from the gymnasium by means of sound-proof doors.

As typical of the exterior appearance of the modern high school, we might select the one done at Greenfield, Ohio, by Mr. William B. Ittner (Fig. 171), probably the most influential figure in the modern development of school design. The general appearance suggests the English perpendicular style, or rather an adaptation of it to modern needs. The material is brick with a stone trim. The windows are placed frankly where they are needed and in a way that satisfies the eye that they are correctly placed. There is a minimum of "ornament," but fine proportions, fine textures, and discreet taste in the handling of economical but pleasant material. The result is a building that reveals its purpose in the frankest way, yet charms the eye.

Mr. Ittner seems to have decided in favour of the centrally placed auditorium and gymnasium, with the two units combined. His Goliad School at Galveston, Texas (Fig. 173), done in collaboration with De-Witt & Lemmon, shows a compact plan, with the cafeteria, stage, and combined auditorium and gymnasium running through its centre. These can thus be reached easily from every part of the building. The combination of auditorium and gymnasium is a great economy, as only rarely is there need of the larger auditorium space, and then the gymnasium floor is easily converted to the purposes of a hall. An adjustable, sound-proof screen divides the stage from the gymnasium. Courts, locker-rooms, and toilets flank the central units, insulating them from the corridors and class-rooms on the outer flanks of the building. The coal and boiler rooms are in a separate wing behind the gymnasium. It would be hard to imagine a saner or more satisfactory plan. The elevation (Fig. 172) shows the simplest treatment of cement and stucco harmonising perfectly with the architectural ideals of the district and offering the utmost in economy without the violation of good taste.

The school problem has been complicated by the easy, cheap, and rapid traffic communication of modern times and the consequent tendency to increase the number of pupils and the size of the plant. It is not unusual to plan for twenty-five hundred or three thousand pupils, and St. Louis has recently completed two schools for an estimated enrolment of thirty-five hundred. It is a question, however, both educationally and architecturally, whether this does not pass the limit of maximum efficiency. An admirable example of the larger school is the East High School of Denver, Colo., by George H. Williamson. The plan (Fig. 175) is H-shaped, with a large auditorium in the centre, preceded by a spacious lobby, with a stage at the back. The gymnasium is moved to a rear wing. The broad wings allow for double lines of classrooms with direct light. Such a plan is admirable, but requires a spacious area and is less economical than that of such a building as the Goliad School. The

FIG. 171. GREENFIELD, OHIO. Edward Lee McClain High School in Foreground. Elementary School in Background. *William B. Ittner, Architect.*

FIG. 172. GALVESTON, TEXAS. Goliad School. *William B. Ittner, Architect;*
DeWitt & Lemmon, Associated.

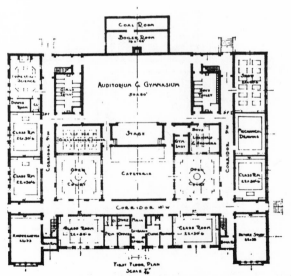

FIG. 173. GALVESTON, TEXAS. Goliad School. *William B. Ittner, Architect;*
DeWitt & Lemmon, Associated.

FIG. 174. DENVER, COLO. East High School. *George H. Williamson, Architect.*

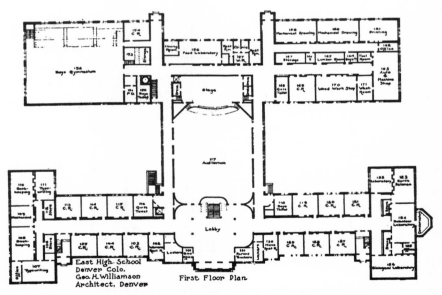

FIG. 175. DENVER, COLO. East High School. *George H. Williamson, Architect.*

192

effect of the exterior (Fig. 174) is a little overpowering, but this is almost inevitable in a building of such scale. The proportions are excellent, however, and the character of the building is properly scholastic, despite its monumental size.

Progress in school design is thus keeping pace with progress in the other fields of architectural activity and the schools may even be considered in the van of specialisation. That the ultimate and perfect solution is reached we should not expect and the problem changes and ramifies with advance in education. The creation of junior and senior high schools complicates the problem. The "platoon system" or "Work-Study-Play" organisation, now supported by many, places further responsibilities on the shoulders of the architect. The private boarding-school, with its arrangements of dormitories for the boys and houses for the masters, demands the skilful combination of many elements which can be ignored in the day-school. Above all, the architect must learn and has learned to collaborate with the head master. Close co-operation between architect, trustees, and masters has produced the best examples of the modern schools, and it is significant that the most successful architects in this branch of the modern field have been the most generous and patient in their willingness to co-operate.

III
ECCLESIASTIC AND MONUMENTAL ARCHITECTURE

III

ECCLESIASTIC AND MONUMENTAL ARCHITECTURE

WE have seen that the tendency of academic architecture is conservative. Even more so has been that of the ecclesiastic architecture of America. This need not surprise us. The Church has always been one of the most conservative forces in society. Most great religions, all radical in their inception, have soon become rigidly conservative, and Christianity has been no exception to the rule. So clearly is this revealed in religious architecture that some would exclude any discussion of it in a treatise on the architecture of to-day, holding that it has lost its hold on the people and represents only a reactionary persistence in repeating the dead formulas of the past. This position is extreme. We have interpreted the architecture of to-day as the architecture that has recently been built and is being built to-day. There are plenty of devout people to whom religion is a living force in present-day society and, correspondingly, there are plenty of churches, recently built and being built, that testify to this fact.

Artistically, they are often among the finest of our monuments. To omit them would not only be a slur on the spiritual force which produces them but would weaken our appreciation of American architecture. That their tendency is conservative, that their historical antecedents are quickly apparent, none will deny. This does not mean that they are unoriginal. If this were generally true, we should have to exclude, in a history of architecture, anything based upon a clearly marked historical precedent. Bramante, for example, would go unmentioned. A *reductio ad absurdum* of this sort shows what a mistake it would be, on account of our interest in modernism, in steel construction, in the vivid commercial building which afford perhaps the most interesting phenomena of our modern architecture, to ignore the churches, which are none the less one of the glories of modern work.

To appreciate them, we should compare them with some of the earlier attempts in America along the same lines. When we do this, when we make a careful study of, let us say, the most recent Gothic, we see that the modern designer has assimilated historic precedent and has learned to design in a style rather than imitate it. The best modern Gothic no more imitates the Gothic of the Middle Ages than did Bramante's St. Peter's imitate the Basilica of Maxentius and the Pantheon on which it was based.

It is nevertheless true that American church architecture has adhered closely to the styles. Of these the favourite has been Gothic, with a tendency to follow English forms more than French, though both have furnished inspiration for American work. The Gothic set in motion by the romantic revival survived the wave of classicism of the nineties and persisted in church architecture. Second in popularity has been the Colonial. Especially in New England, people reverted naturally to the Colonial type and built, and are building, classic churches of brick and limestone or brick and wood, based upon Colonial or early Republican precedents. The New England meeting-house was architecturally congruous, historically American, and based ultimately on the work of Gibbs, Wren, Jones, and others who it was felt designed especially with an eye to the needs of the Protestant ritual. This style often appears in the South, as well, and is by no means unknown in practically all parts of the country.

Other styles have been used, however, with great success, and one cannot but feel that originality increases as the designers get away from Gothic and Colonial. Byzantine antecedents have begun to be influential and Romanesque forms, especially Lombard, are having a vogue. In the West and Southwest, as one might suppose, the Spanish missions have made their influence felt, and the Spanish style has appeared even more strongly and successfully in religious work than in secular. Even the strictly classic styles have been used for church work, and there have been interesting attempts on the part of the modernists to apply their canons of design to churches as well as to secular buildings.

Denominational influences have played their part in determining the character of much of the work. The Colonial church is closely associated with Puritan New England. It is seldom imitated in modern times by the Church of Rome. In America, as in England, Gothic, too, had been pre-empted by Protestants and the Roman Church tended to avoid it, though its attitude in this is now undergoing a clearly marked change. Other more modern and less orthodox sects sought to preserve their architectural independence by using other forms. Thus the Christian Science Temple is usually of classic design and such sects as the Theosophists built templar constructions which would have no association with Puritanism, with England, or with Rome. The Jews naturally avoid styles which suggest Western Christianity and use for their synagogues semi-oriental, nearer Eastern forms, based really upon Byzantine, which Solomon probably would have considered strange, but which call up association with the great temple at Jerusalem. An amusing treatise might be written on denominational reflections in modern architecture.

In our review we can call attention to a very few only of the thousands of fine monuments which embody the various *genres,* and perhaps it will be clearest to begin with the Colonial, or Georgian, churches. These, from the historic point of view, we can perhaps consider the most American. They can be treated with a brevity that ill reflects their charm, for, as a type, they are easily understood. We reproduce first one of the severest of examples, St. Paul's Church, at Newburyport, Mass. (Fig. 176), by Perry, Shaw & Hepburn. It is in a late seventeenth-century style, plain, well proportioned, and avoiding any parade of the orders except in the portico, so small as to be almost a hood, and in the belfry. Such a building well expresses the stern religion of our Puritan forebears and fits with perfect aptitude its New England environment.

Of a somewhat later and more ornate expression is the "meeting-house," the First Congregational Church, at Lyme, Conn. (Fig. 177), by Ernest Greene. Here we find a portico with a temple front and a gracefully designed tower, starting square and carried, in the fashion of the design of Sir Christopher Wren, to a graceful, many-sided polygon with a slender spire. The blocklike body of the church, however, with its double row of small windows and its unobtrusively projecting chimney, shows that we are still viewing a New England meeting-house. The interior (Fig. 178) is simple, but not bare; galleried, chastely white in colour, and filled with high-backed pews. It is charmingly proportioned and is at once old-fashioned, spacious, and worshipful. Indeed, if we hark back to the actual examples of fine eighteenth-century American work which we reviewed in the beginning of our discussion of American

FIG. 177. LYME, CONN. First Congregational Church.
Rebuilt by Ernest Greene, Architect.

FIG. 176. NEWBURYPORT, MASS. St. Paul's Church.
Perry, Shaw & Hepburn, Architects.

Fig. 178. LYME, CONN. First Congregational Church. *Rebuilt by Ernest Greene, Architect.*

Photograph by the Williams Studio, Honolulu.

FIG. 180.   HONOLULU, HAWAII.   Central Union Church.
Cram & Ferguson, Architects.

FIG. 179.   WASHINGTON, D. C.   All Souls' Church.
Coolidge & Shattuck, Architects.

architecture, it is hard to believe that this is not one more true Colonial example and one of the best.

For a still more sophisticated example, we may look at All Souls', in Washington (Fig. 179), by Coolidge & Shattuck.   Here the building is on a really monumental scale.   The portico is deep and dignified.   The tower and spire, large in scale, astride the roof behind the portico, remind one of such a building as St. Martin's in the Fields, London, by James Gibbs.   The interior, too, with its broad arches, barrel and groin vaulted ceilings, galleries, and entablature blocks, is pure Georgian and reminiscent of the best Colonial work.   It is the polished and polite style which aristocratic America, in the second half of the eighteenth century, had learned from England, only in the twentieth century the designer has access to more original material, both in books and photographs.   This is the type that spread far and wide over America.   It is interesting to see it, for example, surrounded by palms and exotic vegetation, in the Central Union Church at Honolulu, Hawaii (Fig. 180), designed by Ralph Adams Cram.   There is no real incongruity in such a building in a semi-tropical country and its presence there bespeaks the American possession of the Island.   It is only one more of the innumerable cases of architecture vigorously voicing history.

Natural as the Georgian style may seem, it has never seriously rivalled in popularity the Gothic.   A thousand associations make people feel that the Gothic is the great church style.   As a result, America is "covered with a fair mantle of churches"; some, it must be confessed, fairer than others, but many of the modern ones showing a grasp of the style of which we can well be proud.   They include all types from small parish churches to ambitious cathedrals and, while they show an assimilation of historic precedent, they cannot be said to be entirely unoriginal.   In any case, they are much in demand and as long as this is so they will continue to be built.   We can congratulate ourselves, therefore, that they are built so well.

As usual, it is hard to select illustrations, when the material is so embarrassingly rich.   For the modest type of country parish church, we might look at All Saints', in Peterborough, N. H. (Figs. 181, 182), another building by R. A. Cram.   The style which inspired it was early.   We sense that we are not far from Romanesque.   The openings are few

Fig. 182. Peterboro, N. H. All Saints' Church.
Cram & Ferguson, Architects.

Fig. 181. Peterboro, N. H. All Saints' Church.
Cram & Ferguson, Architects.

and small, the heavy lantern almost Romanesque despite its Gothic detail. We feel here the influence of Saxon and Norman, as well as Gothic, but imitation of none. The interior is simple almost to bareness, with thick walls, wooden roof, heavy arches, and vigorously splayed windows. By mass and proportion, the designer has won his effect and we feel the honest country parish church in its lines. "Una bella vilanella," Michelangelo might have called it.

The city produces another type of chapel, modest in scale, but lavish in the study of ornament and the rich but refined use of material. A good example is the Leslie Lindsey Memorial, in Boston (Figs. 183, 184), by Allen & Collens. Here again the design has an English flavour—one might almost call the style a purified curvilinear—but the Gothic vocabulary is used to express the designer's own ideas and not to reiterate any given formula of the past.

An exquisitely proportioned piece of Gothic is the First Baptist Church, at Pittsburgh, Pa. (Fig. 185), by Cram, Goodhue & Ferguson. As one studies this monumental work, one feels more and more that American Gothic has originality and beauty and that the modern work shows an *understanding* and deliberate deviation from historic form thoroughly assimilated. This impression will be fortified tremendously by the examination of the Chapel of the Intercession, in New York (Cram, Goodhue & Ferguson, Architects) (Fig. 187). Here the material is variegated and carefully studied. It is unlike any Old World example. The tracery is somewhere between curvilinear and perpendicular. The interior is wooden roofed with great trussed timbers richly ornamented in colour. We know that all mediæval timber roofs were coloured, and plenty of archæological researches have been made and their results incorporated with most damaging effect in modern work. The late Mr. Goodhue probably made archæological researches, but he designed his colour not to be correct so much as to be brilliant, rich, and harmonious. He thus got it correct in spirit, though whether it be correct in fact the writer does not know, nor care. The Intercession is a superb example of the way the modern designer has boldly, skilfully, and sensitively attained the beauty of old Gothic. It would be less ungracious than absurd to accuse him of unoriginality.

As a final example of the Gothic church, apart from the cathedral,

Fig. 184. Boston, Mass. Emmanuel Church:
Leslie Lindsay Memorial Chapel. *Allen & Collens, Architects.*

Fig. 183. Boston, Mass. Emmanuel Church:
Leslie Lindsay Memorial Chapel. *Allen & Collens, Architects.*

Fig. 186. New York, N. Y. Church of St. Thomas.
Cram, Goodhue & Ferguson, Architects.

Fig. 185. Pittsburgh, Pa. First Baptist Church.
Cram, Goodhue & Ferguson, Architects.

207

Photograph by Kenneth Clark

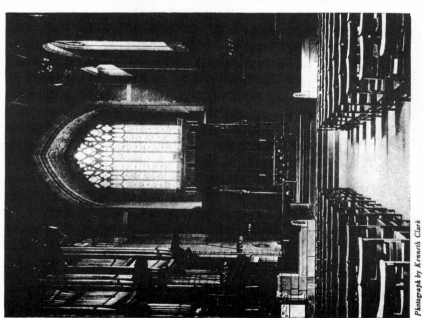

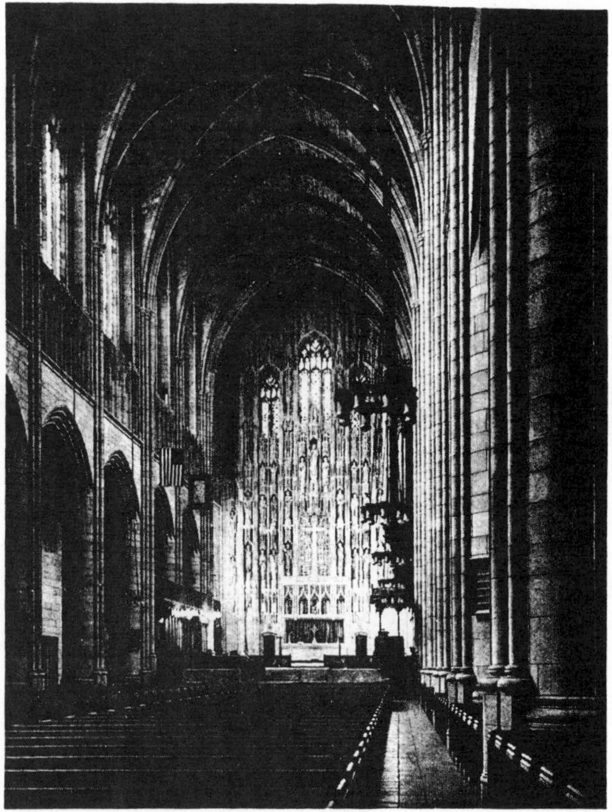

FIG. 187. NEW YORK, N. Y. Chapel of the Intercession.
Cram, Goodhue & Ferguson, Architects.

Photograph by Kenneth Clark.

FIG. 188. NEW YORK, N. Y. Church of St. Thomas
Cram, Goodhue & Ferguson, Architects.

we may look at St. Thomas', New York, by Cram, Goodhue & Ferguson * (Fig. 186). In this case, the influence is frankly flamboyant. The exterior has the lightness and grace which goes with that style and is a consequent dream of beauty. The designer was bold enough and sensitive enough to disregard the purist critics who proclaimed that the only good Gothic was done in the thirteenth century, and frankly recognised the possibilities of flamboyant. Again, however, he varied consistently from flamboyant, so that his building has no appearance of an historic problem in a given style. The interior (Fig. 188) is simple and spacious, with large windows, broad quadripartite vaults, and the quiet verticality which suggests an earlier phase of Gothic and contrasts with the late character of the window tracery.

We must not think that Gothic is the only style, however, which has been adapted to modern church needs. Just as Richardson was tempted into the field of Romanesque, so modern designers have worked in that field with (we say it with due deference and trepidation) as great, or even greater, success. Let us note such a work as the little church of St. John of Nepomuk, in New York City (Fig. 189), by John V. Van Pelt. It is, of course, very archæological in character, being derived direct from north Italian and specifically Lombard Romanesque. It is, however, entirely charming, the designer having attained by a judicious and feignedly haphazard intermingling of stone and brick the picturesqueness and fine surface of an old original. His proportions suggest the original but, it must be noted, are far finer than in many an original of the twelfth century in Lombardy. Of a somewhat different type is the parish church of St. John, in Cambridge, Mass. (Fig. 190), by Maginnis & Walsh. Here again the forms are Lombard, but with more Byzantine feeling. Colour is used tastefully, but not lavishly, and, although one is reminded immediately of Lombard work, one can feel originality as well. The church is Roman Catholic, and this firm, and others, have been very successful in adapting the type to the needs of the Church of Rome and thus differentiating it from its Protestant neighbours, Colonial and Gothic. We must be satisfied with these two examples, remember-

---

* It is not easy, when a work comes from this office, to be sure of the real designer. Both Cram and Goodhue were masters of Gothic, though with different styles. I believe St. Thomas' is largely the work of Goodhue.

Photograph by John Wallace Gillies.

FIG. 189. NEW YORK, N. Y. St. John of Nepomuk. *John V. Van Pelt, Architect.*

FIG. 190. CAMBRIDGE, MASS. St. John's Church. *Maginnis & Walsh, Architects.*

ing that they represent a large and impressive volume of work of the type.

A church that is more generally Romanesque in character, but much more original than anything else, is St. Bartholomew's, in New York (Fig. 191), by B. G. Goodhue. Here the architect was forced to design a church and incorporate with it features of the old church of St. Bartholomew's—especially McKim's fine portico—which the parish wanted to save for artistic and sentimental reasons. Frankly retaining this as a projecting narthex, he built behind a round-arched church in harmony with it. For material, he used a pink brick, intermingled with bits of cream colour and with a white trim. By unerringly skilful composition of material he got one of the finest effects in colour and texture which American architecture has attained. The proportions, too, are unusually fine. For the interior (Fig. 192), he used an enormous barrel vault of brick, skilfully keeping all the pews in the nave and reducing the aisles to lateral passages. Not a seat exists which has not an unobstructed view of the chancel. Above the aisles are galleries with lofty transverse barrel vaults. The design of St. Bartholomew's is so new that many laymen, preferring historically correct Gothic, have misunderstood and condemned it. It is nevertheless one of the most perfect examples of combined modernism and sanity, and we venture to predict that it will come into its own as one of the most beautiful, as well as constructive, of American designs. With the connoisseurs it has already done so.

The strictly classical, as opposed to the native Colonial and Georgian types, has not been especially popular in American church architecture. It has been used most frequently by other than the Protestant sects which have felt that the other styles had been pre-empted by Protestants. The Roman Catholics especially, familiar with the use of the classical styles for church architecture in thousands of examples on the Continent of Europe, have often used the style here; not, we feel, with any conspicuous originality. The prolixity of American Gothic has challenged the ingenuity of American designers to a refinement and originality that has not been called out in the classic ecclesiastical style. Classic work has been more satisfied with correctness and a close relation to European models. A stately and very typical example of this work is the Chapel of St. Catherine, at Spring Lake, N. J. (Fig. 193), by Horace Trumbauer. It is in the classic style of Europe, suggesting the return to stricter models

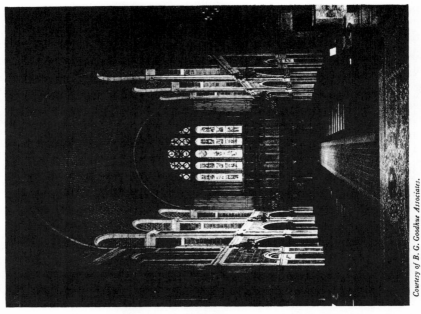

FIG. 192. NEW YORK, N. Y. St. Bartholomew's Church.

Bertram G. Goodhue, Architect.

FIG. 191. NEW YORK, N. Y. St. Bartholomew's Church.

Bertram G. Goodhue, Architect.

FIG. 193. SPRING LAKE, N. J. Exterior of St. Catherine's Chapel. *Horace Trumbauer, Architect.*

FIG. 194. CINCINNATI, OHIO. Temple Ben Israel. *Tietig & Lee, Architects.*

FIG. 195. CHICAGO, ILL. Isaiah Temple. *Alfred S. Alschuler, Architect.*

FIG. 196. CHICAGO, ILL. Isaiah Temple. *Alfred S. Alschuler, Architect.*

after the wave of Italian baroque had spent its fury in the latter part of the eighteenth century.

Occasionally the classic style has been taken over for synagogues. A dignified example is the Temple Ben Israel, in Cincinnati, Ohio (Fig. 194), by Tietig & Lee. Here we have the rich forms of late Renaissance classicism, with suggestions from Labrouste and other free classicists of the nineteenth century. Again, however, we feel that the building is more correct and conservative than interesting. The spark which produced the Gothic of Goodhue and Cram, of the Philadelphia architects and others, is absent.

Generally the Jews have shown more originality in the forms which they have preferred. For obvious reasons of association, these have been especially of a near-Eastern or semi-Byzantine character. Sometimes they have shown a complete lack of assimilation of the styles imitated and atrocious aberrations have been the result. In other cases, good architects have been employed and the buildings have attained not only originality, but impressiveness of mass and beauty of composition. As one example, we reproduce the Isaiah Temple at Chicago (Figs. 195, 196), by Alfred S. Alschuler, having in it almost as much suggestion of Aquitinian Romanesque as Byzantine. The interior, with its huge dome on pendentives, its Byzantine detail, its galleries, and its round-arched windows, is admirably adapted to the Judaic ritual. It fulfils its purpose, avoids any suggestion of the Christian Church, and gives the Jew a religious architecture which he can frankly consider his own.

Another restless sect architecturally has been that of the Church of Christ Scientist. It has striven to house itself in a type of building which would differentiate it from the older religious beliefs, but with more practical than artistic success. As far back as 1905, when Carrère & Hastings designed the First Church of Christ Scientist on Central Park West, New York (Fig. 197), we can trace the attempt at a Christian Scientific architectural originality. Here we have the general mass and silhouette of a Georgian church, with the ornament and superficial expression of the free classic of the nineteenth century. The result is originality and, as desired, the church is "different," but it is by no means æsthetically happy, even though designed by a famous and able firm. More recently, the Christian Scientists have turned to the classic domed type. A good

From "The American Architect."

FIG. 197. NEW YORK, N. Y. First Church of Christ, Scientist. *Carrère & Hastings, Architects.*

Photograph by Paul J. Weber.

FIG. 198. NEW YORK, N. Y. Third Church of Christ, Scientist, Park Avenue.
Delano & Aldrich, Architects.

216

example is the Third Church of Christ Scientist, on Park Avenue, New York (Fig. 198), by Delano & Aldrich. These buildings belong again, however, to the type of the uninspired "correct." The charm of American Gothic and Georgian, the impressiveness of American monumental architecture, the originality and imagination of American commercial building; all seem to have passed them by. One feels that the sect is young and its architecture is still in the stage of experiment.

As we might expect, some charming church designs have been done in the Spanish styles in the West and Southwest. These run all the way from the simplest "mission" chapels to great structures which embody all the glitter and theatric charm of full-fledged Spanish baroque.

A perfect example is the gorgeous Episcopal Cathedral of La Santissima Trinidad, designed by the late B. G. Goodhue, for Havana, Cuba (Fig. 199). Here the forms are of the richest and the truest. The sharp contrasts of plain walls and florid fields of exuberant baroque ornament are as interesting as any work in Spain. The building is not large in scale, but it tells as large on account of its monumental composition, at the same time charming the eye with the wealth and profusion of the ornament. Designed by the greatest master of American Spanish, it must typify for us a host of monuments which many talented Americans have designed and are still designing in appropriate districts in the United States.

Before we leave the subject of American church architecture, we must devote two or three paragraphs especially to the cathedral. Not many cathedrals are being built to-day. A trite commonplace is that this is not a cathedral-building age. Nevertheless, cathedrals are occasionally built, and on a huge scale. Civic and national pride plays its part in this, as it did in the Middle Ages, and it is healthy that this should be so. In the Middle Ages, however, the cathedral was practically the *sole* architectural expression of the wealth, the culture, and the civic pride of the citizens. Now it is rivalled in this respect by many civic monuments and especially great commercial structures which we must admit—whether we like it or not—mean more to the average citizen than do churches. Hence the correctness of the commonplace.

In cathedral, as in other work, the favourite style has been Gothic, though this is not universal. The scale has often varied, but generally when we think of a cathedral we think of a building of generous proportions.

Fig. 199. Havana, Cuba. Trinity Cathedral. *Bertram G. Goodhue, Architect.*

Fig. 200. Washington, D. C. Episcopal Cathedral: Design for West Front.
Henry Vaughan and George F. Bodley, Architects. Work now being carried on by Frohman, Robb & Little, Architects.

A very elaborate and beautiful Gothic cathedral, in process of erection, is the Episcopal one at Washington, D. C., by Henry Vaughan and George F. Bodley. The façade, as planned (Fig. 200), reminds one of French rather than English work, though the general character of the building is English. The interior (Fig. 201), with its longitudinal ridge rib and network of tiercerons, is inspired by English decorated, though the detail has not the floridity which we associate with the decorated style. The east end takes the circular form of the French *chevet*, nervous and graceful, and very un-English (Fig. 202) in character. It is hemmed in by a ring of double flying buttresses. For some reason these are built clear of the church, as piers, with a passageway of lawn between them and the apsidal wall, a feature more original than logical.* It does not spoil, however, the exquisite grace of the apsidal silhouette.

Although not technically speaking a cathedral, under this head we should mention the proposed shrine of the Immaculate Conception, at Washington, D. C., by Maginnis & Walsh, with F. V. Murphy associated. Here, for reasons we have sketched, the Gothic style is abandoned and the great pile is composed in a frankly Byzantine style. In elevation (Fig. 203) it has a portico and lofty nave, reminiscent of Romanesque. The arches are round, the detail Byzantine. Over the crossing is a nicely adjusted dome on pendentives, low, as in the sixth-century Byzantine style, yet not so low as to be unpleasantly saucerlike. It is lighted by windows in the drum. The interior (Fig. 204) has spacious barrel vaults, domes on pendentives, and walls decorated with mosaics. As in the work of all of the very best firms, though the archæological debt is clear-cut, there is no feeling of lifelessness nor copyism, and here again America is to have a monument of which it can be honestly proud.

By far the most elaborate piece of cathedral-building in America is, of course, St. John the Divine in New York. Begun many years ago, like so many of its mediæval predecessors it has suffered changes of style in its construction. The earliest architect, C. Grant La Farge, announced the deliberate intent of keeping away from the archæological point of view and striving for originality and something that was truly American. Some of his details were Gothic, others Romanesque. The massive

* There is, of course, precedent for these, especially in the English Gothic chapter-houses.

FIG. 202. WASHINGTON, D. C. Episcopal Cathedral.
Henry Vaughan and George F. Bodley, Architects.
Work now being carried on by Frohman, Robb & Little, Architects.

FIG. 201. WASHINGTON, D. C. Episcopal Cathedral: Interior.
Original Design by Henry Vaughan and George F. Bodley, Architects.

220

Fig. 203.   Washington, D. C.   Proposed Shrine of the Immaculate Conception: Model.
Maginnis & Walsh, Architects; F. V. Murphy, Associated.

Fig. 204.   Washington, D. C.   Proposed Shrine of the Immaculate Conception: Interior.
Maginnis & Walsh, Architects; F. V. Murphy, Associated.

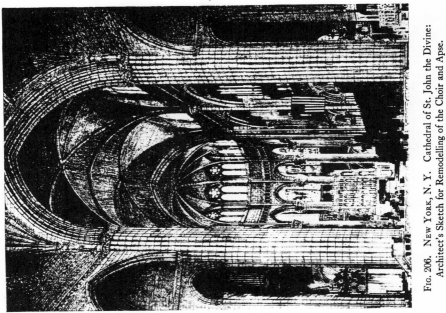

Fig. 206. New York, N. Y. Cathedral of St. John the Divine: Architect's Sketch for Remodelling of the Choir and Apse. *Cram & Ferguson, Architects.*

Fig. 205. New York, N. Y. Cathedral of St. John the Divine: Present Choir. *Heins & La Farge, Architects.*

222

colonnade of cylindrical columns which separate the apse from the ambulatory (Fig. 205) suggests the great east end of Romanesque Cluny. The low apsidal vault of brick was more Byzantine than Romanesque or Gothic. The interior was a stylistic ragout or a clever and individual piece of originality according to the taste and opinion of the observer. It was, however, bitterly criticised, we suspect especially by those whose opinions were formed more by books and theories than the evidence of their eyes. To the writer, though lawless as regards historic precedent, the present (*i. e.,* as yet unaltered) interior is one of the most impressive in Christendom.

For good or ill, however, the first designs for St. John fell before the insistent American cry for Gothic as church architecture. The earlier designers were dismissed and Ralph Adams Cram was employed to restudy the whole problem. That he will create a magnificent building none can doubt. Whether it will be finer, or as fine as the one originally planned, none will ever know. That it will be consistently and truly Gothic, as far as compatible with the use of the present structure (apse, choir, and crossing), might have been assumed and is proved by the architect's published drawings.

The present plans for St. John call for an enormous five-aisled cathedral (Figs. 207, 208). The front, more French than English, will reflect in a logical way the fivefold division of the interior plan. The five-aisled plan, however, calls for a double clerestory, which is not to be reflected in the façade. Over the crossing is to be a huge lantern, crowned with an openwork spire, on a scale rivalling, if not overpowering, the great towers of the western façade. The sexpartite vaulting of the interior (Fig. 206) is to be reflected with admirable logic in the alternately large and small flying buttresses on the exterior, the large piers responding to the major ribs, the small to the intermediate. The apse is to be raised (Fig. 207) and given a steeper and more graceful profile. The non-Gothic ornament of the earlier building is as far as possible to be suppressed. The work is proceeding apace. By a mighty effort, the Episcopal Church has launched a drive, which promises to be successful, to raise fifteen millions of dollars to complete the cathedral. Albeit we are not in a cathedral-building age, the fact that a building costing so many millions is in course of construction is a tribute to the religious spirit, pride, energy, and generosity of the American people. We can argue that the

FIG. 207. NEW YORK, N. Y. Cathedral of St. John the Divine: Sketch of Completed Design.
Cram & Ferguson, Architects.

FIG. 208. NEW YORK, N. Y. Cathedral of St. John the Divine: Projected Façade.
Cram & Ferguson, Architects.

Fig. 209. New York, N. Y. Cathedral of St. John the Divine: Present Apse. *Heins & La Farge, Architects.*

Fig. 210. New York, N. Y. Cathedral of St. John the Divine: Exterior of Apse as It Is to Be Remodelled. *Cram & Ferguson, Architects.*

225

cathedral has no place in American life. The reply is that it is in our midst. The reviewer of modern American architecture who overlooked St. John the Divine would be either biassed or blind.

No buildings show more clearly the wedding of American taste to classical architecture than those civic and monumental. As we have seen, this was made almost inevitable by the country's architectural history and especially by the popularity and success of the Early Republican style. Latrobe, Bulfinch, Walters, and many others so popularised the domed structure in civic work that the average American has come to feel that one can scarcely govern correctly unless from under a dome. The mushroom growth of domes in every State of the Union has not been entirely happy. The sophisticated are getting tired of them. Many embody pomposity rather than impressiveness, and too often domes have been raised by uninspired designers, feebly copying earlier successful buildings, but spoiling their detail and proportion in an attempt to avoid plagiarism. Nevertheless, the domed capitol has become almost a convention in modern American architecture and some of the best have shown great beauty and a haunting impressiveness. As in the case of other types, it is most noteworthy and encouraging that, despite the many fine examples which occur throughout our architectural history, the most modern work has shown the highest average of taste and ability.

We can view the question squarely by examining a few specimens of the American State Capitol. Though built in 1903 and therefore by no means a new building, the Rhode Island State House (Fig. 211), by McKim, Mead & White, is a typical example of the modern State capitol. All such designs go back in inspiration to the Capitol at Washington and thence to the great European examples of domed architecture from Bramante's time. What strikes the eye first is the beauty of proportion. With a little study, however, we see that what distinguishes this building from many of its prototypes is the chastity of its design and the refinements of its detail. This is enhanced by the material, marble, of which it is composed. That refinement of taste, so often condemned by our Continental colleagues as reactionary conservatism, was the inevitable result of the Early Republican style, which first taught monumental architecture to the United States, and of the revolt against the vagaries and stupidities of Victorian romanticism in America. For a civic building, Amer-

FIG. 211.   PROVIDENCE, R. I.   Rhode Island State Capitol.   *McKim, Mead & White, Architects.*

FIG. 212.   ST. PAUL, MINN.   Minnesota State Capitol.   *Cass Gilbert, Architect.*

FIG. 213.   MADISON, WIS.   Wisconsin State Capitol.   *Geo. B. Post & Sons, Architects.*

FIG. 214.   MADISON, WIS.   Wisconsin State Capitol: Plan.   *Geo. B. Post & Sons, Architects.*

ica—both lay and professional—demanded not only power, but restraint. The Rhode Island State House embodied both.

This domical type persisted, and an exhaustive review of our State capitols would lead to redundancy. The Rhode Island State House is, comparatively speaking, on a small scale. That at St. Paul, Minn. (Fig. 212), by Cass Gilbert, impresses one as large. Although certainly not unrefined, it has not the same striking purity that is so noticeable in Rhode Island. Its historical debts are more apparent to the designs for the Capitol at Washington and, in the dome especially, to St. Peter's in Rome. The far-flung wings are impressive, the absence of a pediment beneath the dome happy, and the dome itself a most inspiring vertical. Here again we meet the question of the propriety of a definite historical inspiration. Most would admit that the Minnesota State Capitol is beautiful; many will deny its originality and reiterate the fear that American architecture is being stifled by dependence upon the art of the past. We must consider the charge, but remember at the same time that a similar fear would have prevented Shakspere from writing *Romeo and Juliet*, or Leonardo from painting the *Virgin of the Rocks*.

Examples might be multiplied, but a few tell the story as well as many. We reproduce the Wisconsin State Capitol, at Madison (Fig. 213), by George B. Post & Sons. Here we have a note of originality in plan (Fig. 214). The building is in the form of a compact Greek cross, the crossing crowned with a lofty dome and the arms bound by exedræ. In actual elevation, the dome, with its lofty drum and attic, seems a little overpowering. It is undeniably impressive, however, and especially so when lighted at night.

Oftentimes in the newer capital cities conditions are such that an architect can plan not only the capitol building, but an entire capitol group. Some of our older capitals, especially in New England, are cursed with mid-nineteenth-century buildings, from which they cannot rid themselves, and these in turn are crowded by structures which it is not economical to remove. In the West, however, in many more youthful sites, foresight and energy have prepared for coherent capitol groups. As an interesting example, we might select the scheme made by Wilder & White for the State Capitol buildings at Olympia, Wash. (Fig. 215). Here the designers were blessed with an interesting site. They could place their build-

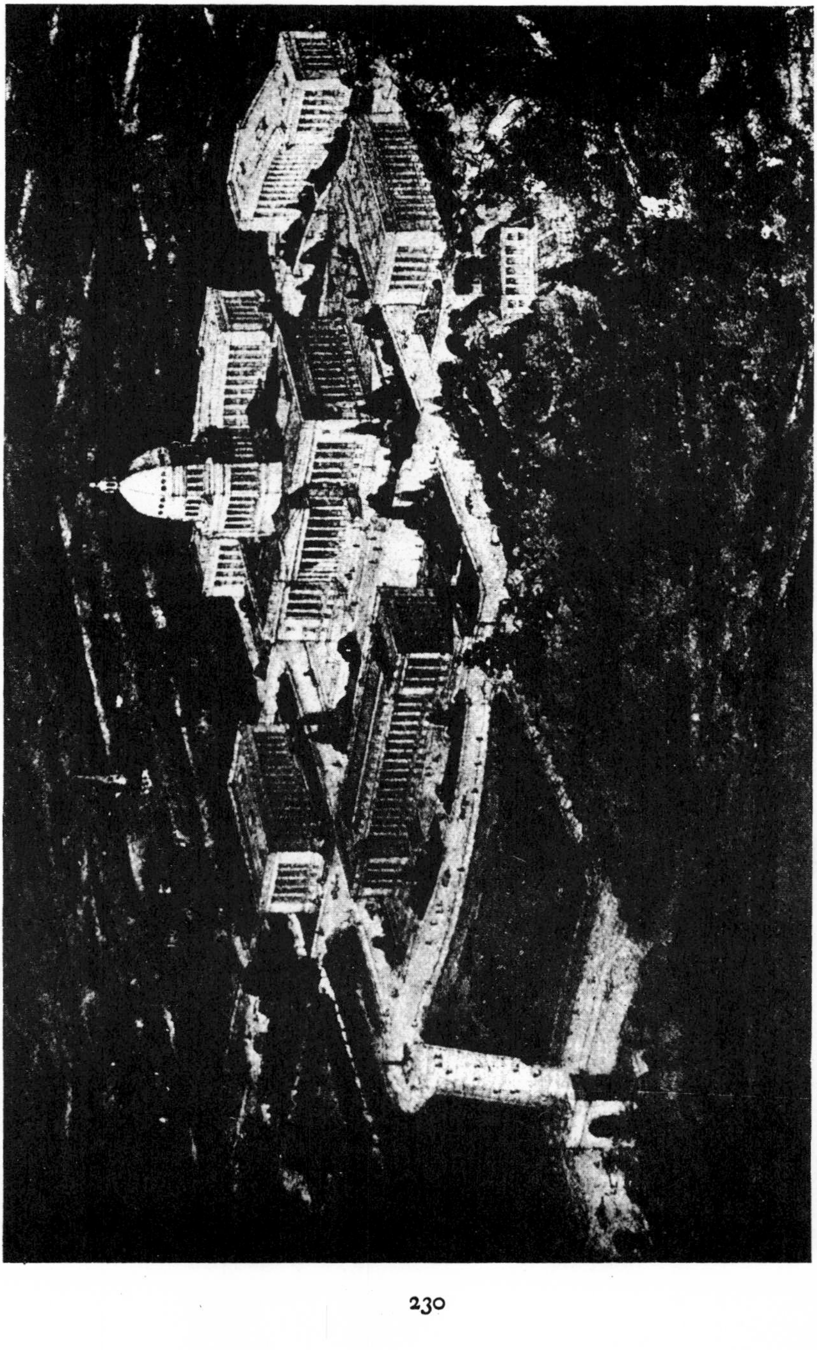

Fig. 215. Olympia, Wash. Capitol Group. Wilder & White, Architects.

ings on an eminence, further beautified by an artificial lake cut off by dams from the sound, and giving the group almost the appearance of an acropolis.   As usual, the central building was domed and designed to tower above the others, which were skilfully placed with reference to it.   The ensemble is unusually happy.   The large means necessary for such a scheme were available through the setting apart, long ago, of State land for State purposes.   Such a work can thus be put through without taxation.

The most interesting recent competition for a State capitol was that for the Nebraska buildings.   Many interesting and beautiful designs were submitted.   The competition was won, however, by a scheme which broke sharply with the past.   Bertram Grosvenor Goodhue submitted a design frankly modern and closely related to the trend of modernistic architectural expression in the Scandinavian countries.   Eschewing the classic vocabulary, using forms that were new without fearing an occasional resemblance to forms that were old, alive to the suggestions in design brought about by the use of steel and the tremendous verticality of much American commercial work, Mr. Goodhue designed a low mass of buildings, telling as one story, with an immense and severe portico in the centre and an enormous tower dominating the whole (Figs. 216, 218).   The windows are rectangular and unadorned with any enframements, classic or otherwise.   The detail of the main portal is as original and simple as it is massive.   The great tower, crowned with a cupola, is slashed with vertical openings which broadcast its steel construction.

The scheme was a bold one; its acceptance by the jury bold.   Usually juries are most conservative in such affairs.   In this case, the jury selected the boldest design, and we can applaud it, since the design is very beautiful.   For America, it is ultramodern.   The building depends for its effect on mass and proportion and these are so nicely adjusted as to be a delight to the eye.   The central tower is a paradox, for it is both massive and soaring, carrying our eyes upward as it impresses us with its bulk.   The feeling of modernism is carried consistently throughout.   The detail of the supreme court, for example (Fig. 217), is entirely modern, though it is designed with taste and skill so that it gives anything but the expression of being by one whose chief motive was to be new.   The relation between this and the modernist movement in Scandinavia we have already stated, and it is so marked that many would call Goodhue's work

FIG. 216. LINCOLN, NEB. Nebraska State Capitol. *Bertram G. Goodhue, Architect.*

FIG. 217. LINCOLN, NEB. Nebraska State Capitol: Supreme Court Room.
Bertram G. Goodhue, Architect.

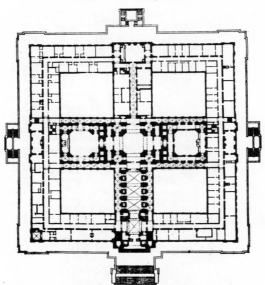

FIG. 218. LINCOLN, NEB. Nebraska State Capitol: Plan.
Bertram G. Goodhue, Architect.

FIG. 220. SAN FRANCISCO, CALIF. Civic Centre as Originally Proposed. As Now Proposed the Positions of the Library and Opera-House Are Reversed. *Drawn by Jules Guerin.*

FIG. 219. SAN FRANCISCO, CALIF. City Hall. *Bakewell & Brown, Architects.*

up to date rather than original. With this we have nothing to do. We can point out one striking difference between this work and the vast majority of the productions of Teutonic modernism. Despite its massiveness, its simplicity, its avoidance of a classic vocabulary, its newness, Goodhue's building has refinement. The same quality that we associate with American classicism we find present in this great monument of American modernism. What the Nebraska State Capitol will mean for the future is pure guesswork. It may be an isolated phenomenon caused by the special interest of one man of genius, or it may break for all time the classic trend in similar State buildings. In any case, if this type of building continues and, at the same time, the new forms persist in the American tradition of harmony of proportion and refinement, we need not fear the future.

A review of the American State capitol buildings suggests immediately the topic of municipal and town halls. Some of these, in the larger cities, rival the capitol buildings in scale and magnificence. Others are very modest and are closer to the realm of domestic architecture than monumental. As an example of the more imposing type, we may look at the huge City Hall of San Francisco (Fig. 219), by Bakewell & Brown. Here, again, we have the favourite domed type, with a central pavilion in the form of a Roman temple, flanked by Doric colonnades on a high basement, that remind one of Perrault's competition drawings for the south façade of the Louvre. The dome, on a high drum, is delicately profiled and has an unusually aspiring lantern. The exterior is majestic and severe, the interior far more ornate. The designers have drawn upon a baroque vocabulary to get the richest and most palatial interior effects.

In connection with the City Hall, San Francisco is planning and has largely put through a majestic civic centre (Fig. 220). This represents another very happy tendency in American architecture. We have seen one example of it in the group planned at Olympia. The San Francisco plans include a great square in front of the City Hall, and the development of an axis which runs obliquely into the important traffic artery of Market Street. Right and left of this axis are grouped an auditorium, an opera-house, a library, and similar buildings for the education and entertainment of the citizens. Planned together, as a unified group, each is able to set off the others and itself receives dignity from them. Throughout America such civic centres are being planned in a number of cities and

Photograph by Paul J. Weber.

Fig. 222. Peterborough, N. H. Town Hall.
Little & Russell, Architects.

Courtesy of Kilham & Hopkins.

Fig. 221. Tewksbury, Mass. Town Hall.
Kilham & Hopkins, Architects.

the success with which they are being put through bears testimony as much to the vision and civic spirit of the citizens as to the skill and grasp of planning of the architects.

It is something of a relief, however, to turn from these monumental, formal, but a trifle oppressive buildings, and look at some of the town halls that grace our smaller communities.   As in the case of domestic architecture, these vary with local taste, material, and geographical and climatic conditions.   To attempt anything like a complete review would mean repeating much that we said in connection with domestic architecture.   A few examples must suffice to suggest the charm and variety of all.   The simplest modern Georgian is embodied in the Town Hall at Tewksbury, Mass. (Fig. 221), by Kilham & Hopkins.   The material is brick.   There is no use of orders or any classic ornament, so that the building has a seventeenth-century simplicity.   The proportions are so fine, however, and the openings so happily placed, that the building is a pleasure to see as well as a most appropriate object in its New England setting.   For a more elaborate example of the New England type, we may turn to the Town Hall at Peterborough, N. H., by Little & Russell. (Fig. 222).   This building, reminiscent of Faneuil Hall, in Boston, though by no means reflecting it too closely, has the Corinthian temple front, carried on a simple, arcaded basement, made possible by the sharp slope of the ground.   The flanks are pierced with simple openings, and the reveals are very shallow, so that the building retains an humble and old-fashioned appearance, in spite of the pilasters on the front.   Again, it would be hard to find a building that fits its environment more happily. The Town Hall at Weston, Mass. (Fig. 223), by Bigelow & Wadsworth, is a far more sophisticated piece of Georgian, but no less successful.   Here we note a lofty, colonnaded portico, windows enframed with classic ornament, and a belfry as light and graceful as any that could be found in a genuine Colonial prototype.

These Georgian New England buildings the writer has selected partly because they are characteristic and beautiful, partly because he is familiar with them.   They are only three of hundreds of such structures, happily reflecting local taste.   Pennsylvania, the South, the West, all have their own which we have no time to illustrate.   By way of emphasising the variety, however, we reproduce the Highland Park City Hall, at Dallas,

Texas (Fig. 224), by Lang & Witchell. Once more the Southwest falls under the spell of Spanish. To be sure, the detail is a little dry and harsh. We do not feel the complete understanding of the style that we have found in some other monuments, but the main characteristics of the style are there, and show how the town-hall type adapts itself to local conditions.

We must not think of all city and town halls, however, as either conventional classic structures with domes, or small buildings reflecting the historic and local taste of domestic architecture. Special conditions and the imagination of architects impatient of the conventional type have evoked unusual and interesting solutions. For example, the City Hall at Oakland, Calif. (Fig. 225), by Palmer, Hornbostel & Jones, departs completely from the older type. From a broad base in three stories, with a colossal Corinthian order, a large rectangular structure, something between an ordinary building and a tower, rises for eleven stories. It is crowned with a cornice and above that contracts into two terraced structures which carry a lantern with baroque detail. Though the vocabulary is classical, the building is a modern and entirely practical one, more closely related to the commercial skyscraper than to the monumental, domical, civic building that we have seen in the capitol and some of the municipal buildings. The designers have conceived of their building as part of the busy environment of the modern city and have brought it into harmony with its surroundings.

The outstanding example of this type of work is the New York Municipal Building (Fig. 226), by McKim, Mead & White. Remembering the classical traditions of that firm, one is not surprised to see that a consistent classic vocabulary is used even in this building, the main mass of which rises for twenty-three stories. At the base is an imposing Corinthian portico, three stories in height. Above and behind is the main mass of the building which connects two wings of equal cornice height with itself. This central bulk, however, is continued up, in stepped masses, cunningly changing from a rectangular to circular form, and terminating in a Corinthian tempietto with a spire and an heroic bronze statue at the peak. The principles evolved by Sir Christopher Wren in the western towers of St. Paul's are here applied to the topping off of a New York skyscraper. For the Municipal Building is frankly that. Its classical treatment and

FIG. 223. WESTON, MASS. Town Hall. *Bigelow & Wadsworth, Architects.*

FIG. 224. DALLAS, TEXAS. Highland Park City Hall. *Lang & Witchell, Architects.*

Fig. 226. New York, N. Y. Municipal Building.
McKim, Mead & White, Architects.

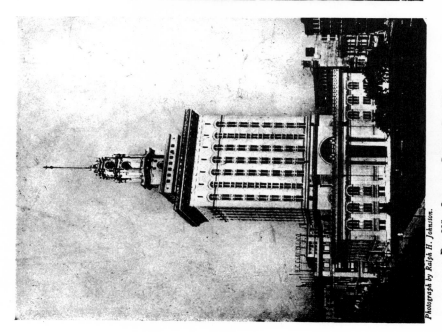

Fig. 225. Oakland, Calif. City Hall.
Palmer, Hornbostel & Jones, Architects.

sobriety temper somewhat its commercial character, but it is frankly designed for lower New York, to be the companion of commercial skyscrapers and to mingle with them on terms of equality. It has their practical advantages, their imagination, their sensationalism, and artistically it must stand or fall with them.

Of a somewhat different function, but belonging to the same general category, is the Court House, designed for New York, by the late Guy Lowell. The architect won a spirited competition, largely, we feel, by the originality of his plan. The competition drawings showed a circular plan, but practical considerations forced a change to the present one (Fig. 228) with a circular interior and an hexagonal exterior. The problem was a very complicated one, and the solution so bold as to inspire first satire, then sincere admiration. The circular central court provides not only a dignified effect, but ideal communication. The subordinate rooms are ranged about it in the happiest convenience and functional position. The eccentric light courts which it imposed, far from being waste space, as at first feared, not only fulfil their purpose, but add interest and variety to the building. The hexagonal form makes a most unusual exterior (Fig. 227). It is probably more successful than the original structure which, not without pertinent wit, was indicted as a *plaza de toros*. Boldness and eccentricity too often produce only an aberration. In the New York Court House they created a building at once interesting, beautiful, and functional.

One of the most interesting types of modern American public building is the museum of fine arts. Thanks to the great wealth of the country and the constantly increasing taste and interest of the citizens, such buildings are being erected all over the country. Even when at times one suspects that little real appreciation of the fine arts exists in a community, civic pride demands that a centre aspiring to metropolitanism must emulate its rivals and have its art museum. Oftentimes beautiful and monumental buildings are erected to house collections of the most indifferent objects. Civic pride too often is appeased by pointing to the building and ignoring its contents. On the other hand, oftentimes new museums are forced into existence by the accumulation of valuable collections and the subsequent inevitable demand that they be suitably housed. In justice to museum directors, one should observe that they are gener-

FIG. 227. NEW YORK, N. Y. County Court-House. *Guy Lowell, Architect.*

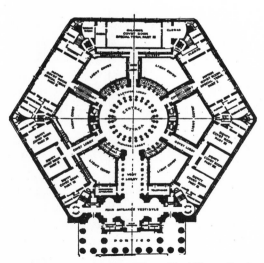

FIG. 228. NEW YORK, N. Y. County Court-House: Final Plan. *Guy Lowell, Architect.*

ally far more interested in their collections than their buildings. With the free funds at their disposal, they generally acquire paintings, statuary, silver, textiles, or whatever most interests them, making hay while the sun shines, realising that the supply is by no means inexhaustible and that what they do not buy now they may never have an opportunity to buy again, confident that the money necessary properly to house and exhibit these objects will be forthcoming when the scandal of their congestion becomes sufficiently obvious. Happily this confidence is usually justified.

From the æsthetic point of view no problem is more delicate and difficult than the design of an art museum. The two chief requirements of architecture appear in their most exaggerated form. The architect must make his building practical and he must make it beautiful. If he falters in either, his building is a miserable failure. In the past, many art museums have been built only to be beautiful. For example, in Hunt's Fogg Museum at Harvard the designer seemed anxious only to make a beautiful monument. The sole magazine space was in the basement, where there was scarcely head room; the only access to this was by stairs, down which it is impossible to carry any large object of art. There was no accommodation for packing and unpacking, the lighting was so poor that, except on the sunniest days, the visitor groped in a Stygian gloom. Hunt built a monument, not an art museum, nor should we criticise him too harshly, for he built according to the ideas of his day. Yet the building which is designed for the exhibition of beautiful objects and in which they cannot be properly shown nor even properly unpacked is a failure, no matter how beautiful it may be in itself.

On the other hand, if an art museum fulfil every functional requirement in the most efficient way and be in itself an ugly thing, it is no less a failure. It is a blatant negation of the very ideal which it is designed to foster. If an architect cannot design a beautiful building which will properly receive, house, and display objects of beauty, his art is useless and he might better turn over his commission to an engineer.

How difficult his task is, few laymen can divine. He must provide such prosaic things as ample and accessible packing-rooms, freight-elevators, and a score of functionalised rooms for photography, restorations, and all that goes with the technical study and care of works of art. He must provide for a most elaborate mechanical plant that will keep temperatures even and maintain a constant humidity. The disastrous frac-tures of delicate ancient panels have taught the necessity of excluding all outer air and supplying the building with only that which has been arti-ficially tempered, filtered, and humidified. The architect must provide not only good light, but light the source of which is arranged with refer-ence to the colour and form of the objects which it is to illumine. At the same time, he must produce broad wall spaces, unpierced by windows, against which his objects may be shown. This imposes large blank walls on the exterior, with a tendency to monotony. With all this, he must usually consider cost and join battle with client and director, jealous of every penny that goes into bricks and mortar, instead of the acquisition of new works of art. All of these conditions he must meet and make his building beautiful, as well. Verily we should judge him charitably, and yet the high standards of his profession enable us to demand his complete success.

In museum design, as in other, there are two problems: one involv-ing the creation of a new museum; the other the modification of, or addi-tion to, an old one. In the latter case, the architect is so handicapped that it is hard to judge his ability, yet the case is very common. In the great-est of American art museums, the Metropolitan in New York, the col-lection has increased so enormously and yet the plant at successive stages has been so valuable that there has been nothing to do but add wing after wing as collections accumulated. In this case, we can hold the architect responsible only for his individual wing, and one could almost trace the development of what we might call the science of museography * in the way the successive wings at the Metropolitan have been handled. On the other hand, a great many of the most modern American museums have been designed homogeneously by one architect. In this case, to other con-siderations he must always add that of the possibilities of expansion.

Obviously, we cannot go into any detailed discussion of the museum problem. We can only indicate it as above, and call attention to a few typical examples of the art museum in America. The Metropolitan, in New York, would require an essay in itself. Much of it would not be pertinent, as a considerable part of the structure we can hardly call "mod-

---

* It is a new but a real science. At Harvard, for example, a whole course is offered, for graduate students, on the museum and museum problems.

ern." If we look at the interior of the wing recently added for the exhibition of classic sculpture, however (Fig. 229), we can see how perfectly an addition is made for the exhibition of a certain *genre* of objects of art. The hall is spacious, the sculptures can be seen well, both close to, from afar, and from all sides, and the flavour of the room is truly classical. Had we time to review the new American wing, we should get a variant of the same successful treatment. On the other hand, though the museum as a whole is an imposing pile, it is hard to imagine anything that would make it truly beautiful.

In Boston the situation was not so difficult. Some fifteen years ago the trustees decided to move the museum to roomier quarters, so that the old museum on Copley Square was abandoned and the plan and erection of a huge new plant on Huntington Avenue and the Fenway was intrusted to Guy Lowell. He produced an interesting mass, with Ionic pavilions and wings, two-storied, with the upper the most important and carried on a rusticated basement (Fig. 231). The material was granite and the whole expression was severe. Imposing as the work is now, it is but a fragment of what is planned. One can criticise it in detail. For example, the rich play of light and shadow in the Evans Wing has been got by a deep profiling which unduly darkens the interior, and the designer has laid himself open to the old charge of forgetting the objects of art in the attempt to make his building itself an artistic success. On the other hand, some of the interiors are masterpieces of proper exhibition, and especially the oriental rooms (Fig. 230), in lighting, in colour, and in arrangement, are an achievement unsurpassed in American work or, for the matter of that, abroad.

In Philadelphia a great museum of art is under construction, but not far enough along for us to judge it critically. The architects' sketches (Borie, Trumbauer, and Zantinger, associated) (Fig. 232) show an impressive elevation. One of the interesting innovations is to be a daring use of colour in, full intensities. The form is strictly classical, and the use of colour in keeping with classic tradition. Just what classic colour was like, however, we cannot tell, though archæological researches have been painstaking on the subject. It is to be hoped and expected that the architects in Philadelphia will not be tempted by the will-o'-the-wisp of archæological correctness, but will select their colours boldly from the

Fig. 229. New York, N. Y. Metropolitan Museum: Pompeian Court.
McKim, Mead & White, Architects.

Fig. 230. Boston, Mass. Museum of Fine Arts: Japanese Court. *Guy Lowell, Architect.*

FIG. 231.   BOSTON, MASS.   Museum of Fine Arts.   *Guy Lowell, Architect.*

FIG. 232.   PHILADELPHIA, PA.   Museum.   *Horace Trumbauer, C. L. Borie, C. C. Zantzinger, Architects.*

FIG. 233.   CLEVELAND, OHIO.   Art Museum.   *Hubbell & Benes, Architects.*

247

point of view of what brings out the best and most decorative qualities of the architecture. In so doing, they may erect a mile-stone in the history of American art. Even more interesting is the use of "architectural refinements," planned in consultation with the late Professor Goodyear, of the Brooklyn Institute. Following a Greek precedent, but not imitating a Greek formula, every line in the building is curved. The designers thus hope to avoid, as McKim, Mead & White have often avoided, the lifelessness that so often mars otherwise admirable modern buildings.

One of the finest and most successful of American art museums was erected in Cleveland (Fig. 233) in 1916, the architects being Hubbell & Benes. Here the designers met their problem frankly and fearlessly. For exterior windows in the façade they had no need, so they were omitted. On the other hand, by the use of fine marble, a central Ionic pavilion with flanking subordinate ones, and quiet but beautifully studied proportions, they made their building a work of art worthy of its purpose and the treasures of which it was to be guardian. Within is a court, admirably suited for the exhibition of sculpture, and round it are galleries with varied functions. The scientific and practical needs of the art museum have been studied with conspicuous success.

Comparable to the Cleveland Museum is the Freer Gallery of Art (Figs. 234, 235), recently erected in Washington by Charles A. Platt, to house the collection left to the nation by the Detroit connoisseur of Whistler and oriental art. Here, again, the front was left unpierced, though the treatment of channelled ashlar is bolder and the parapet perhaps a little false in scale. Within is a beautiful court, with rooms round it specially designed for the type of objects, chiefly oils by Whistler and oriental painting on silk, which were to be shown. Again, the scientific requirements have been carefully studied. In the same general class is the beautiful Memorial Art Gallery of the University of Rochester, New York (Fig. 263), by Foster, Gade & Graham. These buildings show that the frequent necessity of designing blank walls in an art gallery may be an æsthetic asset as well as a handicap. Indeed, McKim showed the way in his design for the Walker Art Gallery of Bowdoin College, Brunswick, Maine. The materials, brick and limestone, were inexpensive, but the proportions are so fine and the detail so delicate, that the building might have been designed by Raphael. A more orthodox classic design,

FIG. 234. WASHINGTON, D. C. Freer Art Gallery. *Charles A. Platt, Architect.*

FIG. 235. WASHINGTON, D. C. Freer Art Gallery: Courtyard. *Charles A. Platt, Architect.*

but a very beautiful building, well adapted to its purpose, is the Minneapolis Museum of Fine Arts (Fig. 237), also by McKim, Mead & White. Here the façade is pierced on the main story, while a second story, lighted from above, is masked on the façade. A basement, lighted with low windows, provides extra exhibition space and rooms for instruction and the manifold technical functions of the museum. The centre is dignified by a fine Ionic portico, raised above the roof of the wings.

A building, technically designated as a library, which belongs definitely in the museum category is the Morgan Library, in East 36th Street, New York, by McKim, Mead & White (Fig. 238). In this case, a client of refined taste and unlimited means commissioned a great firm to design a modest building, sparing nothing to make it fine. Though figures are not available and it would be impertinent to ask them, there is probably no building in America that cost more per cubic foot than the Morgan Library. There is none that would give less of an effect of ostentation. The ashlar is of the finest, cut with the precision of the craftsmen of Ictinus and joined, without cement, in the Greek manner. Every detail is as carefully studied and as delicately carved as though it were itself a jewel, yet everything is quietly done. An exquisite sense of proportion is maintained between the unpierced walls and the porticoed front, with its *motif Palladio*, the favourite of the small museum. Probably no building of its size was ever designed to house so many such precious objects. The architects designed it deliberately to be worthy of its charges.

The classic style has been the overwhelming favourite for museums and certainly seems the most apt and congruous. On the other hand, not all museums exhibit this style. In New Haven, Day & Klauder have just finished the Peabody Museum of Natural History (Fig. 239), in the Gothic style. To be sure, this is not an art museum, and the problems of exhibition in a museum of natural history are far simpler than in an art museum. In the former we are more interested in the quantity than the quality of light, while the designer of the art museum is equally interested in both. The lofty Gothic windows of the Peabody Museum are, therefore, no handicap from the practical point of view. To design a Gothic art museum, however, where large blank walls are demanded, will tax the ingenuity of the architect. An ingenious architect might accomplish it, but at the cost, we suggest, of an uneconomical effort.

FIG. 236. ROCHESTER, N. Y. University of Rochester: Memorial Art Gallery.
Foster, Gade & Graham, Architects.

FIG. 237. MINNEAPOLIS, MINN. Museum of Fine Arts. *McKim, Mead & White, Architects.*

An interesting example of the university museum just completed is the Fogg Museum of Art, at Harvard (Fig. 240), by Coolidge, Shepley, Bulfinch & Abbott. Here the problem was unusually involved, as the museum had to be not only a work of art in itself and well adapted for the favourable exhibition of works of art, but also a laboratory of the fine arts for the university department. It had to include lecture-rooms, large and small; drafting-rooms; a small working library of the fine arts; storage-rooms for photographs; facilities for the taking of photographs, both common and X-ray; for chemical research in pigments, and for the restoration of works of art; in short, for the score of functions that appear when a museum is combined with a working department of the fine arts, interested in history, theory, and practice. The problem was complicated by limited funds. The building is of brick with a lime-stone trim, no orders, and depending for its effect solely upon refinement of detail and carefully studied proportions. Its success is gratifying and it is a most interesting example of the type embodying the collaboration of the architect with a long-established department of fine arts, well aware of its needs.

In the Southwest, the Spanish styles have been found peculiarly well adapted for museum purposes. The broad, blank walls, the small openings, the massed ornament; all lend themselves to easy solutions of the museum problem. We reproduce a detail of the façade of the Fine Arts Building in Balboa Park, San Diego (Fig. 241), by W. T. Johnson. For Spanish, it is very restrained work. As a stylistic performance and as a work of art, it is most creditable and, at the same time, it is ideal from the practical point of view.

A most interesting example of local architecture in museum work is the Santa Fé Museum (Figs. 242, 243), by J. H. Rapp and A. C. Hendrickson. This is a combination of what we might call the Spanish and the Pueblo styles. The two have much in common. If we look at a characteristic piece of Pueblo work, such as the oven at Taos, we note the heavy, thick-walled construction, with a tendency to batter the walls, and the otherwise smooth face enlivened by slashed shadows produced by projecting beams. This is the simplest and crudest of construction; one can hardly call it architecture, or imagine it inspiring architecture. If we look at a group of Pueblo buildings, as at Taos (Fig. 56), we see

FIG. 238. NEW YORK, N. Y. Morgan Library. *McKim, Mead & White, Architects.*

FIG. 239. NEW HAVEN, CONN. Yale University: Peabody Museum. *Day & Klauder, Architects.*

Fig. 240. CAMBRIDGE, MASS. Harvard University: New Fogg Art Museum.
Coolidge, Shepley, Bulfinch & Abbott, Architects.

Fig. 241. SAN DIEGO, CALIF. Fine Arts Building. *William T. Johnson, Architect.*

that the ensemble has an architectural impressiveness. The repetition of a number of units of the same shape produces dignity and harmony. The recurrent shadows cast by the beams make the whole sparkle. In the Santa Fé Museum many of the details are Spanish, but designed and cut with the naïvete of early Spanish work, when the actual craftsmen were usually Indians with the scantiest technical training. The exterior is derived from pure Pueblo work. It is bound to be criticised on the grounds of crudity. On the other hand, it is a most interesting example of the combination of historical influence and rampant modernism. Its sources can be guessed by a study of Taos and, let us say, the old Governor's Palace at Santa Fé (Fig. 16). Its outline, its point of view, its philosophy of design will be accepted, however, by the extremist in Teutonic modernism.

A different and probably a significant phase of modernism is embodied in B. G. Goodhue's building for the National Academy of Sciences, Washington, D. C. (Fig. 244). Modernist tendencies appeared, as we have seen, in this great artist's work in Nebraska. At the same time we have noted the refinement, so charming in his Gothic and Spanish, carried over into modernism. The same is true in the building for the Academy of Sciences. Its functions are unusual and manifold. It is at once a scientific museum, a building for instruction, and a monument. Placed on a vital and conspicuous point in the Washington plan, it could not be designed without reference to the Capitol, the Washington Monument, and the Lincoln Memorial—all whole-heartedly classical. The architect's bent caused him to reject a classical design, his exquisite taste led him to adopt one that would not be out of harmony with the classic monuments. For material he selected a beautiful, white marble. His forms are the most blocklike and simple, showing off the marble at its best. His detail is new and unclassical, but his effect of horizontality, dignity, and easily grasped geometric form are in perfect harmony with classic design. In short, he has demonstrated that one can be new and not eccentric; modern, and refined. For his interiors (Fig. 245) he used broad vaults and a new and colourful system of ornament, developed by himself. None was better fitted to do so, for this architect was a book illuminator of charm and ability and he had colour mastery at his finger-tips. The National Academy of Sciences is unquestionably a landmark in American

FIG. 242.   SANTA FÉ, N. M.   Museum of Art.   *Rapp & Rapp and A. C. Hendrickson, Architects.*

FIG. 243.   SANTA FÉ, N. M.   Museum of Art.   *Rapp & Rapp and A. C. Hendrickson, Architects.*

Fig. 244. Washington, D. C.   National Academy of Sciences.
Bertram G. Goodhue, Architect.

Fig. 245. Washington, D. C.   National Academy of Sciences: Central Hall.
Bertram G. Goodhue, Architect.

257

architecture. It does give one, however, a little the impression of an exquisite idea not entirely thought out. One of the greatest losses to American architecture was the death of Mr. Goodhue, preventing him from taking the step forward beyond this design that we should not have looked for in vain had he lived.

Another special set of problems in connection with the public building is involved in the library. These vary from huge, complicated, and ornate structures, like the Library of Congress or the New York Public Library, to the small town libraries, often the gifts of some well-to-do and public-spirited local citizen. Like the museum, the library is something of a gauge of cultural progress in America. Like the museum, however, too often it is the result of civic pride, or the desire of some prominent citizen to commemorate himself in a beautiful monument, rather than an indication of a real interest of the community in books. The memorial library, with its pretentious front and its indifferent collection of unread volumes, is none the less rapidly becoming a thing of the past. A teacher in a university is often surprised to see how frequently, when a reading prescription has caused a temporary demand for some standard book, his students will find copies of it in a half a dozen neighbouring libraries with small but well-chosen collections.

Like the museum, too, the practical needs of the library are essential and, if not attained, make the building a failure no matter how beautiful it may be. These requirements are simpler than those of the museum. The public library, large or small, must be well ventilated, provided with a reading-room, with good light by day and night; must have clean and adequate stack-room, with a chance for expansion; and must be fireproof. The most complicated problem is that of circulation. The communications from the multifold stacks must lead easily to the delivery desk. These lanes must not cross those of persons coming to the desk for books. The main reading-room must be easily accessible to the desk and yet so placed that the readers will not be disturbed by those who come to get books to take away. In a library of any scale, the reading-room must have an attendant whose desk should command the ingress and egress as a precaution against theft. This is the more important since most reading-rooms of any size are provided with books on shelves, standard works and books of reference, which may be taken down and perused without being signed for. In a really great library, there are the problems of the card catalogue, accessible to the delivery desk, the specialised rooms for the many special collections that all such libraries accumulate, and a score of other considerations peculiar to a given example. The chief idea in America, and we may be proud of it, is to make as many books as accessible as possible to as many people as demand them. This ideal, in any of our great libraries, is attained at the cost of frequent loss or mutilation of volumes. To any one who has worked in a Continental library where, by paying a large deposit, one may be entitled to demand, say, three books at a time on one day and receive them on returning the next, the gain is worth the sacrifice. All these things the architect must keep in mind and still must make his building beautiful.

The largest library in the United States, and the second in the world, is the Library of Congress, by Smithmeyer & Pelz and E. P. Casey (Fig. 246). In elevation it is classical, with a high basement and a colonnaded pavilion in the centre. It is dominated by a low dome, which covers the main reading-room. The plan is interesting, the central polygon being flanked by exedralike rooms which give it the form of a St. Andrew's cross, while it is bisected by a lateral axis with stack-room and corridors. The main desk is situated in the centre, under the dome, and is thus accessible to the stack-rooms on all sides which feed up to it from below. The main room is more convenient for delivery than for reading. Much of the building is treated in a very monumental way and indeed was designed as much as a national monument as the nation's great storehouse and delivery centre for books. Great halls and staircases, elaborate coloured marbles, and variegated painting adorn it (Fig. 247), but taste has changed since it was completed in 1897, and nowadays it looks more ostentatious than we generally consider compatible with the serious, intellectual purpose for which it is supposed to be designed. It cost $6,180,000, but it looks its cost a little too obviously.

A rather more successful contemporary was the Boston Public Library, by McKim, Mead & White, completed in 1895 (Fig. 248). In this building nothing was spared which might give it practicality and beauty. Designed to house one of the largest collections of books in the world, and a collection that, though carefully selected, was intended steadily to grow, the problems of stack space, communication, and cataloguing

FIG. 246. WASHINGTON, D. C. Library of Congress.
(*1*) *D. C. Smithmeyer & Pelz, and* (*2*) *Edward P. Casey, Architects.*

FIG. 247. WASHINGTON, D. C. Library of Congress: Grand Stair Hall.
(*1*) *D. C. Smithmeyer & Pelz, and* (*2*) *Edward P. Casey, Architects.*

were carefully studied and admirably solved. The exterior was richly designed, but kept massive and dignified, the ornament having that refinement which so frequently appears in American work. For inspiration, McKim went frankly to Labrouste's Bibliothèque St. Geneviève, in Paris. He has been accused of a lack of originality in so doing. On the other hand, most people will admit that he improved upon the original and this is the commonest way in which great architecture has been achieved. If the charge of plagiarism has any ground, it should be applied equally to Labrouste, who went as frankly to Bramante and Leon Battista Alberti for his ideas. The interior of the Boston Public Library was decorated with paintings by Abbey, by John Singer Sargent, and by Puvis de Chavannes. The latter, especially, created a colour scheme for the great staircase as exquisitely in tone with the marble architecture as any work in fresco of the late Middle Ages or Renaissance. The cost of the Boston Public Library was slightly under two and one-half millions. It gives the impression of unlimited wealth handled with the taste and restraint of intellectual good breeding.

Following these came the New York Public Library (Figs. 249, 251), completed in 1911 by Carrère & Hastings. Again, built to house the combination of three enormous collections and destined to grow, it offered its designers the most tremendous technical problems. These they overcame forcefully, though occasionally at some artistic sacrifice. For example, the enormous reading-room, beautifully proportioned, with a magnificent ceiling, is seriously marred by a delivery desk which cuts it squarely in half and prevents the eye from grasping its true proportions and enormous scale. On the other hand, the way the stack-room is handled and lighted from behind is not only practical and ingenious but an exquisite artistic success as well. The front shows a fine Corinthian colonnade, broken by a vigorous entrance pavilion, carrying an attic. The impression of that pavilion to-day is a trifle too heavy, a defect that is admitted by Mr. Hastings, the surviving member of the firm. We reproduce a photograph of a modified façade (Fig. 250), with the angles of the central pavilion broken and two more columns added, making three pairs of two columns instead of two pairs of two and single columns at the angles. This has been designed by Mr. Hastings and represents an enormous improvement on the present façade. It is interesting to note

FIG. 248. BOSTON, Mass. Public Library. *McKim, Mead & White, Architects.*

that the architect has made provision in his will for the means to carry out the change. The conditions under which an artist considers he may rest in peace often differ from those imagined by a layman! As at Boston, the detail of the New York Public Library is of great refinement, and the monument is one of which Americans should always be proud.

The libraries of Congress, of Boston, and of New York are the three particularly outstanding examples of the type in recent American architecture. Many other great examples have recently been erected, however; indeed, so many that we could not chronicle them all in so general a review. A few will call attention to the group and the excellence of the work as a whole. For Detroit, Cass Gilbert did a very magnificent library, using a simple plan and a rich but not ostentatious exterior (Fig. 252). Not unlike it in general character and scale, and one of the most dignified and gracious in effect, is the St. Paul Public Library, done for the capital of Minnesota, by Electus D. Litchfield. Both these examples favoured the blocklike elevation and the avoidance of the elaborate colonnade and the colossal order.

A separate group might be made of university libraries. Here the problem is apt to vary slightly with the need for larger reading-rooms, for greater shelf space for reserved volumes, for rooms for special study, and in many other ways. The university library must always plan for growth, but it can control its growth better than many other libraries and is usually able to exclude all books of a frivolous or ephemeral appeal. Generally, too, the university brings all the pressure it can in favour of the maximum expense for the efficiency of the plant and the minimum for the adornment of the building. Materials are apt to be simpler and the exterior effect less monumental than in the case of the public or national library. This is true in the face of the fact that, as far as the size of the collection is concerned, the university library may rival that of the municipality, or even the nation.

One of the earliest of the great modern university libraries was that done by McKim, Mead & White for Columbia, in New York (Fig. 253). It is a great domical structure, of the central type, and is purely classical. Unlike most of the work of the firm, however, it is a trifle cold and uninspiring. Nor does it seem entirely felicitous from the practical point of view. The main reading-room is not very well lighted nor very

Fig. 249. New York, N. Y. Public Library. *Carrère & Hastings, Architects.*

Fig. 250. New York, N. Y. Public Library: Façade as It Is to Be Remodelled by Mr. Hastings.
Carrère & Hastings, Architects.

FIG. 251.　NEW YORK, N. Y.　Public Library: Rear View.
Carrère & Hastings, Architects.

FIG. 252.　DETROIT, MICH.　Public Library.　*Cass Gilbert, Architect.*

conveniently arranged. There is little provision for the expansion of the collection, and one senses that the ambition to make an imposing monument has overshadowed the study of practical needs. When one compares this with the Boston Public Library by the same firm, one feels that the seriousness of the problem of the university library is not yet wholly appreciated.

As an example of the problem more practically solved, we might observe the Harry Elkins Widener Memorial Library of Harvard University (Fig. 255). Here a princely gift made possible the erection of a proper building not only to house, but in every way to make accessible, a great university collection. The architect was Horace Trumbauer, and the library was dedicated in 1915. The conservative at Harvard dreaded the erection of an enormous pile which would dwarf the older buildings in the Harvard Yard, but it is hard to see how one could place profitably a university library anywhere but in its centre and, if any building in a university is to dwarf the others, the library is surely the most appropriate one to do so.

The scale, perforce, was enormous. Although not all, the great majority of the books of Harvard were to be housed in the new building and Harvard's general collection is the fifth largest in the world, being preceded only by the Bibliothèque Nationale, the Library of Congress, the British Museum, and the New York Public Library, which rank in that order. As far as size is concerned, therefore, the problem was as grave as could confront any library. In addition were peculiar conditions involving accessibility of the books for large numbers of students and the most liberal possible accessibility in the very stacks themselves for graduate students, members of the faculty, and accredited scholars engaged in research. The reading-room (Fig. 256) had to be made large, well lighted, and well aired for the hordes of students who would be using it all day. Enormous provision had to be made for the increase of the collection and, even with the allowance made, at the present rate of growth, the stacks will be filled in ten years' time. In the stacks, cubicles with tables and chairs were placed for graduate students, and opening into the stacks were private rooms allotted to members of the faculty. For a serious student, engaged in research, the Widener Library is like the private library of an individual. The writer has taken

FIG. 253.   NEW YORK, N. Y.   Columbia University Library.
McKim, Mead & White, Architects.

FIG. 254.   NEW YORK, N. Y.   Columbia University Library: Reading-Room.
McKim, Mead & White, Architects.

FIG. 255. CAMBRIDGE, MASS. Harvard University: Widener Memorial Library.
Horace Trumbauer, Architect.

FIG. 256. CAMBRIDGE, MASS. Harvard University: Widener Memorial Library, Reading-Room.
Horace Trumbauer, Architect.

268

a hundred and more books in a day from the shelves to his study, having them charged to him merely by filling out little cards which he dropped in a slot in his study door. When one compares this with the difficulties involved in the use of libraries elsewhere, and especially abroad, one feels that the scholar must be poor, indeed, whose work does not progress in such a library. It is the heart of the university and, by the number, quality, and accessibility of its books, one can best judge the health of an institution of learning.

A very interesting example of the university library is soon to be erected at Yale (Fig. 257). The architect is James Gamble Rogers, and, consistent with his other work at Yale, the library is to be Gothic. The problem is in all respects similar to the one at Harvard. The academic conditions are the same and the collection is second only to Harvard's in size. On the other hand, the use of Gothic, with especial emphasis on verticality, is a bold innovation. The theory seems to be that with steel construction and the efficiency of the modern elevator, vertical communications are as easily handled as horizontal ones. Even in a great library horizontally composed, many tiers of stacks are imperative and numerous automatic elevators are required. The wisdom of stressing their use only time can tell. Unless a considerable number of roomy lifts with human operators are included there will be bound to be irritating delays. Other things being equal, it seems better to communicate horizontally than vertically, but this may be the retention of an old-fashioned idea. In any case, the experiment at Yale is courageous and interesting, and the perspective designed by the architect is undeniably very beautiful.

All these have been libraries on a very large scale. We must not forget, however, the hosts of charming and efficiently designed small libraries that are appearing all over the country. They remind one of the similar class of art museums which we have already reviewed. As a wholly satisfactory example, selected frankly because it is familiar to the writer, we might observe the public library of Waltham, Mass. (Fig. 258), by Leland & Loring. Agreeable proportions, refinement of brick and stone, could hardly go farther, nor could we find a monument more perfectly expressive of American taste in architecture. Again, we may be proud when we realise that this is not an isolated example, but merely one of a numerous class.

FIG. 257.　NEW HAVEN, CONN.　Yale University: Proposed Sterling Library.
James Gamble Rogers, Architect.

FIG. 258.　WALTHAM, MASS.　Public Library.　*Leland & Loring, Architects.*

For an entirely different type, but much the same in scale, we may turn to the building, as modest as it is charming, designed by W. T. Johnson, for La Jolla, Calif. (Fig. 259). Here, using the simplest means and the most economical materials, the designer has created an appropriate, intimate, and graceful work. It, like the library at Waltham, must symbolise an army of small buildings which add lustre to the American architecture of to-day.

There are, of course, important monumental buildings in the United States which are not monuments pure and simple, and yet which cannot be classified under the head of libraries, art museums, or in similar general categories. Perhaps the most conspicuous and interesting of these is the building, designed by Kelsey and Cret, for the Pan-American Union in Washington, D. C. It was completed in 1910. It is a pity that we cannot study it in detail. Few buildings have shown as good taste, as careful study, as rich a use of variegated material, and as much constructive imagination as the Pan-American building. The problem was an unusual one. There were practical considerations, such as the housing of a library, but the chief consideration was to create a monument worthy to symbolise the great cause of amity between the American nations and, at the same time, to suggest that it was a monument to North and South America and to all of the nations of both continents. The exterior (Fig. 260) is both rich and chaste. Using a fine marble and without breaking violently from ordinary architectural speech, the designers created something that immediately announces itself as different from the other buildings in Washington. There is happily no attempt to imitate any specific South American style—historic or otherwise—yet the architects, with infinite finesse, have given the elevation just that exotic touch which bespeaks a work designed for two continents and many nations. Within, archæological research and historic study have assisted imagination until, detail by detail, the mind moves to Mexico, to Central America, and to the republics of the South. Imagination has spiced archæology, however, so that never are we oppressed by that sense of pedantry which so often accompanies an archæological effort. The patio (Fig. 261) is frankly southern. It has a fountain in the centre, an open staircase at the back, Spanish windows which look down upon the flower-filled court, and a movable glass roof which can protect the court in winter and yet be rolled

FIG. 259.   LA JOLLA, CALIF.   Public Library.   *William T. Johnson, Architect.*

FIG. 260.   WASHINGTON, D. C.   Pan-American Union.
Albert Kelsey and Paul P. Cret, Architects.

FIG. 261. WASHINGTON, D. C. Pan-American Union.
Albert Kelsey and Paul P. Cret, Architects.

FIG. 262. WASHINGTON, D. C. Pan-American Union: Ballroom.
Albert Kelsey and Paul P. Cret, Architects.

273

back and open to the sky when nights are balmy and fair. Its carvings in interesting and precious materials recall the civilisations of the Aztecs, the Mayans, and other great races of the South before the Spanish Conquest. In the upper story, at the back, is one of the most beautifully designed and proportioned ballrooms (Fig. 262) which the writer has seen in any country. Here the exotic and playful is properly excluded and nothing breaks the refinement of cool, white members, perfect proportions, and aristocratic formality. Behind the building is a beautiful garden and pool in keeping with the whole.

Another important building, not purely a monument, yet none the less belonging to the general category of monuments, is the Temple of the Scottish Rite, at Washington, by John Russell Pope. It was dedicated in October, 1915. Here, again, the problem was a very special one. The building had to be adapted to a ritual and had to embody monumentality, beauty, and mystery. The style chosen was classic, yet different from the ordinary classic design (Fig. 263). Upon a very lofty base the architect carried an exquisite Ionic colonnade. This carries an attic, above which towers a stepped pyramidal roof. The effect is that of a temple, but certainly not the conventional Greek temple. One is reminded more of a great monument like the Mausoleum of Halicarnassus. The material is fine limestone, which can reveal the delicacy and beauty of the detail. The floor plan, with its spacious walls and its apsidal termination, suggests both the church and the temple, though it cannot be said to be designed strictly for either. Lofty windows, rectangular and severe, partially shrouded in curtains, admit sparse light to an interior of mystery (Fig. 264). Here again the problem was difficult, unusual, and the architect has risen nobly to a noble opportunity.

When we turn from these to buildings intended purely as monuments, we consider still another phase of modern American architecture. Since men have first built, they have tended to commemorate great events and great characters in architecture. The memorial building is often the architect's noblest creation; it has, on the other hand, often been the unhappiest. Sometimes memorials have been erected with a useful purpose in mind. Indeed, one school would hold that the finest memorial must be of some practical benefit to mankind and have some function other than pure beauty to justify its existence. Another school believes that a commemorative monument is a sacrifice, that to confuse with it a mundane function is to lower its dignity and cloud its true purpose.

With these conflicting beliefs we need not trouble ourselves. It is quite conceivable that a commemorative building might have a useful purpose and still be a fitting and inspiring memorial. On the other hand, a memorial building which has beauty certainly needs no other justification. On one point only should we insist: such a monument must be beautiful, more beautiful, if possible, than any other type of building. It may be costly or simple, imposing or modest, but beauty it must have, or it is a negation of its purpose and an architectural abomination as well. A serious danger attaches to projects for such monuments. Their erection is an act of sentiment, a fine sentiment usually, but sentiment none the less. Admirers of a great character may want to glorify him with something ostentatiously costly and thus pitifully defeat their purpose by a vulgar display. Small communities of limited means may determine to exalt their heroes when they have neither the money to erect fine work, nor the taste to demand it. America was scourged by a pest of memorials after the Civil War, many a pretty village common being ruined by a stock-made granite soldier in forage cap and baggy trousers, pathetically attesting the patriotism, the civic pride, the fine spirit, and the execrable taste of the inhabitants. The little villages of France to-day are pockmarked with hideous memorials, oftentimes the exact model being purchased, like stock mantles, for many towns, placed there by tiny and poor communities through motives which thrill us too deeply for expression, but with a taste that fills us with an equal compassion. In deciding on a memorial building, above all, we must tread softly, remembering that, whatever our motives may be, a building that is ugly or mechanical or in any way meretricious is an insult to the cause or the character that it purports to glorify.

We have no space here to consider large numbers of war memorials that are being built or planned for different parts of the country. They run from the simplest tablets to great buildings which cost millions. It is enough to note that they are as yet fewer than those projected in the years immediately after the Civil War, and on the whole very much more appropriate and tasteful.

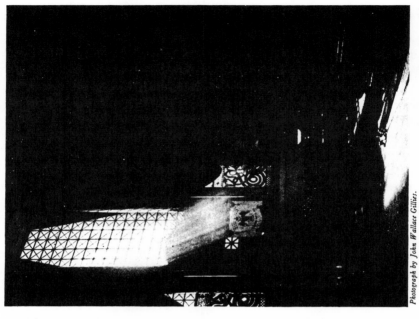

FIG. 264.   WASHINGTON, D. C.   Temple of the Scottish Rite.
John Russell Pope, Architect.

FIG. 263.   WASHINGTON, D. C.   Temple of the Scottish Rite.
John Russell Pope, Architect.

This should not lull us to ignoring the danger, however, and be luke-warm or indifferent in our fight against the shoddy war memorial. As we might imagine, most memorial monuments show a bent for conservatism, for tranquillity, and for refinement. They are almost invariably classical and, since Bernardo Rossellino first demonstrated the superiority of classic to Gothic in a sepulchral monument, the bulk of mankind have preferred the reposeful style for monuments which are intended to stimulate a feeling of reverence. The excursions into Gothic in this field, like the Albert Memorial, have but thrown into bolder relief the superiority of the classic. Modernism has occasionally offered a substitute, but nothing which has yet weaned the great mass of Americans from what they seem to consider the national style for this work.

As a very characteristic example, we may look at the first prize design (Fig. 265), submitted by Walker & Weeks, for the Indiana War Memorial Competition. Preceded by an obelisk, carried on a terraced base, a great rectangular masonry mass is reared. Its angles are solid, its façade opened by a colonnade of four Ionic columns. Above is an attic and above that a pyramidal stepped roof. The design is conservative, even conventional. The effect must depend upon the undeniably fine proportions and the refinement of detail which is the birthright of the American architect. In theory, a more original scheme, attaining the same successes of proportion and refinement, would be better. Practically, however, the commission sought a monument restrained, reposeful, impressive, and beautiful, and they got it. The story of the Indiana competition is the story of many other similar attempts to attain worthy designs for such a purpose, and it is a story destined to be told many times again.

One of the most important and most discussed of the great monumental designs of to-day is the Liberty Memorial at Kansas City, Mo. The competition was won by H. Van Buren Magonigle. The winning design (Fig. 266) showed a soaring shaft springing from a vigorous base, a part of a lofty terrace, with classic buildings symmetrically placed on either side. The terrace was broken for the base of the shaft so that it stood free of the lateral walls. The shaft was moulded to give it roughly the form of an irregular polygon. Near the summit it was embellished with heroic figures in rather low relief, breaking slightly the vertical line of the profile, and at the top was an urn from which it was planned to permit lighted steam to issue, making a pillar of cloud by day and a pillar of fire by night.

As actually built (Fig. 267), the scheme was radically changed. The break in the terrace wall was eliminated and the shaft set back so that it was on the axis of the lateral buildings. This produced an uninterrupted terrace wall, which the architect planned to decorate with a long sculptured frieze. At the same time, it must be admitted that this caused the shaft to spring somewhat abruptly from the terrace and destroyed the happy feeling of transition from the horizontal base to the vertical shaft which the competition drawing displayed. It is hardly fair to judge the effect, however, without the frieze. The most pleasing view at present is from the terrace above (Fig. 268), where a magnificent vista leads to the shaft, and the eye is not disturbed by the emphasised horizontality of the terrace wall.

It is a little too early to judge the success of the Liberty Memorial. It has been harshly criticised and as forcibly defended. The stock complaint is that it bears too close a resemblance to a chimney, and this criticism was the more wide-spread on account of the pyrotechnic display which was designed to issue from its summit and which has, for reasons of economy, been abandoned. The relief of the figures near the top is so low that they are not very legible at a distance and thus do not play a major part in emphasising the monumentality of the shaft. It is fair to say that the monument is more impressive in a close view than at a distance. It is, however, bold, original, monumental in material, and exquisite in craftsmanship. Many may deny it complete success, but most will welcome it as a refreshing attempt to get away from the trite and conventional in monumental design.

The greatest, the most typical, and the most famous example of the type in modern America is the Lincoln Memorial in Washington (Figs. 269, 270), by the late Henry Bacon. Here, an architect of the greatest refinement and the most profound sense of monumentality was given the responsibility of designing for America the shrine of one of her two universally acknowledged greatest characters. He was given at the same time one of the most dignified and beautiful sites in the world, as well as one of the most conspicuous. On a hill overlooking the Potomac, across the river from Arlington Cemetery, on the axis of the Capitol

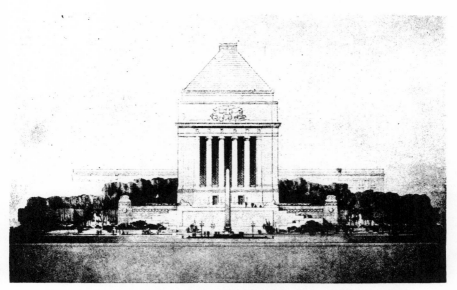

FIG. 265.   INDIANAPOLIS, IND.   Indiana War Memorial.   *Walker & Weeks, Architects.*

FIG. 266.   KANSAS CITY, MO.   Liberty Memorial: Winning Design; North Elevation.
H. Van Buren Magonigle, Architect.

FIG. 267.   KANSAS CITY, Mo.   Liberty Memorial: The North Front.
H. Van Buren Magonigle, Architect.

FIG. 268.   KANSAS CITY, Mo.   Liberty Memorial: South Front from the Mall.
H. Van Buren Magonigle, Architect.

FIG. 269. WASHINGTON, D. C. Lincoln Memorial. *Henry Bacon, Architect.*

FIG. 270. WASHINGTON, D. C. Lincoln Memorial. *Henry Bacon, Architect.*

and the Washington Monument, he was invited to rear a monument worthy of the place which Abraham Lincoln had attained in the hearts of the American people. He reverted to the classic temple form. He could hardly have done anything else. Proportion, fine material, beautiful detail, honest craftsmanship were the aids he called to express his ideal. Soundly avoiding all suspicion of elaborate ornament, he turned to severe Doric for his great exterior marble colonnade. Above it, an entablature incorporates a modified Doric frieze with the arms of the States. Above that is a simple and perfectly proportioned attic. Within is an hypæthral court, with the colossal statue of Lincoln by Daniel Chester French. A little colour is added by some painting in low intensity. Right and left, beautifully lettered, are the Gettysburg and Second Inaugural addresses. The statue looks out past terraced steps and across a thousand-foot architectural lagoon, to the Washington Monument and the distant dome of the Capitol. It would be hard to imagine anything simpler, finer, or more exquisitely appropriate. The universal acclaim which the monument has had has been a proof of the success of its designer and the taste of its admirers. In 1923 * the American Institute of Architects staged a colourful yet dignified pageant before the monument and, in the evening, as the building was bathed in soft artificial light, in the presence of the President of the United States and representatives from all the architectural organisations of the country, presented the designer with the Gold Medal of the Institute. In all the throng there was no jealous voice to call it undeserved.

Before we leave the subject of the national memorial, there is one very important building projected which should be mentioned. This is the Roosevelt Memorial, for Washington, the competition being won by John Russell Pope. The backers of the scheme selected as the site the place opposite the White House, across the long axis which connects the Lincoln Memorial, the Washington Monument, and the Capitol. It is probably the most conspicuous and important site yet available in Washington, and opposition has been raised to using it for a figure recently deceased—even so great a figure as that of Theodore Roosevelt. Whether the monument will ever be placed there is uncertain. Whether the monument which won the competition would be suitable, if placed somewhere

* The monument was actually completed in 1922.

Fig. 271.   Washington, D. C.   Proposed Roosevelt Memorial: Model.
John Russell Pope, Architect.

Fig. 272.   Washington, D. C.   Proposed Roosevelt Memorial: Model of Colonnade.
John Russell Pope, Architect.

283

else, would of course depend upon the character of the new site. All we can do, therefore, is to examine the architect's winning design, which will assure him the commission for the building, whether it be this one or another, and see what more it tells us of the tendencies of American monumental design. Though it is more unusual and original than the Lincoln Memorial, it confirms what we have observed (Fig. 271). It is severely classic, exquisitely refined, and gets its effect by monumentality and proportion. It is, however, distinctly novel in conception, being a colossal fountain. In the centre of a beautifully designed architectural pool one enormous jet is projected upward to the height of a hundred and more feet. The pool is framed by paths and by two quarter sections of a circular Doric colonnade (Fig. 272), leaving the view open through half the area enclosed. About the area is a parkway, formally treated.

The unique feature of the scheme is its combination of restraint and imagination. The low colonnades do not screen the view of the Virginia hills from the White House, and are themselves of the quietest and severest design. The pools are tranquil and reposeful features. Only the enormous jet, aptly symbolising the terrific vitality and force of the man commemorated, contrasts with the refined tranquillity of the ensemble. Itself a striking feature, it marks an essential axis without concealing a vista. There are obvious mechanical difficulties in the way of completing and continuing such a monument. With these we have no concern, nor with the argument about the site. It is enough to note one more example of refinement, of classic tranquillity, in a great American monument, designed as a permanent and dignified memorial.

IV
COMMERCIAL ARCHITECTURE

IV

COMMERCIAL ARCHITECTURE

WHEN we turn from the monumental to the commercial buildings of modern America we approach a problem the most complicated and in some ways the most interesting in our review. The mass of material is so enormous that we can only examine a few examples as characteristic of tendencies, and much of the field must remain untouched. At the outset we meet the difficulty of the relation of the architect and engineer. Just what constitutes architecture? A large office-building or department store is almost invariably built by an architect and may properly fall within our domain, but should we so classify a power-plant, built by an engineer with no architect associated? A monumental memorial bridge, such as McKim, Mead & White are now designing for Washington, is obviously architecture. Is the same true of a steel railway bridge, purely functional and entirely unadorned, and designed by an engineer whose sole aim has been a structure which can carry trains adequately, efficiently, and safely?

The word architecture comes from the Greek ἀρχιτεκτονια, or "chief building," as the word architect comes from the Greek ἀρχιτεκτων, or "chief builder." Thus, if we regarded the derivation, we should include under architecture all building. On the other hand, the modern word has come to have a more restricted meaning. Perhaps the best definition is the simplest; architecture is beautiful building. Since beauty is an abstract concept, and often a matter of opinion, this definition is not so helpful as it should be, but it is the best we have. Under it we have, without saying so, excluded many works that would ordinarily be called architecture. Under it, in turn, we may accept works that normally would be termed engineering, for many great factories and plants have an undeniable beauty despite the severely practical aim of the designers. If an engineer, meeting a special problem in a purely scientific way, produces a building of beauty, he has produced architecture. He may do it unconsciously, he may even resent the implication that he has done it at all, but he cannot escape the fact. This does not mean that all fac-

Fig. 273. East St. Louis, Mo. Cahokia Power Station.
Mauran, Russell & Crowell, Consulting Architects.

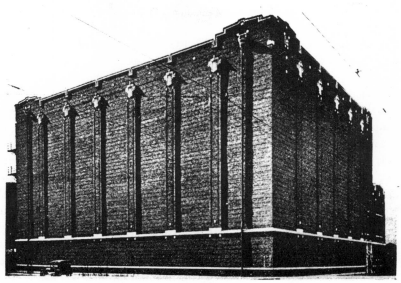

Fig. 274. White City, Colo. Cold-Storage Plant. *S. Scott Joy, Architect.*

tories are beautiful. Alas, the great majority of them are hideous, but there remain many, designed by engineers, by engineers and architects associated, and even by great architects in full control, which have the element of beauty as well as practicality and which we can be proud to include in the category of American architecture.

To begin with the severest and most intensely practical, let us consider the question of power-plants and factories and see if they may not be admitted creditably to the architectural class. Some are by well-known architects, and one of the most encouraging aspects of the art to-day is the way clients are beginning to realise that the architect's knowledge of planning can save him money in designing a factory.* One of the most important functions of an architect is to plan ingeniously to meet special conditions and, if an engineer does this in a building, he becomes—temporarily, at least—an architect. Moreover, the conditions of air, light, orderly arrangement, make for beauty and, as we have seen, even the commercial value of beauty, for its effect on client, employee, and casual observer is more and more being recognised.

Let us look, for example, at the Cahokia Power Station, near East St. Louis, Mo. (Fig. 273), by McClellan & Junkersfield, Inc., engineers, and Mauran, Russell & Crowell, consulting architects. Built up from the river in terraces of steel and ferroconcrete, vertically buttressed with great concrete strips that increase in scale with every block, pierced with great verticals of glass and crowned with four pairs of enormous chimneys, it would be difficult to find a more impressive structure. Call it engineering, if you will. Gustave Doré would have revelled in it, and the American who, on account of its purely utilitarian purpose, denies it a place in the great architecture of his country, is a man of small taste and less vision.

A power-plant has a certain romance, however, for those who have imagination. It suggests the titanic forces of nature controlled by the genius of man and, if it be on a large scale, it can hardly lack a certain grandeur. Let us look, therefore, at a still less promising type. Nothing less romantic could be imagined than a cold-storage plant, yet, if we observe the one designed by S. Scott Joy for the White City Cold Storage

---

* For a most illuminating discussion of the whole problem, see a series of articles by George C. Nimmons in the *Architectural Record*, 1918 and 1919.

FIG. 275. CHICAGO, ILL. Pennsylvania Freight Terminal.
McLanahan & Bencker, Architects.

FIG. 276. CHICAGO, ILL. Pennsylvania Freight Terminal.
McLanahan & Bencker, Architects.

Company, Colorado (Fig. 274), we cannot deny its architectural character. Here are no soaring chimneys, no picturesque terraced masses, no great windows with flashing glass. The building is a great block, but its buttressed walls, its enormous sense of scale, give it an inspiring power. Two lines of white to mark the base, spots of white to accent the bases and the tops of the buttresses, and a simple, white moulding at the top of the wall are all the "ornament" the designer has used. Their cost was negligible but they accent exactly the functional construction of the building. Again, we are conscious of the sternest practicality and a certain real beauty as well.

Another building of the most prosaic purpose and the most practical design is the Chicago Freight Terminal (Fig. 275), by McLanahan & Bencker. It is low, designed in simple masses, heavily buttressed, and pierced with small windows. The material is brick and all conventional ornament is avoided. The result is not bareness, but a fortresslike dignity. The great tower (Fig. 276), which has a functional purpose, adds to the forceful effect of the whole. The pile is severe, even forbidding, but no one would call it dull. Yet we seldom associate a freight terminal with architecture.

From this we may turn to the office-building of the Hudson Motor Car Company, at Detroit (Fig. 277), by Albert Kahn. Given a large area, the design is a horizontal one in two stories. The inner steel construction is frankly admitted. The angle piers are channelled, the friezes —if we may give them so academic a name—of the shallow pavilions are decorated with medallions in low relief. The attic (again we use the old term in lieu of a better) is topped with a simple parapet, and its under edge is picked out with rectangular blocks like the old Greek dentil range. Everything is in keeping, everything quiet, and the ornament is consciously designed for the expression of a practical structure. Economy is manifest at the first glance, but not poverty, either of means or of imagination.

We do not wish to stress the work of any one man, but it is hard, at this point, not to mention the building for the Detroit *Evening News* (Fig. 278), again by Albert Kahn. This is a typical example of revealed steel construction in a building of the horizontal and not skyscraper type. The ground story is arcaded, with buttresses between, which run up to the attic and mark the course of the main steel columns. Above are rows of windows in pairs of three, corresponding to the arcades below.

FIG. 277. DETROIT, MICH. Hudson Motor Car Company Office Building.
Albert Kahn, Architect.

FIG. 278. DETROIT, MICH. Detroit Evening News Building. *Albert Kahn, Architect.*

FIG. 279.   CHICAGO, ILL.   Donnelly & Sons' Printing Plant.   *Howard Shaw, Architect.*

FIG. 280.   SOUTH BROOKLYN, N. Y.   U. S. Army Supply Base.   *Cass Gilbert, Architect.*

The proportions of arcades, windows, and attic are exceptionally fine. The ornament, classic in feeling, but modern in design, is sparing and appropriate.   One senses immediately the lightness, airiness, and functional practicality of the work, while one delights in its proportions and refinement.   It avoids any archæologising and lavish parade and attains the finer art.

Another superb example of the same type is the R. R. Donnelley & Sons Co. Printing Plant at Chicago (Fig. 279), by the late Howard Shaw.   Here the material is reinforced concrete with dark-red brick and Indiana limestone for the exterior.   Once more the main steel lines are emphasised and great windows are opened from base to cornice between the rhythmic buttresses.   The angles are reinforced with what appear as rugged pylons, but flush with the wall, their use as isolated passages for vertical communication revealed by the windows on one side.   The building is topped with an arcade, far more effective than the old-fashioned cornice.   The arches are pointed, but it would be as absurd to call the design Gothic as it would be to call the Cahokia power-plant classic because of its accent on horizontality.   The modern designer has not only passed beyond archæology, he has even overcome the fear of being accused of it, and is free to get his ideas from any source, provided only that they be appropriate to the work in hand.

We cannot linger too long over this very practical type of architecture.   One more example will be illuminating, however, to prove what an effect sheer mass, coupled with fine proportion, can do in a building so sternly practical as almost to parade its desire not to be regarded as a work of art.   We refer to the U. S. Army Supply Base, at South Brooklyn, N. Y. (Fig. 280), by Cass Gilbert.   This is purely in reinforced concrete.   Every detail of ornament, every suggestion of the amenities which we associate with the fine art of architecture is ruthlessly excluded.   Mass it has, and line, and fearless honesty.   These it could have and still be ugly, but these are used not only to permit it to fulfil its function but to make it beautiful as well.   We should look in vain for refinement; indeed, that quality would be incongruous in an army supply base.   On the other hand, we look in vain for coarseness, or vulgarity, or the blatant revelation of a crass commercialism.   The building has dignity, power, and a self-sufficiency that is neither boastful nor unconscious.

Bridges offer a difficult subject in our review.   They may be divided into those, the point of view of which is purely engineering, and those that are primarily monumental. If these categories were clearly marked the problem would be simple, but they overlap. As we have seen, the railroad bridges of the engineer often have beauty and the most purely monumental bridge has its traffic function to solve, without which it would be an absurdity. Indeed, one of the beauties of any bridge is the observer's feeling that it is satisfying a need. No matter how monumental it may be, Sir John Vanbrugh's bridge at Blenheim will always be laughable in that it is designed in scale for a Roman army and crosses one shallow arm of a body of water that it makes appear no larger than a duck-pond. All that we can do is to examine one or two examples of the general types, showing how the engineer's work may be beautiful, how the architect's may be practical, and how the two types tend to merge. The engineering type is apt to be of suspension or cantilever design, the monumental supported on piers of masonry and the spans arranged on the principle of the true arch. The rule is not invariable, however, and oftentimes our modern reinforced concrete affords the appearance of the latter and not its fact. In such case we are dealing not with an architectural deception but the appropriate use of a new medium.

The era of great bridge-building opened, we might say, with the Brooklyn Bridge in New York. This engineering triumph, achieved in 1883, by John A. Roebling and W. A. Roebling & Sons, was justly hailed as an epoch-making work. Attention was concentrated naturally upon the physical aspect of the bridge, the tremendous difficulties overcome, and the miracle of science which it embodied. There were not lacking many, however, who were conscious of the extraordinary beauty of the structure, the power of its mighty piers, the swinging curve of its huge cables, and the lacelike pattern of its web of supporting antennæ. Here, if ever, a bridge was a great work of engineering and of art. It set the type and, since then, a number of great suspension bridges have been designed,* equal triumphs in engineering, though sometimes not the peers of the original from the æsthetic point of view. Any such bridge, however, by the very nature of its scale and construction cannot but be impressive and have grace as well.

* Witness the Williamsburgh Bridge (1903), the Queensboro Bridge (1909), and the Manhattan Bridge (1909), all in New York. To Palmer & Hornbostel belongs the lion's share of credit for these works.

Fig. 282. Camden, N. J.   Delaware River Bridge.
R. Modjeski, G. S. Webster, and L. A. Ball, Engineers; Paul P. Cret, Architect.

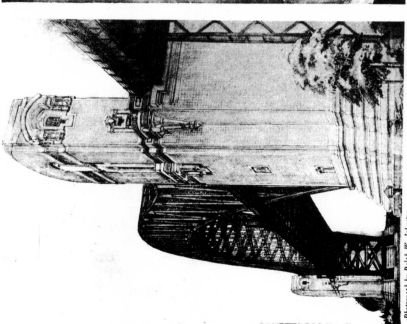

Photograph by Ralph W. Johnston.
Fig. 281. New York, N. Y.   Hell Gate Bridge.
Gustav Lindenthal, Engineer, with Palmer & Hornbostel, Architects.

FIG. 283. BOSTON, MASS. Proposed New Harvard Bridge.
Andrews, Jones, Biscoe & Whitmore, Architects.

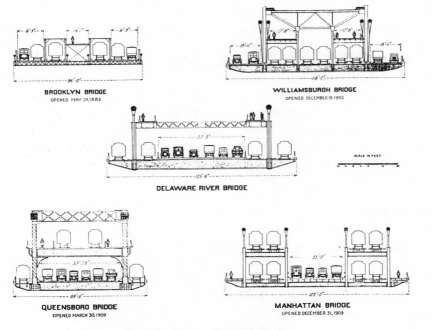

FIG. 284. Comparative Bridge Designs.

For a more intensely practical and severe modern work we might turn to the Hell Gate Bridge across the Harlem River in New York, designed by Gustav Lindenthal, with Palmer & Hornbostel as architects (Fig. 281), and opened in 1917. It was built purely for train service. Cantilever construction was used, and the striking feature was the great steel arch thrown across to span the entire river. We may be assured that that arch, costing millions, and constructed to carry the traffic of several railroads, was designed with an eye to engineering efficiency and not to beauty. Here was a case, if ever, where art would have to wait on science; yet when the bridge was done it was a very beautiful thing. It is a mistake to suppose that engineering efficiency imposes a functional and accidentally a graceful line and mass. Works of sound science and proved engineering efficiency, yet atrocious to the eye, exist in dismal numbers. Good engineering may, however, produce great art, and is the more apt to do so as the scale increases. Indeed, we suggest, though it cannot be proved, that *the best* engineering will produce work of beauty. In any case, we insist that the Hell Gate Bridge, a work with no pretense to other than engineering expression, is a thing of beauty.

Were we to follow the line suggested by this work it would take us too far afield and we must confine our attention to bridges of a more strictly architectural character. For the simplest type we have already seen how effective can be the concrete bridge, with bare piers and arches and practically no ornament at all, when we observed the bridge which spanned the ravine leading to the grounds of the San Diego Exposition (Fig. 52). Goodhue had designed a more elaborate structure, but reasons of economy imposed the simpler construction.

Examples of the concrete bridge built along the lines of the older, true-arched type are legion. At random we select one by Andrews, Jones, Biscoe & Whitmore (Fig. 283), designed to replace the present ugly steel Harvard Bridge which joins Boston with Cambridge, Mass.* Here the basin is shallow, the interval to be spanned very wide, and water traffic limited to small boats. Consequently the designers have suggested a low bridge of nine arches, built out from artificial promontories treated as parks. The flattened arches are given a graceful parabolic curve, so

* It has recently been decided, for reasons of economy, to retain the old bridge, so the design we reproduce will probably never be more than one on paper.

that, with the greatest economy of material, the roadway may be kept level. Suggestions for such designs are found in large numbers in Europe. We have in mind particularly Ammanati's Ponte Trinità at Florence, the father of a numerous progeny. Such a type lacks the grandeur of the lofty and wide arch, and has been called derisively the frozen caterpillar bridge, but under the conditions outlined it is entirely appropriate and can be made very graceful and beautiful.

One of the most ambitious designs for a modern great suspension bridge is the one just constructed to span the Delaware River from Philadelphia, Pa., to Camden, N. J. It is designed both for motor traffic and street-cars and rivals the Queensboro and Manhattan Bridges in New York in the volume (Fig. 284) which it carries. Unlike these two, however, it is not double-decked, so its roadway has to be very broad.* It carries six lanes of motor traffic and four of street-cars. The piers are 60 feet wide, a span of 1,750 feet from centre to centre of the piers is required, and the floorway at any point may be called upon to bear a moving weight of 30 tons. The board of engineers who reported on the work were Ralph Modjeski, George S. Webster, and Lawrence A. Ball. The actual architectural design was done by Paul P. Cret. A general sketch of the bridge (Fig. 282) shows its breathless daring and its great grace as well. The anchors (Fig. 285), massive as fortresses, would seem frail were it not for the tenuity of the great steel antennæ which they restrain. The architectural details are bold, yet once again they show that refinement which is such a precious thing in American architecture. Unlike the older type of the Brooklyn Bridge, the central pier supports are of steel, giving additional lightness to the whole design. The sketch reveals this and suggests, as well, the tremendous daring of the span.

To conclude our discussion of bridges with one of an entirely different type, we turn to the beautiful classic design made by McKim, Mead & White for Washington, D. C. (Fig. 286). It is to cross the Potomac, near the Lincoln Memorial, and will be one more monumental addition to the great ensemble of architecture in the Capital. Here dignity, repose, and the feeling of permanence were essential. No modern steel, no suspension work could adjoin the Lincoln Memorial. As a result the bridge

---

* One hundred and twenty-five feet six inches. The Manhattan Bridge, its nearest rival in this respect, is 123 feet broad.

FIG. 285.   CAMDEN, N. J.   Delaware River Bridge: Philadelphia Anchorage Looking Northwest.
R. Modjeski, G. S. Webster, and L. A. Ball, Engineers; Paul P. Cret, Architect.

FIG. 286.   WASHINGTON, D. C.   Arlington Memorial Bridge.
McKim, Mead & White, Architects; Colonel C. O. Sherrill, Chief Engineer.

is low, of many arches, segments of hemispheres to keep the roadway low and level. The detail is to be crisp, but the design is chastely simple. Statuary will appear, sparingly used, to mark the great piers. Otherwise the line of the roadway will be unbroken. These two, the Delaware and the Arlington Bridges, can stand for the two types of daring engineering with architectural beauty and of pre-eminent monumentality with perfect functional fitness.

Nothing is more inspiring in modern American architecture than the way the railroad-station has been developed. Not long ago it would have been considered absurd to attempt to make a railroad-station beautiful. The public was used to smoke, gas, dirt, gaunt steel beams, befouled glass, and dingy platforms, and considered these the logical concomitants of the railway terminal. For a long time the designers were so preoccupied with the problems of getting the trains in and out safely and of loading and discharging passengers that the thought of beauty never entered their heads. This attitude still prevails in some parts of the country and is common in Europe. Generally in America, however, a determined effort is being made to make our railway-stations beautiful as well as convenient, and to give the entering stranger a first impression which will charm and not repel. So elaborate are some of our greater terminals that we have been accused of vulgar lavishness in commercial enterprise. Such criticism, naturally, we can ignore, and anything which will tend to make more beautiful the surroundings in daily life of a million citizens we can welcome with enthusiasm.

The difficulty of the problem makes its successful solution the more creditable. Many trains must be brought in and out swiftly and on scheduled time. Vast numbers of passengers must be allowed to enter and depart without the traffic lanes crossing one another in a confusing manner. Ticket-offices must be conveniently placed to handle not only normal sale but rush orders, when hordes of impatient travellers arrive simultaneously and must be provided for immediately or miss their trains. The bureau of information must be placed where none can miss it. Large waiting-rooms must exist for those who come early or wait between trains. Elaborate and roomy communication must be arranged for those who come and go, either as pedestrians or in vehicles, and everything must be done with an eye to the greatest speed and the least confusion, for our Ameri-

Fig. 288. New York, N. Y. Grand Central Station.
Warren & Wetmore, Architects.

Fig. 287. New York, N. Y. Pennsylvania Station.
McKim, Mead & White, Architects.

302

can citizen of to-day, either from necessity or force of habit, is always in a hurry. When one considers the complicated physical difficulties in the design of a railway-station one wonders that beauty ever came to be considered at all.

Bearing this in mind, let us look at the grand concourse of the Pennsylvania Railroad Station at New York (Fig. 287), by McKim, Mead & White. One is almost awed by its spaciousness, its dignity, and its vast scale. Its design is Roman classical, recalling directly the baths of Caracalla, and it has often been attacked as being too archæological. Here again, if a Roman bath can suggest a design most apt for a terminal concourse, it is hard to blame an architect for adopting the suggestion. A far more pertinent criticism would attack the congruity of the original for a bath. Whatever the source, the designers have given us one of the most impressive interiors in the country and one that will stimulate the imagination and elevate the mood of every passenger who enters it. On the other hand, as planning, the Pennsylvania Station does not live up to the promise of its concourse. The multiple exits discharge the passengers easily and quickly, but any one who has tried to meet an incoming friend will know how confusing they are. The long promenade from the façade to the concourse is also of dubious value.

New York's other great station, the Grand Central, finished in 1913 by Warren & Wetmore, is an even greater achievement. Its exterior is not so imposing as that of its rival, and the scale of the central group of statuary is disturbing to say the least. The planning, however, is far superior. Trains enter, load and unload, and depart with clocklike regularity. Multitudes of passengers come and go with so little confusion that their numbers seem few. The most absent-minded can find his train without hesitation, and every incoming train with its exit is so neatly handled and clearly announced that one can meet a friend almost without effort on the most crowded day. The chief glory of the Grand Central is its concourse (Fig. 288). Here there is no archæology. Enormous square piers, without capitals, go up to support a cornice and a huge plaster vault. The vault is painted light blue, with the signs of the Zodiac in light dull gold for decoration. The scheme is daring in the extreme and as successful as it is bold. In the centre the information bureau, circular so that it can be approached from all sides, advertises itself as one enters from any direction. The details of ticket-offices, check-rooms, telegraph-offices, etc., are in fine marble, as crisply and simply designed as possible. The whole interior is original in conception and of the greatest beauty as well. The writer was never prouder of his country's architecture than one day when he entered this concourse with a cultivated young Englishman and heard his delighted comment that at last he had found a race that had not only the taste, but the sense, to make a railway-station as beautiful as a palace or a cathedral.

We must not imply, however, that the great railway-stations are confined to New York. One of the greatest and one of the best planned is the Union Station in Chicago, by Graham, Anderson, Probst & White. Its exterior (Fig. 289) is both pleasing and practical. A long, Tuscan colonnade dignifies the façade and offers instant shelter for any one entering the building. The waiting-room (Fig. 290) is treated simply, but with reasonable richness, by a Corinthian order and a great steel and glass skylight. As at the Grand Central, the information desk is in the centre, this time not of the concourse, but of the waiting-room. The thing that impresses one particularly is the frank revelation of the steel. No attempt has been made to clothe the steel in another material (Fig. 291). It springs from the marble floor and rises to support a steel and glass roof, yet it is graceful in its lines and curves so that one is not disturbed by its harshness or engineering frankness but accepts it as a beautiful part of the design. Here, again, we have the union of the practical and the beautiful.

These have all been stations on a large scale, in great metropolitan centres, erected at the cost of millions. Were they the only creditable railway-stations being erected in the country we could not be so optimistic as we are. The same taste, however, which has produced so much beauty in the greatest terminals is producing the same sort of thing in a more modest scale elsewhere. Let us look, for example, at the Union Station at Richmond, Va., by John Russell Pope. Its exterior (Fig. 292) is a charming composition with a central Doric colonnade and attic, simple, well-proportioned wings, and a dome in the centre, low and harmoniously related to the rest of the building. Such a work is a beautiful monument and a credit to the city. As one enters the waiting-room (Fig. 293) one has the same impression of restful charm and dignity. The

FIG. 289. CHICAGO, ILL. Union Station: Canal Street Façade.
Graham, Anderson, Probst & White, Architects.

FIG. 290. Main Waiting-Room.

FIG. 291. Secondary Concourse.

CHICAGO, ILL. Union Station. *Graham, Anderson, Probst & White, Architects.*

glory of the American station is that it seems to take care of the hurrying, bustling passenger *noiselessly*. It envelops him, it informs him, it expedites his movements, but its spacious interiors swallow the noise he makes and its great scale reduces his nervous rushing about to a trifle. There is no place, short of the stock exchange, where nerves are more on edge than in a railroad-station, and it is the more remarkable and happy that these are being designed not only to function perfectly but to quiet and to soothe.

Had we the time we could see the same good work extended to stations all over the country. Many ugly ones are still designed, of course, but better and better work is being done and, what is more encouraging, many of the old atrocities are being remodelled. In conclusion, we might glance at a southwestern example just to remind ourselves of how aptly the Spanish style is being used in this type as well. It is the attractive little station at Ajo, in Arizona, by Kenyon and Maine (Fig. 294)—a well-planned, well-composed, and entirely appropriate building. Here once more the West shows its local individuality and falls into harmony with the general tendency to make the railway-station an object of beauty as well as utility.

Any discussion of American commercial building must include a reference to shops, both great and small, but here the subject is so vast that it would require a separate volume to begin to do it justice. Nothing is more characteristic of America than the department store. There are such stores abroad, but in nothing like the numbers in America, and usually based upon the American type. A building for one of these great shops must almost house a community. In designing it, the architect must think of light, of air, of window display, of varying proportions of rooms and stories to assist the sale of various kinds of objects. Obviously, one can sell gloves in a room that would not be suitable for the sale of tapestries, but the shopper rarely stops to consider the fact. Were it not considered by the architect, we should soon be aware of it, however, and would probably shop elsewhere. As always, communications are important and large areas of the building, of which the shopper is blissfully unaware, must be devoted to services for receiving, unpacking, and shipping goods. All this must be arranged for rapid, smooth handling. One parcel misdirected often means a lost customer and the man-

Fig. 292. Richmond, Va.
Union Station.
John Russell Pope, Architect.

Fig. 293. Richmond, Va.
Union Station.
John Russell Pope, Architect.

Fig. 294. Ajo, Ariz   Railroad Station.   *W. M. Kenyon and M. F. Maine, Architects.*

307

agement and the architect are aware of this fact. Rooms of all sorts must
be devised; lunch-rooms, for example, with their kitchen service; so that
the problem approaches that of the hotel. The best big stores provide
lunch-rooms, rest-rooms, and recreation-rooms for the employees. Indeed, the architect of the great department store is almost a community-
planner.

Examples of the type are so common and so well known that it almost seems superfluous to quote them. Any inhabitant of a large American city is aware of one that he can study and, if he will enter it with an
eye to understanding its architectural problems, instead of merely to purchase goods, he can learn a great deal by observation.

As a modern, a refined, and orderly example we might select Lord &
Taylor's (Fig. 295), in New York, by Starrett & Van Vleck, completed
in 1914. Here the steel supports are revealed, though they are scarcely
an integral part of the design. At the base they are broken by broad horizontal windows for display. The masses of smooth masonry right and
left of the arched entrance and the masses at the angles give the eye a
sense of support for the upper stories. The detail is refined, and in this,
as in so many other types, we note that steady trend of American architecture away from the coarse, the careless, and the florid.

A very different type is the great addition to Macy's (Fig. 296), in
New York, made by Robert D. Kohn & Associates. Here we meet a
new type of design, caused by the New York Zoning Law, of which we
shall have more to say later. It is enough now to note the scale, the picturesque relation of masses, the economy and practicality yet the fine effectiveness of the design. The problem is the old one but it is met in a new
way and the department store falls into line with the most up-to-date tendencies of the architecture of New York.

Certain stores by their function require a more dignified and refined
appearance than others. When a firm of jewellers like Tiffany & Co.
moved to new quarters, they commissioned McKim, Mead & White to
design their building. As might be expected, the design was dignified,
refined, and severely classical (Fig. 297). A firm selling precious jewels
and works of art, catering to a wealthy and discriminating clientèle, required a building which should be monumental, itself a work of art, and
marked by refinement. It called in artists who could fulfil this ideal and
created an aristocrat among shops.

FIG. 295. NEW YORK, N. Y.
Lord & Taylor's Building.
Starrett & Van Vleck, Architects.

FIG. 296. NEW YORK, N. Y. Addition to
Department Store of R. H. Macy & Co.
Robert D. Kohn & Associates, Architects.

FIG. 297. NEW YORK, N. Y. Tiffany Building.
McKim, Mead & White, Architects.

FIG. 298. NEW YORK, N. Y. Macmillan Building.
Carrère & Hastings and Shreve & Lamb, Architects.

Of much the same refinement, though greater originality in treatment, is the Macmillan Building, in New York (Fig. 298), by Carrere & Hastings and Shreve & Lamb. Here, again, a dignified and long-established publishing house would want to avoid vulgarity and ostentation. At the same time, it would welcome the cultivated expression of fine material finely used, and would be glad of a certain up-to-date originality in its dwelling. This it got. Fine stone is used for the exterior, but its lines reveal that it clothes steel. The base is heavy, pierced with large windows, and dignified on the Fifth Avenue side by two pairs of Ionic columns. The angles are marked by pierlike walls of smooth ashlar, flanked by broad strips of superposed windows. Between the angles the windows are narrower, and slender piers of stone, obviously concealing steel, are carried through to the roof-line. The cumbrous cornice of a generation ago is happily suppressed in favour of a simple parapet. The result is a dignified and refined structure, yet smart and up-to-date. Such a work once more emphasises the modern American tendency towards refinement and restrained richness in architecture, as well as originality and the elimination, after due thought, of illogical features inherited from the past.

From this we can turn to the smaller shops, or shop fronts. Here the varieties are bewildering and the tendencies legion. A few, however, it is easy to analyse. One noticeable thing is the attempt, often conspicuously successful, to reveal in the front of the building the character of the goods it offers. Obviously, a store for jewelry, flowers, or candy should not have the same character as one for the sale of sporting-goods or books. Another tendency is to take advantage of modern steel construction to allow a plate-glass front to display the goods and tempt the purchaser. Sometimes this is got at an apparent denial of support to the upper stories, which is disturbing. Too large areas of glass are hard to handle but, when well composed, these great first-story windows can be fine. This is especially so when they have been designed intelligently to allow the shopkeeper to make his window display a work of art properly enframed. A good window display is a work of art. The windowdressers of such a firm as Yamanaka, in New York, show their Oriental cunning in colourful and harmonious arrangement and are true artists. It is to the credit of the public taste that the window display which is an artistic success is also a commercial one. It sells goods. Here the architect can give his client material aid, while exercising his talent as well; nor should he, nor any one else, ever despise a commission to do a shop. The "commercialisation" of art in America is one of its happiest features.

Another characteristic which we might observe is the tendency towards "modernism" or vice versa. A small shop is not like a church, or even a bank; it does not take itself too seriously. Oftentimes it is willing to be eccentric for the advertising value of eccentricity. One often, therefore, gets effects of originality in shop fronts that one will find nowhere else. Sometimes these are vulgar, sometimes laughable, but often interesting and fine. On the other hand, there are shops that are conservative, that lean towards the historic styles and seek to prove themselves a part of an ancient community of inherited traditions and respectability. These and a hundred other conditions go to make the variety of the type which we can examine only in a few random examples, noting several ways in which the problems are solved, several of the tendencies which we have sketched, and, above all, the improvement in design, refinement, thought, and imagination which the shop fronts of to-day show over those of a generation ago.

For the exquisitely refined and conservative type, we might select the building for Chickering & Sons, in Boston (Fig. 299), now unfortunately remodelled, by Richardson, Barott & Richardson. It is of brick and limestone, frankly in the Early Republican style, and is as delicate and charming as a dwelling. One feels distinguished merely to enter it. For an old, established firm, engaged in the manufacture and sale of pianos, nothing could be happier. Moreover, when one notes the attention that the building attracts from those persons who might have the means to buy pianos, one is inclined to add that nothing could be shrewder. For the same sort of thing in an entirely different style, we reproduce a building in Los Angeles, by Morgan, Walls & Clements (Fig. 300). It is designed as an art shop, and the Southwesterners have selected their beloved Spanish style. It expresses perfectly the function of the building, gives it prestige, and makes it a work of art to house the works of art which it is its function to sell.

As an example of more modern treatment but one in which the greatest stress is laid upon refinement and the clean-cut, chaste use of fine material, we might select an art shop in East 56th Street, New York, done by Trowbridge & Ackerman (Fig. 301). The building is narrow. In

Photograph by Thomas Ellison.

FIG. 299. BOSTON, MASS.
Chickering Building, as It Formerly Appeared.
Richardson, Barott & Richardson, Architects.

FIG. 300. LOS ANGELES, CALIF.
Van Nuys Building.
Morgan, Walls & Clements, Architects.

FIG. 301. NEW YORK, N. Y.
Art Shop. 56th Street.
Trowbridge & Ackerman, Architects.

FIG. 302. NEW YORK, N. Y.
Maillard's Shop.
Cross & Cross, Architects.

the centre one great window with fine glass displays a sparing number of works. Right and left are doors, without mouldings or enframements, which set off the beauty of the finely cut stone. Above are windows, without enframements, and a delicate gallery on corbels. The proportions of such a building are early Republican, the actual design entirely modern.

Another type can be illustrated by the façade designed for Maillard's candy store (Fig. 302), in New York, by Cross & Cross. Here a monumental wall of fine ashlar is left plain, and the shop front, in two stories, is broken through it and composed entirely in metal and glass. One could criticise the design on account of a lack of relation or binding element between the shop front and the wall. On the other hand, the whole front is treated as a great window and this explains itself and needs no further enframement.

An interesting example of the extensive use of glass and steel is Child's shop on Fifth Avenue, New York, by William Van Alen & Severence. This building (Fig. 303) turns the corner not with a sharp angle but with a curve. This curve is filled with glass at each window level, so that when viewed from slightly up-town each story seems to be supported at the edge only by the frail curved pane of the plate glass below. The effect is rather terrifying and fascinating at the same time. The building certainly attracts attention and in detail and material it is fine. Its function allows for a certain playful fancy and one might justify its violation of organic feeling on this ground. Its design was a bold experiment, however, and one feels that it flirts with, rather than solves, the problem of the maximum glass area for display.

A much more exuberant shop front is that which we reproduce by Shape & Brady, done for the Edison Company, in New York (Fig. 305). Here there is a distinct splaying of the opening to produce a welcoming effect and draw the visitor in. In the centre a broad window displays the wares and right and left are a window and a glass door. Above the splay of the archway, the *voussure*, is filled with exuberant relief in stone and terra-cotta. Here restraint and dignity are sacrificed to gaiety and the whole design resembles a pretty stage with proscenium and stage proper arranged for the wares as actors.

Finally, as an example of out-and-out modernism, handled in a sprightly way, we may look at the front of E. Weyhe's book-shop on

Lexington Avenue, New York (Fig. 304), designed by Henry S. Churchill. The client was interested not only in books but in post-impressionist painting. His architect gave him modernism without extravagance, framing the door and main window and marking the baseboard with a chequered pattern in brilliant colour. The wall he left plain and the windows above he set off merely with a narrow fillet. There is no suggestion here of anything of the art of the past and the crude but striking colours accord with the taste that one notes so often in ultramodern painting. The design is bold, by no means unpleasing, and certainly challenging to the eye. It advertises the shop and at the same time gives some indication of the character of the wares and the taste of the shopman.

One might go on multiplying such instances indefinitely. The main things to note are, however, the great variety of work of this sort, its imagination, and above all its tremendous improvement on similar work of a generation or two ago. Though we have drawn most of our material from New York, this was done *de convenance,* and the types could be illustrated successfully in any great city of the United States. The greatest bulk of material and the most interesting is, however, to be found in the richest and largest metropolitan centre.

Among the strictly utilitarian buildings of America to-day, no genre is more important nor interesting than the hospital, and none has shown greater progress in design. On the other hand, in a book of this sort, only the briefest mention of the type is possible. The problem is such a special one that it is difficult to discuss it at all. It is well for the layman, however, to try to grasp the amazing difficulties which the architect must overcome to reach even a reasonably successful solution of the hospital problem. Probably no task in architecture is more appalling. Indeed, it would seem to demand an architect who was also a physician, or vice versa. Certain architects, or members of certain firms, have made an intensive study of hospital designs and certain physicians with a flair for planning and administration have devoted much research to the architectural side. The collaboration of these individuals has produced the modern hospital, an affair as different from the house of the sick of fifty years ago as Robert Fulton's steamboat is different from the *Leviathan.*

The layman hardly knows what the problem means. If one suggests the word hospital, he thinks instinctively of a general hospital. It does

FIG. 303. NEW YORK, N. Y.
Childs Building, Fifth Avenue.
William Van Alen and Severance, Architects.

FIG. 304. NEW YORK, N. Y.
Weyhe's Book-Shop.
Henry S. Churchill, Architect.

FIG. 305. NEW YORK, N. Y. Edison Shop; Now Demolished. *Shape & Bready, Architects.*

not occur to him that even the general hospital is not so "general" as he supposes. A modern general hospital, for example, does not provide for the treatment of the insane nor the tubercular nor the victims of many other types of illness. It must be equipped for diagnosis of all diseases, but be prepared to transfer certain classes of patients immediately to other hospitals specially designed. These offer other problems, each of which might take many chapters to itself. If one wanted an optimistic gauge of the progress of humanity, one could find it in comparing the hospitals for the insane of to-day with the prisonlike horrors that were used for the purpose in an age less scientifically enlightened. The study of the causes and cure of a disease like tuberculosis has evolved a type of building with considerations of placing, site, altitude, light, and air that is unique in architectural history. The designer of such a building must study not only architecture but tuberculosis and the specialist in hospitals must further specialise in a type.

However much relief may be given by special hospitals, the complexity of the general hospital must remain a fearful thing. The architect must consult with the physician and decide, for example, how much space must be devoted to the surgical unit and how much to internal medicine. This will vary with the location and with the clientèle, and future possible changes in the proportion of variation must be considered. The out-patient department must be studied and brought into a proper relation with the other divisions. Provision must be made for special types of treatment such as X-ray and radium. Laboratories for analyses are required and, in a modern hospital of any size, for research. A unit must be devoted to emergency cases and first aid, and the district must be studied to permit an estimate of the volume of such cases to be expected. Even though contagious cases are transferred to other hospitals, they are bound to be met in a general hospital, and the designer must co-operate with the physician as to the best means of averting cross-contagion.

All of the ordinary problems which beset the designer of a large building in which many people dwell are exaggerated and made formidable in the hospital. Kitchens and food service must be provided, but a host of special problems in dietetics must be considered. Service becomes vastly more difficult when special foods must be provided and meals served largely to patients in bed. A laundry is essential, but it must be even more efficient than that provided for a hotel. Means of incineration are necessary, yet the architect must discover, for example, how completely dressings will be incinerated and what proportion the hospital authorities will try to reclaim. Communications, always important, become vastly more so in a hospital. Nurses' steps must be saved, quick communication between laboratory and ward is essential. The entrance of any great building is apt to be confused. It must not be so in the hospital. Incoming patients should not mingle with outgoing. Visiting friends must be cared for courteously and swiftly, but must not be allowed to interfere with the reception of patients or the more important activities of the staff.

Forms, ornament, materials, all must be selected specially. As in the schoolroom, the architect must try to give his patients agreeable and cheerful surroundings. The most material physician will admit their therapeutic value. On the other hand, the hospital at best is an extremely expensive thing. Rigid economy must be observed. At the same time, considerations of germ elimination, the possibility of easy, rapid, and thorough cleaning will change the architectural forms. Economy enters in the decision as to the size of wards and the placing of beds. For the sick, the ideal arrangement is a separate room for each patient. Expense renders this ideal impractical, yet there must be many separate rooms for those who can afford them, or whose condition entitles them to special treatment. The number of individual rooms again must be decided in consultation with the medical staff. Moreover, it is possible to compromise between the individual room and the great open ward. Units with four beds are possible and often chosen. Alcoves may be used, or units with a few beds communicating, but partially screened, one from another. In any case, isolation must be obtainable for the very ill, the violently delirious, and the moribund. Every feature—from the large ones of placing and planning to the details of material—heat, light, plumbing, fixtures, garbage disposal, and all the manifold things that go into the consideration of any building, must be studied anew as they enter into hospital design.

The problem of expansion is graver in a hospital than probably any other form of building. Magnificently as many are endowed, all will probably need to expand. In the beginning, architect and staff must often meet the question of whether they will content themselves with an in-

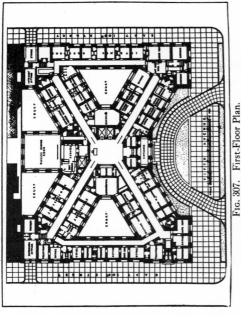

FIG. 307. First-Floor Plan.

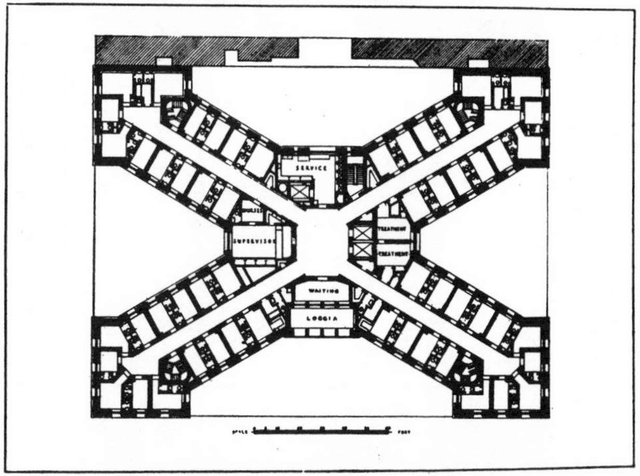

FIG. 308. Fourth-Floor Plan.

FIG. 306. NEW YORK, N. Y. Fifth Avenue Hospital.
York & Sawyer, Architects.

318

adequate unit or eliminate it entirely until such time as they can afford
an adequate one. They must consider when the necessity for expansion
is likely to come and where it will be most needed, arranging the building so that its first structure will not interfere with additions when the
need becomes imperative and the funds available. Indeed, so thorny are
the difficulties that hem in the hospital designer that one wonders not
only that he ever solves his problem but that he ever has the courage to
undertake it. In view of this, the great modern hospital becomes one
of the most inspiring things in architecture to-day.

As in the case of many other types of building, it is hard to mention
specifically any one hospital without seeming to do an injustice to the able
designers of hundreds of others. Perforce we must limit ourselves to
two or three and regard them as illustrations of the complexity of the
problem and the ingenuity with which it has been met. One of the most
modern and interesting is the Fifth Avenue Hospital, New York, by
York & Sawyer. In elevation (Fig. 306) it is eccentric, showing a lofty
central mass connecting wide-flung wings, nine stories in height. Economy, as so often, has eliminated all superficial ornament and permitted
a superb effect of mass and silhouette. The building bespeaks its function without attempting to parade it. Fine as is the exterior, however, it
is the plan (Fig. 307) that interests us most. From the central unit there
radiate four wings in the shape of a St. Andrew's cross. These are connected on the first two floors with lateral wings parallel to the main axis,
producing two triangular courts. Above the second story (Fig. 308) the
St. Andrew's cross rises clear, giving the maximum of light and air to
the single rows of rooms on either side of the central corridor in each
wing. It would be hard to conceive of a plan more admirably adapted
to roominess and light, with the easiest communication and central control. It shows how boldly the architect throws aside previous notions
of planning and meets new difficulties in a new way.

Another very ingenious solution of the hospital problem, in this case
a special one, is the Lying-In Hospital at Boston, Mass., by Coolidge &
Shattuck (Fig. 309). Here again economy enforced simplicity. The
mass is built up in great horizontals with an interesting proportion and
relation of part to part. Even so prosaic a feature as the water-tank on
the roof takes its place as an integral part of the design, yet that, too,

with the maximum of practicality. Accidentally, or rather functionally, the designer attained something of the modernist expression that we associate with the work of Sullivan and Wright, though he would probably deny, indignantly and correctly, that he had any such aim in mind when he created the work. Most ingenious of all is the treatment of the possibilities for expansion and rearrangement. In any scientific building the rooms of to-day may be obsolete to-morrow. In the Lying-In Hospital partitions are so arranged and constructed that they may be changed with minimum expense and damage to the permanent structure of the building. At the same time, every possible chance is allowed for the addition of units without interfering with the scheme of communication or central control. The building is thus assured of a far longer permanent usefulness than is the case with most specialised buildings for scientific purposes.

Probably the most ambitious hospital building, or rather group of buildings, in America to-day is the Columbia-Presbyterian Medical Center in upper New York (Fig. 310). It is an enormous pile, a veritable "fortress against disease," and a glance at its mass will perhaps bring home more vividly than anything else the magnitude of hospital design. The architect is James Gamble Rogers. There are many unusual and almost revolutionary features about the Medical Center. In the first place, it is organised with an emphasis on the theory that the duty of the hospital is even more to keep people well than to cure the sick, so that the out-patient department, clinics, and means of providing attendance and instruction for the not too acutely ill are multiplied. The scheme is so large that the Center is not really one great hospital, but thirteen small hospitals placed one above the other, with central service. To a considerable extent, this reverses the procedure as developed in the ordinary modern hospital. Instead of one central laboratory for the whole, there is one for each unit. This means that responsibility can be fixed with ease. Instead of one huge central kitchen, there are two diet kitchens for each unit, so that the nurses can attend personally to the preparation of trays for the patients and see that the food is served invitingly and at proper temperature. In short, the Medical Center studies anew the problem of centralisation, how far it is an advantage, and wherein it is liable to become unwieldy and break down. Central control is essential, but if the organisation be large enough many features are better decentralised.

FIG. 309. BOSTON, MASS. Lying-In Hospital. *Coolidge & Shattuck, Architects.*

FIG. 310. NEW YORK, N. Y. Columbia-Presbyterian Medical Center, as Seen from the New Jersey Shore. *James Gamble Rogers, Architect.*

Certainly the Medical Center is tremendous in scale. The buildings now standing cover 84,000 square feet, or nearly two acres. The height from the ground to the main roof of the hospital is 253 feet and to the top of the hospital tower is 306 feet. The hospital building will contain at opening 743 beds, 122 infants' cribs, and accommodations for a complete personnel of 400. There will be a daily service for 2,500 outpatients. Perhaps to the layman the scale may be grasped by the homely details that the dietary department is planned to serve 4,115 meals daily and the laundry department to turn out 35,000 pieces every eight hours. Be it remembered that the building we describe is only part of that designed to go up on the site! Expansion is provided for and expected in the near future. In the face of a scheme of such immensity the layman may well gasp, but it is salutary for him to know something about it and to consider the work that not only the physician, but the architect, is doing for his health and that of his fellow citizens.

Another interesting phase of modern American architecture involves theatre design. The modern tendencies are manifest in various ways. One of the happiest is the elimination of the fatty exuberance of ornament which formerly seemed to be regarded as absolutely necessary to the expression of theatre design. Theatres are meant to entertain and to our ancestors this seemed to mean that they should flare and glitter with all the gold, tinsel, ruddy colour, and obese ornament that could be applied. The stage was regarded as a picture, to be enframed in a most ornately carved and heavily gilded setting. Actors were a florid, a strange, and a rather dangerous race, and they were housed and supposed to appear in a setting which revealed their characters. Now this is changed and the era of the "Bird-Cage Op'ry House" is gone, we trust, forever. Designers and public have realised that a reasonable restraint, proportion, harmonious and not blatant colour, is just as important in a theatre as in anything else. Properly, a theatre will always lend itself to a more playful and fanciful treatment than buildings of another type, but the extreme vulgarity which marked the old-time theatre is now rejected.

The most interesting phase of modern theatre design we have not the time nor, to confess it frankly, the technical knowledge to review. This is the mechanical development which modern invention in machinery and electricity have made possible. The stages of modern theatres have deepened and broadened. Arrangement has been made for the setting of one scene while another is being used, the set stage later being put into place by a moving platform. Few people realise that the part of the modern theatre devoted to the stage and its accessories is as large, occupies as much cubic space, as that devoted to the auditorium. Scientific lighting has gone hand in hand with mechanical development, pigments have been studied in their relation to rays of certain qualities, so that some rays will be absorbed and others reflected, and a whole scene, costumes and set, may be changed in the twinkling of an eye by switching on a light of different colour. Light and machinery make ocular effects undreamed of by our ancestors. Full orchestras rise and disappear at will, whole scenes sink and are replaced by others without the creaking of a wheel. If the illusion demands it, the whole theatre itself may be transformed, as the Century Theatre in New York was changed into a mighty and impressive cathedral for the performance of *The Miracle*. These are the real wonders of modern theatre design, into which we cannot go.

Reverting to more purely architectural considerations, we may note in the legitimate theatre the two types of large, formal, impressive work, like the Century, and the intimate, small theatre that has become such a common phenomenon in New York and other large American centres. Though the large theatre is, of course, more opulent than the small, both have the comparative restraint and refinement that we have come to look for in all modern American work. To these categories must be added a peculiarly American type, the motion-picture theatre. Nothing is more striking in modern America than the growth of the motion-picture industry. Even comparatively young people remember the age of the "nickel" theatre, arranged in some fire-trap over a store, and can realise the difference between that and the enormous theatres, capable of seating thousands, with rich ornament, carefully studied light, perfect ventilation, and every mechanical device known to the modern theatre, which are the temples of the industry to-day. Wealth has poured into the industry and is as lavishly poured out. All classes of people attend the "movies" nowadays, so that the designers of the theatres have begun to use real discrimination as well as wealth. It seems to be felt, however, that the "movie" audience is less cultivated than one which attends the spoken drama, and the motion-picture theatres are more lavishly decorated, have less refinement, and show a more unrestrained imagination than do the theatres of the legitimate stage. It is understandable and not inappropriate that this should be so.

As an example of the elaborate modern theatre on a large scale, we may look at the New Theatre, now the Century, in New York (Fig. 311), by Carrère & Hastings. This was the result of an elaborate venture, in which many people of means were interested, to produce the best possible plays in the most artistic manner. No expense was spared. The architects produced a palatial ensemble, reminiscent of the style of Gabriel and the period of the Place de la Concorde. Relief was bold, play of light rich, but all was dignified and refined. The interior (Fig. 312) was most impressive. Here more colour was used, the ornament was richer, and one felt something of the gilded setting that is associated with the theatre of olden time. Precious materials were used lavishly, but under control, and the effect was extremely rich and yet dignified and even formal. The scale was immense and, though every one admired the building, a good many found it somewhat oppressive. One had the same feeling in it that one has so frequently at Versailles. One could do with a little less grandeur, even a grandeur aristocratically under control.

In the sharpest possible contrast to this we might turn to the Neighbourhood Playhouse, on Grand Street, New York, by Ingalls & Hoffman. The scale is tiny. The front (Fig. 313) is a brick and limestone composition, recalling the American Colonial, with crisp detail simply handled. The brick runs up for two stories, where it is stopped by a quiet cornice and a parapet with the simplest of balustrades. Above that, stepped back, is an attic third story, with low windows. The entrance sign and billboards are small and quaintly designed in the manner of signs on a Colonial shop. No flaring posters, no glaring lights advertise a theatre that consciously strives for modesty and refinement. The designer's aim has been to be distinguished, rather than vociferous, and to cater to that quiet taste which is more and more insistent in our modern style. The interior (Fig. 314) echoes the same taste. Florid and especially curved lines are avoided. The colours are generally cream whites and greys. The walls and balconies are panelled in simple rectangles

Fig. 311. New York, N. Y. Century Theatre. *Carrère & Hastings, Architects.*

Fig. 312. New York, N. Y. Century Theatre: Interior. *Carrère & Hastings, Architects.*

325

FIG. 313. NEW YORK, N. Y. Neighbourhood Playhouse.
Harry C. Ingalls and F. Burrall Hoffman, Architects.

FIG. 314. NEW YORK, N. Y. Neighbourhood Playhouse: Interior.
Harry C. Ingalls and F. Burrall Hoffman, Architects.

FIG. 315. CHICAGO, ILL. American Theatre. *Mahler & Cordell, Architects.*

FIG. 316. ROCHESTER, N. Y. Eastman Theatre.
Gordon & Kaelber, Architects; McKim, Mead & White, Associated.

and the ceiling is broken and cleverly given depth by two sunken circular panels of the slightest reveal. The details of the lobby and other parts are carried through in the same consistent, generally early Republican detail, so that the interior has the intimacy of a distinguished dwelling with the practical conveniences of a well-planned theatre. The Neighbourhood Playhouse must serve us as a single example of a very numerous *genre* which appears in New York and elsewhere. Its group is a militant reaction against the extreme floridity which has marked theatre design in the past.

As usual, we do not want to dwell entirely on the more conservative types. Modernism appears in theatre design, as in everything else, and in passing we note the American Theatre in Chicago (Fig. 315), by Mahler & Cordell. A glance will show its relation to the styles of Sullivan & Wright. Some of the forms are more conventional, the break with the past is not so abrupt, but the attempt is clear to make an original design, thinking in masses and planes and avoiding the vocabulary of the past.

The motion-picture theatre is even more interesting than the older type and in a sense more characteristic of modern life. Here the problems differ, though not so much as one would expect. To be sure, the stage need not be so elaborate for a drama that requires only a screen, but in most of the elaborate examples the building has been designed not only for the cinematograph but for concerts, vaudeville, and even complete dramatic performances, so that the problems of stage design do not vary. The motion-picture theatre, however, tends to be much larger than any other but grand-opera and concert halls. In a drama the eye can see satisfactorily much farther than the ear can hear, so that there is no objection to assembling large audiences, and many of the buildings are enormous.

One of the finest and most interesting is the Eastman Theatre, at Rochester, N. Y. (Fig. 316), by Gorden & Kaelber, with McKim, Mead & White as associates. The local firm planned the building, the New York firm being called in later. It is somewhat misleading to call this a motion-picture theatre. It is quite as much a concert hall and a dramatic theatre, but the aim of the donor was to bring as many people as possible to hear good music and see good performances, and one of his means was to include good motion-pictures. The exterior of the Rochester Theatre is eccentric, following a curve and taking advantage of every available inch of space. One enters at the angle into an oval lobby, fine in itself, but awkward in that the entrance to the theatre is not opposite the entrance from the street. Within, one finds oneself in a spaciously designed theatre, with every mechanical means studied for the comfort of the audience. Even the mezzanine (Fig. 318) is provided with padded armchairs for every visitor, which would be a luxury in a drawing-room. The most conspicuous thing of all is the colour. It is not too much to say that the colour feature is epoch-making in American architecture. A group of young men, trained in the American Academy in Rome, where a great point has been made of the collaboration of the arts, and where the finest ancient examples of polychromy in architecture are available, worked together at Rochester to add one more to these great polychromatic designs. We reproduce one wall with paintings by Barry Faulkner (Fig. 317). It means little in black and white. In colour, judged by the standards of any period, the harmony of painting to stone is a masterpiece. We have seen how necessary in America is the comprehension of the possibilities of colour in architecture. The Rochester Theatre gives us an object-lesson. All the details of the work are exquisite. As intended, it is a monument to the elevation of the public taste. In one part of the building is the Kilbourn Hall (Fig. 319), a small theatre for concerts, as restful to the eye architecturally as it is acoustically a scientific masterpiece. The whole building is of its kind one of the most important monuments in the country.

We must not expect all the motion-picture theatres to have the artistic distinction of the Eastman. Generally they are exuberant in design, a trifle ostentatious, and imposing chiefly on account of their enormous scale, ingenuity of planning by which all of a thousand and more seats have an unobstructed view of the screen, and skill and cleverness of the lighting system. As characteristic of many, we reproduce the auditorium of the Capitol Theatre, New York (Fig. 320), by Thomas W. Lamb. If it lacks the supreme distinction of Rochester, it is by no means vulgar, is overpowering in scale, and has one of the most perfectly planned great auditoria in the country.

Other effects are purposely much more fanciful and exotic. Another

FIG. 317. ROCHESTER, N. Y. Eastman School of Music: Barry Faulkner's Murals in Theatre.
Gordon & Kaelber, Architects; McKim, Mead & White, Associated.

FIG. 318. ROCHESTER, N. Y. Eastman School of Music: Mezzanine in Theatre.
Gordon & Kaelber, Architects; McKim, Mead & White, Associated.

FIG. 319. ROCHESTER, N. Y. Eastman School of Music: Kilbourn Hall.
Gordon & Kaelber, Architects; McKim, Mead & White, Associated.

FIG. 320.   NEW YORK, N. Y.   Capitol Theatre.   *Thomas W. Lamb, Architect.*

Photograph by Winslow.

FIG. 321.   CHICAGO, ILL.   Capitol Theatre.   *John Eberson, Architect.*

example on a large scale is the Capitol Theatre at Chicago, Ill. (Fig. 321), by John Eberson. Here the designer has deliberately made the auditorium to appear as located in an Italian garden. So perfect is the illusion that in a photograph it is almost impossible to believe that the theatre is not out-of-doors. An exotic effect of a different sort is the Fifth Avenue Theatre, Seattle, Wash., by R. C. Reamer and the Robert E. Power Studio (Figs. 322, 323). Here the designers have selected the architecture of China as a source of inspiration. On the West coast such a selection is natural. The details are heavy, the ornament florid, the colour as variegated as possible and in full intensity. The brilliance of the colour is enhanced by carefully studied polychromatic lighting. From the description one would imagine the building to be vulgar. Actually it is a fairy-land, inviting and compelling the visitor to accept its imaginative and exotic point of view.

Recently an elaborate motion-picture theatre has been opened in Boston, the Metropolitan, the chief designers being Blackall, Clapp & Whittemore. This is an interesting example of the combined theatre and office-building, the rentals of the ten-story office-building supplementing the profits from the theatre. The combination has imposed a rather dull exterior (Fig. 324), blocklike and offering little stimulus to the imagination. The interior, however, is gorgeous, if not wholly refined. The enormous entrance foyer (Fig. 325) is as impressive as Versailles. The staircase makes one feel, in ascending it, that one should be wearing at least silken breeches and a clubbed wig. The auditorium and stage are enormous (Fig. 326), the latter provided with a platform which disappears and can slowly be lifted into place, carrying a full orchestra, playing the while. Even so elaborate a work as this, however, seems insignificant when compared to the most recent and ambitious motion-picture theatres. For example, the recently opened Roxy Theatre, in New York, with its capacity of 6,000, its three organs appearing or disappearing while simultaneously being played, its rising full orchestra, drives home most vividly the power, the wealth, the vulgarity, the scale of modern Rome. These theatres are typical of the tendency in American motion-picture-house design. There is something jarring in the sight of commonplace crowds in overshoes hurrying across a lobby which, despite its occasional use of spurious materials, is worthy of Mansart, while the elegantly dressed visitors to the Boston Opera-House stroll during the entr'actes

FIG. 322. SEATTLE, WASH. Fifth Avenue Theatre.
R. C. Reamer and the Robert E. Power Studio, Architects.

FIG. 323. SEATTLE, WASH. Fifth Avenue Theatre.
R. C. Reamer and the Robert E. Power Studio, Architects.

333

along a corridor scarcely more imposing than that of the city jail. None the less, this is typical of America and perhaps not an unhealthy phenomenon.

Among the commercial buildings of America few types are more interesting than the hotel. The extraordinarily high standard of living in this country, its enormous resources, and the demand, of even comparatively humble folk, for luxury as by a right, have produced a development of hotel design far more elaborate than any in other countries. As in the case of the theatre, we could not possibly examine all the technical points involved in the problem. The chief thing to note is that the great modern hotel is a self-sufficient community. It must provide not only bedrooms, efficiently run, and all sorts of restaurants with their attendant service, their problems of communication with the serving-rooms and kitchens, but must have a police force, a detective force, medical attention, a hospital, baths of all sorts, even swimming-tanks, squash-courts, and, in some instances, a chapel. Thanks to steel construction and the high-speed elevator, unlimited space can be provided vertically, and often one plan will do for many floors above the main and mezzanine. On the other hand, the problem of arranging efficiently for the service of thousands of guests, so that everything will run smoothly, rapidly, and yet leave an impression of ease and beauty, is one of the most difficult that the architect can approach. If a layman wishes to get an idea of the complexity of the difficulties, let him peruse one of the pamphlets issued by the Statler Company. A few pages will be an eye-opener.

We can concern ourselves only with the appearance of American hotels, confining ourselves to a few of the important examples which show different tendencies in modern design. Perhaps as typical and impressive an one as we can find is the Commodore, New York (Fig. 327), by Warren & Wetmore. Built before the zoning-law restrictions, it piles up in an enormous mass, U-shaped for the admission of light above the main lower stories. Some twenty-five stories high, the cornice is eliminated, and the upper four stories are given a separate treatment which makes them a crowning feature of the building, without the absurdity of the projecting cornice which earlier design tried to bring into scale with the height of the building. The window-openings are regularly placed and there is no attempt in the exterior design to express the steel construction. The building has a fine-cut, distinguished air, but is neverthe-

Blackall, Clapp &
*Whittemore; C. H*ᵤ. -
ard Crane, Kenneth
Franzheim, G. N.
Meserve, Architects.

Fig. 324. Boston,
Mass. Metropolitan
Theatre.

Photograph by Paul J. Weber.

Photograph by Paul J. Weber.

Fig. 325. Grand Lobby.

Photograph by Paul J. Weber.

Fig. 326. Auditorium.

Boston, Mass. Metropolitan Theatre.
Blackall, Clapp & Whittemore; C. Howard Crane, Kenneth Franzheim, G. N. Meserve, Architects.

335

FIG. 327. NEW YORK, N. Y. Hotel Commodore. *Warren & Wetmore, Architects.*

FIG. 328. NEW YORK, N. Y. Hotel Commodore: Lobby. *Warren & Wetmore, Architects.*

336

FIG. 329. NEW YORK, N. Y. The Shelton Hotel. *Arthur Lewis Harmon, Architect.*

FIG. 330. NEW YORK, N. Y. The Shelton Hotel: Entrance Loggia.
Arthur Lewis Harmon, Architect.

337

less somewhat blocklike and rigid. The interior shows much more imagination. The lobby (Fig. 328) is one of the most attractive in modern
American work, low, two-storied, with unadorned and heavy round arches
in the Spanish manner, but with no archæological feeling whatever.

Of the same generally classic character, but of a more interesting silhouette, is the Savoy-Plaza Hotel which McKim, Mead & White have
just erected at Fifth Avenue and 58th Street, New York (Fig. 63). This
shows the effect of the zoning law upon a building which might otherwise have been much more like the Commodore. Here again no attempt
has been made to express the steel; the terra-cotta envelope appears as
a self-sustaining wall, or a covering for the steel, according to the common sense or the lack of it of the observer. The mass, however, with its
projecting wings and its regular terraces and setbacks, is exceedingly interesting. The very bareness of the walls helps us to appreciate the mass
and we feel that the "conservatism" is here a deliberate aid to modern
expression.

One of the most interesting and powerful effects of the zoning law
is embodied in Arthur Loomis Harmon's Shelton Hotel, New York
(Figs. 329, 330). This is a combination of club and hotel, accommodat-
ing permanent dwellers and transients. It is of brick, deeply recessed in
the centre, and towering skyward, stepping back twice to a massive rectangular central tower. The material is brick and cut stone and architectural ornament is restricted practically to the base, where a beautiful
colonnade gives both dignity and scale. In this building the lines reveal
the steel construction without insisting upon it. Pure mass is the key-
note of the style, and we seem to be in the presence of some titanic result of the forces of nature rather than a building by the hand of man.
The mass seen at dusk is as impressive as Gibraltar. The boldness of the
scheme frightens and awes and at the same time commands admiration.
It is such work as this that one finds in America and nowhere else in the
world.

Although it is not a hotel, such work draws our attention to the Philadelphia Athletic Club (Fig. 331), just completed by Zantzinger, Borie
& Medary. It is an example of perfect sanity in modernism. The technical problems were much the same as at the Shelton, though of course
more was made of the several functions of the building. Here no zoning
law imposed the masses, but a fire law interfered with the design and

FIG. 331. PHILADELPHIA, PA. Athletic Club. *Zantzinger, Borie & Medary, Architects.*

FIG. 332. LOS ANGELES, CALIF. Biltmore Hotel: Main Lobby. *Schultze & Weaver, Architects.*

339

was skilfully made an asset instead of a liability. The isolated fire-escapes at the angles were used to bring variety and harmony into the masses, so that they form one of the chief elements in emphasising the majesty of the silhouette. The building is huge and the detail as forceful and rugged as the design demands. The cornice is courageously suppressed and the design immensely improved thereby. Most daring of all, the colour, a salmon pink, is selected entirely with an eye to beauty and without regard to anything that has been done before. It lightens the mass without destroying its dignity and may be regarded as one more triumph in colour in American architecture.

The variety, richness, and imagination of American hotel design tempts one to linger unduly over the subject. One likes to go afield and look at such work as the Los Angeles Biltmore (Fig. 332), by Schultze & Weaver. The lobby of this hotel is one of the richest, most ornate, and at the same time most satisfactory designs in the American-Spanish style. It is a precious monument, open to criticism on the ground only that it is too fine for a hotel, a flattering condemnation which the architects will probably be glad to accept.

In Albuquerque, Trost & Trost have designed the Hotel Franciscan (Fig. 333), applying the principles of the pueblo style to hotel architecture on a large scale. This is modernism rampant, yet finely done. All detail is consciously crude. Angles are blunted, the mass of material is emphasised. Blocklike ornament with heavy cast shadows takes the place of the vocabulary of the historic past. The effect is cubistic, but cubism under definite intellectual control. Paradoxically, the building is full of harsh harmonies. It is closely related to the modernist productions of the German and Scandinavian peoples, by whom it has been acclaimed, but the ideas which it embodies, the forms which it displays, are taken from the pueblo style of the district in which it exists. It is thus a work of ultramodernism with an archæological basis, is appropriate to its setting, and represents an original experiment in American architecture, as well. Incidentally, its thick walls, and especially its heavy reveals, have a great functional value in a climate like that of New Mexico, where high winds are frequent and constantly impregnated with sand.

This reminds us of another example with a modernist expression, probably less consciously attained: the Hotel Traymore, at Atlantic City

FIG. 333. ALBUQUERQUE, N. M. Hotel Franciscan. *Trost & Trost, Architects.*

FIG. 334. ATLANTIC CITY, N. J. Hotel Traymore. *Price & McLanahan, Architects.*

(Fig. 334), by Price * & McLanahan. Here the scale is tremendous. The building is broken into pavilions, in turn accented with verticals in the form of superposed bays. This continues to the tenth story, where a balcony, flung wide on corbels, makes a powerful horizontal. Above that an attic, stepped-in masses, and domes produce a sky-line of rare picturesqueness and force. The Traymore is really the old, picturesque seaside hotel, purged of its gimcrack and filigree, translated into the terms of stern modernism, with its picturesqueness preserved.

The outstanding example of modernism in hotel design will take us far afield, to the Hotel Imperial in Tokio, by Frank Lloyd Wright. We have seen something of the architect's domestic work and know generally what to expect. At Tokio, however, he was called upon to design a huge building in a country where European classicism has no home and for a race with a very high artistic sensibility. His philosophy was peculiarly apt for the problem and he went ahead in full determination to evolve forms which were new in architecture, harmonious, and expressive of his ideals. The physical difficulties were great. The enormous mass had to be carried on a boggy foundation, so that actually the hotel is supported on concrete piles, driven into the silt, and carrying a platform of concrete on which the building rests. The success of the construction was revealed dramatically in 1924, when the city was largely destroyed by an earthquake which left the Imperial Hotel unscathed. Other buildings, by German engineers, similarly constructed, bore the earthquake with equal security.

Our first impressions of the Imperial Hotel are exotic. As we look into the garden courts (Fig. 336) we see the horizontality, the composition in blocklike masses, the wide overhangs with dark shadows, and the sharp rectangularity of the architect's work in this country. Everything is, however, on an amazing scale, and we are struck, too, by the brilliance of the colour. When we examine one of the garden pools we feel the fine spirit of the Japanese rock garden, though there is not the slightest attempt to repeat any Japanese design. It is the abstract philosophy of the fine art that produces a similar effect in both cases. If the ornament displeases, it is on account of its ruggedness. A view of the Sunken Garden (Fig. 335), North Bridge, and Social Group, brings this out. Were it not for the planting, the detail would all be repellently harsh. This we feel especially in the interiors. A view of the main promenade (Fig.

* I believe the late William L. Price is responsible especially for the original design.

FIG. 335. TOKIO, JAPAN. Imperial Hotel: Sunken Garden, North Bridge, and Social Group.
Frank Lloyd Wright, Architect.

FIG. 336. In the Gardens.   FIG. 337. Interior, Main Promenade.

TOKIO, JAPAN. Imperial Hotel. *Frank Lloyd Wright, Architect.*

343

Fig. 339. New York, N. Y. Bowery Savings Bank.
York & Sawyer, Architects.

Photograph by Wurts Brothers.

Fig. 338. New York, N. Y. The Knickerbocker Trust Co., Before Alteration.
McKim, Mead & White, Architects.

337) reiterates the effect of harsh angles, overpowerful mass, and crushing weight. Not even the colour can entirely relieve this feeling. It is hard to judge such a building and we are probably too close to it to do so intelligently. That the artist's philosophy, his aims, are entirely admirable, all will agree. Whether the forms that he has evolved actually express his ideals is more open to question. We leave this to individual opinion and to posterity, emphasising only the facts that here we have, at least, originality, courage, and confidence in a philosophy of æsthetics independently reached. We should note, too, that among the modernists of Europe this work has attracted more attention and elicited more approbation than anything in its class that America has produced to-day.

Another phase of modern American architecture is shown in the design for banks. Banks, like churches, are conservative, but their conservatism takes a different architectural form. A bank must be strong, solid, rich, respectable; and architects have vied to give it a character which would inspire confidence in its solubility. A fine bank is a good advertisement, most people regarding a solid and rich architectural display as a proof of financial impregnability. Only a few of us, and those the most ungracious, pause to consider that the money that is not put into building may be put into securities. At least, we should not blame an enthusiastic president and board of directors of an old and powerful institution for wanting to house that institution in a building worthy of its importance. If we deplore the fact that this is not a cathedral-building age, let us at least encourage our commercial magnates in the current tendency to put a substantial part of their earnings into the creation of beautiful and monumental business structures.

Until very recently all banks were classical, and even to-day this remains the favourite style. The classic orders, especially the Doric, were rich, ancient, strong, and conservative, and they were taken over practically without dissent as the inevitable adornment of a respectable bank. Magnificent designs in the classic style have been made for banks and must be familiar to every one. As a famous example, we might note the Knickerbocker Trust Company, in New York (Fig. 338), issuing from that stronghold of classicism, McKim, Mead & White. Big in scale, graceful in proportion, rich in form and play of light, massive and solid in expression, it perfectly expressed the ideas of permanence, wealth, and security that a bank demands. It is one of the tragedies of architecture

Fig. 340. New York, N. Y. Bowery Savings Bank. *York & Sawyer, Architects.*

that the failure of the Knickerbocker Trust Company not long after the erection of the building forced it to be used for another function, and the increase in land values decreed its transformation to a loftier building.

In very recent years classicism has begun to weaken in bank design. Other styles, semihistoric or entirely modern, have often taken its place, and there has been a tendency to combine the bank with an office-building above. This was inevitable when banks are bound to be placed on the busiest of sites, where land values are at their maximum. No matter how wealthy the institution, it cannot afford to cover land worth a thousand dollars a foot with a low building. As an example of this combination, and of fine modernism in bank design, we may note the Bowery Savings Bank, in New York (Fig. 339), by York & Sawyer. The detail here is more Romanesque than any other historic style, but is really modern. The entrance is a massive arch, in a monumental ashlar wall, with fine detail which emphasises the scale. Above, the vertical steel lines are emphasised for nine stories, where a colonnade occurs, and above it another small one, crowning the building very satisfactorily, without resort to a cornice. The last story is plain and slightly stepped back. The interior (Fig. 340) is one of the roomiest and most majestic ever designed for such a building. Every convenience is included, with the most lavish provision for air and light. The thing to note especially is the amount of waste space, or rather the amount of space used purely for considerations of beauty. There is probably no land in the world more valuable per square foot than that on 42d Street, New York, opposite the Grand Central Station. Whether or not an architect or a bank is justified in using sixty feet of it to make a monumental approach to a great banking hall is a question we must consider. From the point of view of sound economy it is shocking. From the point of view of beauty it is a complete success. For those who invest "savings" in such an institution, the lavishness of the design and the preciousness of the material open a vulnerable avenue of attack. On the other hand, we can sympathise with and applaud a great and wealthy institution which has so high a regard for beauty and so enthusiastic a self-respect as to call such a monument into being.

It is a relief to find the classicism of the last generation beginning to go. We get banks like the Seattle National (Fig. 341), by Doyle

& Merriam, in which the detail is still classical, yet the massing and arrangements so new and so obviously imposed by modern conditions that the effect is of an architecture of to-day with no great reference to the past. We find designs like George G. Elmslie's for the Merchants Bank, at Winona, Minn. (Fig. 342), in which the attempt is made to obtain the necessary dignity, power, and richness, using the vocabulary of pure modernism. Classic banks will continue to be designed and we are glad of it. On the other hand, we can look forward to a continuation and probably an expression of the monumental phase of bank design, with an infinitely greater variety and independence of study and expression.

Under factories we have reviewed briefly the buildings of large scale and broad cubage made possible by modern steel construction. To this we should add a word more about the enormous loft buildings, used for offices and for a hundred other purposes, which are springing up in all the great cities of the United States. Oftentimes they have little architectural pretense, yet tell as mighty monuments on account of their huge bulk and soaring verticals. As an example, we might cite the General Motors Building, in Detroit (Fig. 343), by Albert Kahn. Four enormous rectangles, springing from a fine base and topped with an equally fine colonnade, rise for fifteen stories. Three light courts separate them and they are joined at the back by the bulk of the main building. Though the detail of the entrance and lower colonnade is architectural and fine, the overpowering effect of the building is produced by the simplest and most logical arrangement of enormous masses.

A building of a more elaborate architectural treatment, but of the office-building rather than the pronounced "skyscraper" type, is the Cunard Building, in New York, by Benjamin Wistar Morris. Its exterior is good, but it is not that which we want to emphasise here. Admirably planned as the building is throughout, it is the great ground-story hall that makes it unique. Here we have another of the great colour designs in American architecture. Many of the same men worked upon it who decorated the theatre at Rochester, and the results are as fine, or even finer. The interior (Fig. 345) is vaulted, with domes and barrel vaults carried on stout piers. The stone is travertine and unadorned in colour up to the main impost. There colour begins, the transition made so skilfully between the clear monotone of the stone below and the full colour

FIG. 341. SEATTLE, WASH. National Bank. *Doyle & Merriam, Architects.*

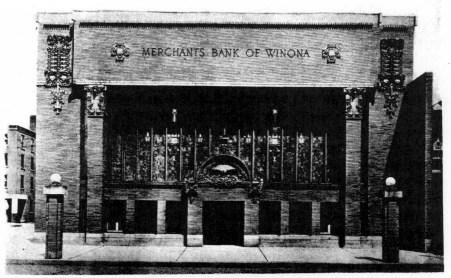

MERCHANTS BANK OF WINONA

FIG. 342. WINONA, MINN. Merchants Bank of Winona. *Purcell, Feick & Elmslie, Architects.*

of the upper part of the vault that at no point is the eye annoyed by a disjointed break. The vistas are superb (Fig. 346). Seldom in the history of art have architecture, sculpture, and painting collaborated so successfully, and the number of academicians employed in it is a triumph for the American Academy in Rome and a vindication of its insistent policy of making its students of all arts collaborate annually in a special problem. As in the case of the Bowery Savings Bank, the Cunard Building is an example of what a great and wealthy corporation can do when it decides to build in a manner worthy of its position and reputation and has the taste and fortune to call in a group of men who can use its resources to create a great monument of art.

When we turn from this to the Marshall Field Building, at 200 Madison Avenue, New York (Fig. 344), by Warren & Wetmore, it is hard to know whether to classify it as a loft and office building or directly as a commercial skyscraper. It is both. Different functions for parts of the building have produced different effects, such as the horizontality of the windows on Madison Avenue and the verticality of those of the central block. The New York zoning law is responsible for the setbacks and here, as at the Shelton Hotel, an opportunity in design has been created by a legal requirement. No building could be more severely practical, yet its mass is interesting and dignified.

Let us turn, therefore, to a more detailed consideration of the "skyscraper." It represents probably the most interesting phase of American architecture and certainly the most truly national. It was developed in this country, and nothing like it exists abroad. It was the result of American invention, American daring, and American engineering skill, and it expresses in the most modern way the American genius in architecture. Stormed at by critics on many counts, impermanence not the least of them, sneered at by the conservative, the reactionary, the intellectually smug, as ostentatious manifestations of vulgar commercialism, the skyscrapers are none the less beginning to be recognised as one of the most beautiful and original phases of American art. The book-made æsthete who, Byron in hand, rhapsodises about Venice "rising from the sea" and, returning to New York and entering the harbour, views the city sky-line unmoved, is living in a darkness in which we had better leave him, for surely if we turned on the light we should find him blind.

Fig. 343. Detroit, Mich. General Motors Building. *Albert Kahn, Architect.*

Photograph by Dwight P. Robinson & Co.

Fig. 344. New York, N. Y. Marshall Field Building. *Warren & Wetmore, Architects.*

Fig. 346. New York, N. Y. Cunard Building.
Benjamin Wistar Morris, Architect.

Fig. 345. New York, N. Y. Cunard Building.
Benjamin Wistar Morris, Architect.

In our first chapter we have said something about the steel construction which has made this art possible and something about the development of the vertical design. It took some time, as we have seen, to get used to the conception of a building composed of beams with walls hung on them instead of walls carrying beams. Even to-day, when we look at an unfinished building like the one we reproduced (Fig. 60) and see what is apparently a solid wall of eighteen stories resting on a hole, we are apt to gasp. Yet regularly the lower part of a skyscraper wall is left incomplete to the last for the easier admission of material. When we look at the base of McKim, Mead & White's great apartment-house on Park Avenue and see that its mighty wall seems to rest on a crack, we are given pause. Reflection quickly tells us that the crack is to prevent the wall from being jarred by the vibrations of the traffic in street and subway beneath, that the wall is hung to the steel, and that the steel goes down to the living rock where no vibrations can occur, and we begin to realise the point of view of steel construction. Whether the steel structure be expressed in the design, or no, the new medium was bound to produce a new art and promptly began to do so.

Into the structural conditions which were creating this new art was injected, in 1916, a new factor of immense importance: the New York zoning law. This was called into being by the unbelievable congestion which occurred in the district of high buildings. Once the possibilities of steel were grasped and corporations realised that literally the sky was the limit in vertical design, there began an orgy of skyscraper building, especially in lower New York. This was partly to take full advantage of the extraordinarily valuable land, partly for the advertising value of lofty buildings and the prestige of having created them, and partly on account of the quickly recognised desirability of offices high in the air, exposed to breezes and far from the noise and the dust of the street. All this was attainable as long as the skyscrapers were few and scattered. The moment two or three were erected in juxtaposition, they cut off one another's air and light. What usually occurred was that a skyscraper of modest dimensions, say fifteen stories, would be built and, after a year or two, one of twenty-five would be erected adjoining it, cutting off its view, its light, and completely undermining its prestige as a lofty building.

At the same time, street congestion became a menace. The new buildings accommodated thousands, when the old ones had accommodated hundreds, but the width of the streets and the amount of traffic they would take remained the same.   Moreover, the immense cost of the new buildings effectually prevented the widening of streets, since that would have involved the destruction of the buildings themselves, erected to take advantage of every inch of space, and abutting the legal limit of the edge of the street.   Distressing conditions appeared and grew worse with no prospect, if let alone, of growing better.   Something had to be done and finally, in the face of opposition from capitalists, from believers in *laissez-faire,* from many artists, and others, the New York zoning law was passed.

We need not repeat here, in technical language, the terms of the law. Its principle is simple and easy to understand (Fig. 347).   The require-

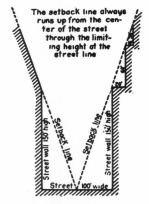

The setback line always runs up from the center of the street through the limiting height at the street line

Street wall 150 high

Setback line

Setback line

Street wall 150 high

Street 100' wide

FIG. 347.   Diagrammatic Explanation of New York Zoning Law.

ments vary with the district, allowing greater verticality in some parts of the city than others, but the principle is as follows.   The walls of the building are permitted to be carried up vertically to a given distance, say one and one-half times the width of the street upon which the building abuts.   Then an imaginary line is drawn from the middle of the street to the point at which the limit of direct verticality is set.   Obviously, this line will slope inward and, carried on beyond the point of the limit of direct verticality, it defines the point beyond which the mass of the building may not project.   After a certain distance, however, the restriction is removed, so that the building may have a central tower of any height, a feature of the law which is open to criticism, since it permits a spire of telescopic form, if the advertising value of height is allowed to overcome good taste in design. In this way, what is called technically the mass envelope of the building is established. Its form, if full advantage of allowed cubage were taken, would be that of a pyramid on a square base, with a vertical shaft of indeterminate height in the centre.

Obviously, no building can take advantage of the full spatial area allowed. It would be neither convenient, nor structural, to construct buildings with steeply sloping instead of vertical walls. Moreover, provision must be made for light and air in the mass of the building. Inevitably, therefore, the law imposes a series of verticals with setbacks at given levels. Infinite variety is left to the designer. He may, at a given point, set his mass back deeply and then carry it high, or he may have a slight setback and carry it a short distance to another, or he may compromise between the two. For practical as well as artistic considerations he must break up the mass, and this he may do in as many ways as his imagination suggests. He is untrammelled except for the very important restriction that he must not let any part of the building project beyond the mass envelope prescribed by the law.

We reproduce four ingenious drawings by Mr. Hugh Ferriss showing, mathematically designed, a mass envelope and the way it is transformed into an architectural possibility.* The first (Fig. 348) shows the mass envelope as prescribed by law in a city block 200 by 800 feet. The second (Fig. 349) shows its appearance after the architect has assumed a plan and begun to make it pass downward through the original envelope. The third (Fig. 350) gives the appearance of the mass after the elimination of the sloping planes, in this case setbacks being imagined at every second story. A tentative limit has also been placed on the tower. The structure has now reached the point where it would be perfectly possible to build it, but it is still unstudied, not very practical, and as yet unpleasing to the eye. The fourth (Fig. 351) shows the building after the setbacks have been made to conform to a reasonable steel grillage and the pinnacles have been truncated at the highest floor level which

* The writer is indebted to Mr. Ferriss for most generous permission to reproduce these, as well as for many suggestive ideas as to the effect on architecture of the zoning law.

would contain a practicable floor area. The mass has now assumed a truly architectural form, has beauty, both of silhouette and of proportion of mass to mass, and is ready for a real architectural articulation.

The effect of the zoning law is the most interesting single phenomenon in American architecture to-day. A restriction, imposed for purely utilitarian considerations and seemingly stifling to freedom in design, has been seized upon by modern designers and made a great architectural asset. Indeed, its acceptance and recognition, when we consider it, were inevitable. A skyscraper must depend for its effect upon its mass and silhouette. It must be interesting in outline and harmonious in relation of mass to mass. It must insist on its verticality and make the most of its great height. Detail or any form of small adornment counts for little and must be subordinated to the main effect. The zoning law taught practicality and suggested design as well. In no other way can the desired effect be got so completely, and the best proof of it is the number of skyscrapers that have been designed in accordance with the scheme of the zoning law in cities in which no such law exists.

To illustrate the immediate effect of the zoning law, we may examine such a monument as the Heckscher Building, in New York (Fig. 352), by Warren & Wetmore. In this case, the designers have used detail of the early French Renaissance, but have been forced to conform in mass to the envelope as prescribed by the law. As a result, the building is designed in receding blocks and finally crowned with a tower. It is an imposing pile, though not wholly successful in that the horizontals are overemphasised and there is nothing to bind any of the main masses to those above or below.

A more interesting and instructive example is the Barclay-Vesey Building, in New York, by McKenzie, Voorhees & Gmelin (Fig. 353). Here the steel verticals are expressed from top to bottom. The lines of the central tower are carried to the ground between the terraced corners. The detail is not historic; indeed, there is scarcely ornament on the building in the historic sense. The designers have met a modern problem in a modern way and produced one of those entirely new structures which are the glory of our architecture. Their building is practical, honest, and infinitely majestic as well.

Having reviewed the zoning law and its effects, we are now in a po-

FIG. 348.   First Stage.

FIG. 349.   Second Stage.

FIG. 350.   Third Stage.

FIG. 351.   Fourth Stage.

A Mass Envelope.   *Sketches by Hugh Ferriss.*

357

sition to examine a few of the great American skyscrapers, both those which conform to it and those which do not. Before we leave the direct consideration of the law, however, we should inquire into its adequacy. Certainly it is an improvement on the old policy of *laissez-faire*. Certainly it has prevented the "hogging" of air and light by certain buildings and produced an infinitely more agreeable and orderly sky-line than existed before its passage. Many, however, assert that it does not restrict enough. A whole school is opposed to the skyscraper on account of its tendency to concentrate population and produce congestion in small areas. The problem is a serious one. We reproduce some photographs, made from the air, of the congested districts of New York (Figs. 354 and 355), Detroit (Fig. 356), and San Francisco (Fig. 357). Each tells the same story. A forest of skyscrapers thrust their bristling verticals upward in restricted areas, daily calling hundreds of thousands of people into these areas. Even a zoning law like that of New York is powerless to prevent this congestion and many cities have no zoning laws at all. Contrast this with a city like Paris, of low buildings laid out in broad areas, and the appearance of the American metropolis has much that is ominous.

It has been urged that the skyscraper was forced upon New York by the narrow limits of Manhattan Island and has no place in a city like Detroit, where there is no natural limit to lateral expansion. This entirely misses the point. Men build skyscrapers because they like skyscrapers. They concentrate them in a district because they like so to concentrate them. There are plenty of places in restricted Manhattan where there is room for skyscrapers, yet none is built. In the Western cities, where expansion is unlimited, the skyscrapers are none the less concentrated in small areas. Such concentrations are the result of the wishes of the community and of natural growth. This we must recognise and meet the question fairly as to whether they are to be permitted or prevented by law.

The disadvantages are obvious. Already in New York it is quicker to do one's shopping or go to the theatre on foot than in a motor. Traffic congestion is appalling and is steadily becoming worse. Unquestionably something must be done. At the outset we announced that we were reviewing the present and not prophesying the future. We venture to

Fig. 352.   New York, N. Y.
Heckscher Building.
Warren & Wetmore, Architects.

Fig. 353.   New York, N. Y.
Barclay-Vesey Building.
McKenzie, Voorhees & Gmelin, Architects.

Fig. 354.   New York, N. Y.   Air View of Lower Manhattan.

FIG. 355.   Part of the "Crater of New York."   33d to 43d Streets between Sixth and Ninth Avenues.

FIG. 356.   DETROIT, MICH.   Air View.

FIG. 357.   SAN FRANCISCO, CALIF.   Air View.

forecast, however, that whatever is done it will not take the form of abolishing the skyscraper by law. Men have always congregated in cities and they always will. Within the city there have always been congested business districts, and there probably always will be. No matter how improved conditions of light, air, communication, and even reposeful design may be, one can hardly look for the time when the president of a bank will tolerate the thought of taking his motor to drive two miles in one direction to a neighbouring trust company and two miles in another to the stock exchange. On the contrary, buildings will probably grow higher and congestion will increase. No matter how much we may disapprove, we can no more stop the growth of a city like New York than we can slow the revolution of the earth on its axis. The means to meet the new conditions will probably take the form of double, triple, and quadruple tracking of the traffic lanes, of viaducts and steel communications from building to building, and of other expedients that seem like figments of the imagination of H. G. Wells and yet the beginnings of which we can already see. To destroy this new growth would be futile and one is tempted to say criminal, if it were possible. Control it we must, and the zoning law is our first great instrument of control, working for the good of humanity, of science, and of art.

We have gone far afield in abstract discussion. Let us return to look at some of the modern skyscrapers, both those that are "zoned" and those that are not, those that are designed with reference to revealed steel construction, and those that revert to plain walls. Some are in New York, others elsewhere. Some we have already reviewed in our first chapter, buildings like the Singer and the Metropolitan Life (Fig. 61), experimental monuments in the new expression. One of the greatest in height, with 57 stories, is the Woolworth Building, erected 1911–13 (Fig. 358), by Cass Gilbert, and built before the zoning law, though its mass has something of the effect of a zoned building. Its detail is frankly Gothic. Another of the most successful of New York skyscrapers, the Bush Terminal (Fig. 359), by Harvey Corbett, uses the same vocabulary. The effect here, however, is much less archæological. The Woolworth Building looks like an enormous and very beautiful Gothic tower. The Bush Terminal looks like a soaring and very beautifully composed modern skyscraper. One has to make a real effort of observation to realise that its detail is Gothic. The old vocabulary is completely transformed as it is applied to modern conditions.

This really states the tendency in modern skyscraper design. Although very beautiful ones have been made using historic ornament, and even using directly an historic style, the majority, and on the whole the most successful, have avoided archæological suggestion. Such a structure as the Chickering Building, in New York (Fig. 360), by Cross & Cross, has details which suggest Gothic, and even specifically perpendicular Gothic, but other details have different associations and the total effect is entirely modern. Here colour, got by terra-cotta, has been used with conspicuous success. Particularly, we can congratulate the designers on transforming the water-tank (Fig. 362), that disagreeable adjunct to the city building, into an object integral in the design, playfully charming in colour, and successful as an example of refined advertising.

One of the latest and most sensational of skyscrapers is the American Radiator Building, in New York (Fig. 361), by Raymond M. Hood. This is one the general shape of which is determined by the zoning law. The daring innovation was to build it in black brick and then to pick out its upper details in pure gold. The effect is theatrical to a degree that opens it to the charge of vulgarity. Nevertheless, although one feels that the building could have been improved by a more extensive study, one cannot deny that it is a magnificent piece of work. Especially at night, when it is artificially lighted, when the black bulk disappears and the gilded upper portions seem miraculously suspended one and two hundred feet in the air, the design has a dreamlike beauty. And if we think it a trifle crude, remember that it is designed to house a radiator company and not to commemorate a war hero nor glorify a saint.

Thus far we have observed skyscrapers only in New York. They appear there in the greatest number and in the most up-to-date design, but many interesting and beautiful examples appear elsewhere to which we must pay the tribute of a glance. One of the most beautiful of the type derived from historic precedent is the Chicago Tribune Tower (Fig. 363), by Hood & Howells. It was the successful design in one of the most sensational competitions in the last decade, and its selection was a triumph for conservatism. Certain restrictions, as the finlike mass on the back and the reduction of area above a certain point, were imposed, but

FIG. 357. NEW YORK, N. Y. Bush Terminal Building.
Helmle & Corbett, Architects.

FIG. 358. NEW YORK, N. Y. Woolworth Building.
Cass Gilbert, Architect.

364

Fig. 360. New York, N. Y.
Chickering Building.
Cross & Cross, Architects.

Fig. 361. New York, N. Y.
American Radiator Building.
Raymond M. Hood, Architect.

Fig. 362. New York, N. Y. Chickering Building: Detail of Top. *Cross & Cross, Architects.*

the designer was fairly free. That he was largely inspired by the Tour du Beurre of the Cathedral of Rouen is undeniable. That so close a reliance on historic precedent is unprogressive may be urged. That the Tribune Tower is one of the most beautiful buildings in America few will deny.

In Philadelphia are interesting skyscrapers, among which we may mention the Elverson Building (Fig. 364), by Rankin, Kellog & Crane. This building is composed of blocks with set-backs, almost as though imposed by the zoning law, though none exists in Philadelphia. The steel construction is expressed and the whole treatment is a frank study in the expression of modern material. There is perhaps not quite so much imagination as in some skyscraper designs, but the general composition is none the less fine.

In St. Louis the Southwestern Bell Telephone Company called upon Mauran, Russell & Crowell to do their Administration and Equipment Building (Fig. 365). This firm produced one of the most interesting designs yet achieved, with light wells and set-backs suggested by the New York zoning law type and a vertical accent, with the inexorable carrying through of all vertical steel lines, that was first clearly shown in Eliel Saarinen's fine, if unsuccessful, competition drawing for the Chicago Tribune Tower (Fig. 62). The detail and the whole conception are entirely modern.

San Francisco has just produced a magnificent skyscraper in the Pacific Telephone and Telegraph Building (Fig. 366), by Miller & Pflueger. Like the design we have observed in St. Louis, this attacks the modern problem in an entirely modern way. In order to study the effect of the building upon its site and in its surroundings, the architects resorted to the ingenious device of constructing an exact model, photographing the site, photographing the model at the same scale, and printing from the superposed negatives. We show a photograph of the building as it appears (Fig. 367) and a photograph of the model superposed upon the site (Fig. 368). It is practically impossible to tell which is the building and which is the model. By means of studies of this sort, architects can attain a complete knowledge of the appearance of a building after it is built though the site be still actually empty, and details and masses can be modified while the design is still in the paper stage. The

Photograph by Trowbridge.

FIG. 363. CHICAGO, ILL. Chicago Tribune Tower. *Hood & Howells, Architects.*

Fig. 365. St. Louis, Mo. Southwestern Bell Telephone Company Building. *Sketch by Hugh Ferriss. Mauran, Russell & Crowell, Architects.*

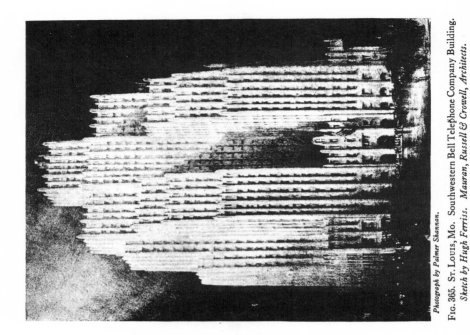

Fig. 364. Philadelphia, Pa. Elverson Building. *Rankin, Kellogg & Crane, Architects.*

detail of the San Francisco Telephone Building is unusually interesting and, especially in the interior (Fig. 369), the designers have experimented happily in exuberant colour in full intensities. This is what we might expect in California, but it gratifies us to find it none the less.

These are only a few of America's great skyscrapers, though they include some of the best. The possibilities of this design are unlimited and we may well feel that we are on the threshold of wonders. This appears most vividly when we observe some of the designs, perfectly possible and constructible, which have been made but, for one reason or another, not carried out. For example, the proposed Office and Convocation Building, by Goodhue, for Madison Square, New York (Frontispiece), was never built, but might have been. Had it been constructed it would, in the opinion of the writer, have been the most beautiful and the most thoroughly modern skyscraper in the world. It would have been new, daring, aspiring, and refined, symbolising the boldness and the taste of American architecture of to-day. Similarly, we reproduce an imaginative design by Hugh Ferriss (Fig. 370), perfectly buildable, and yet pushing verticality to extremes as yet unrealised.

In this connection we reproduce a design by the late Donn Barber which is now being built (Fig. 371). It is the scheme for a Broadway Tabernacle, combining in the most daring way the church and commercial building. Its conception came from a consideration of land values and the difficulty of supporting a church in a congested district. Though shocking to the conservative, the idea developed that both logic and taste might permit the design of a church which, with adequate provision for its own functional needs, might incorporate with itself a hotel or office-building which should assist in its support. If the design were well done, the combined buildings could be made beautiful and dignified, and no feeling of irreverence need ensue.

The lower part of the building is given up to the church and its huge auditorium. It is, of course, entirely unconnected with the building above. It is also, be it noted carefully, designed to have no interior columns or supports of steel in the auditorium. Above it, literally on its back, is reared a skyscraper of some twenty-five stories, *carried on the transverse trusses* over the auditorium. It will be a miracle of construction, but modern science works miracles complacently. Give an engineer money enough

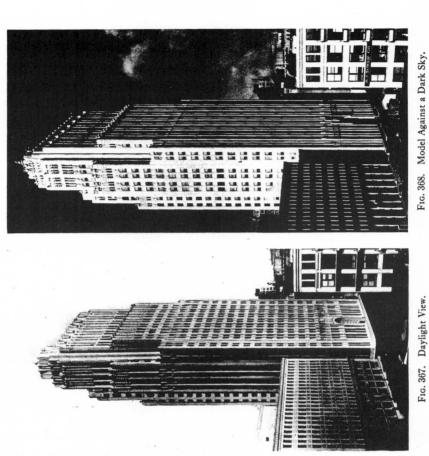

Photographs by Gabriel Moulin.

Fig. 366. Night View.

SAN FRANCISCO, CAL. Pacific Telephone and Telegraph Building. *J. R. Miller and T. L. Pflueger, Architects.*

Fig. 367. Daylight View.

Fig. 368. Model Against a Dark Sky.

Photograph by Gabriel Moulin.

FIG. 369. SAN FRANCISCO, CAL. Pacific Telephone and Telegraph Building.
J. R. Miller and T. L. Pflueger, Architects.

FIG. 370. A Skyscraper Design by Hugh Ferriss.

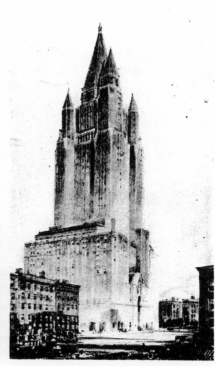

FIG. 371. NEW YORK, N. Y. The Broadway
Tabernacle. *Donn Barber, Architect.*

371

and room enough and he will construct cross-girders that can support a skyscraper. It is intriguing to consider what bearing such a building has upon our theories of architectural design, notably that which would have us believe that the real beauty of the steel building depends upon a truthful expression of its structure in its design. Should we, in this case, express to the unhappy worshippers that the unobstructed ceiling under which they sit is supporting a skyscraper above their heads? The idea is amusing, but seriously it forces us to consider again not only the possibilities of steel but the æsthetic expression which should go with its use. Whether we realise it or no, we are still applying to steel æsthetic formulas which were developed in connection with stone and brick, and the process leads only to confusion.

It is fascinating to toy with the possibilities of the future. Speculation is futile, but of one fact we can be sure: the era of steel will work a transformation in the physiognomy of our cities which will make its marvellous beginnings look pallid and weak. In conclusion, we reproduce some imaginative drawings of Hugh Ferriss. One shows New York a Babylonian composition of terraces and ziggurats (Fig. 372). Another shows a city composed according to the principles of the zoning law, but retaining its classical character and crowning its great masses with Roman temples, amphitheatres, and colonnades (Fig. 373). A third (Fig. 374), a night scene, avoids all suggestion of historic architecture and dimly indicates the great masses and the decked traffic communications which the future may evoke. None arrogates to itself oracular accuracy. They are intended solely to stimulate the imagination and make us think of the possibilities of the future.

We have forsworn prophecy, however, and are concerned with the present. Our review has shown it interesting and stimulating enough. The phenomena have run from the utmost conservatism to modernism unrestrained. We have seen the modern building constructed and designed according to the tenets and even the practice of Ictinus; we have seen the new steel and concrete which represent one of the most stupendous innovations in the history of architecture. Building by building and type by type, we have noted the improvement of the work to-day over that even of a generation ago. Without definitely stating the fact, we have sensed that American architecture is just entering upon a Renais-

FIG. 372. A Drawing by Hugh Ferriss.

FIG. 373. A Drawing by Hugh Ferriss.

373

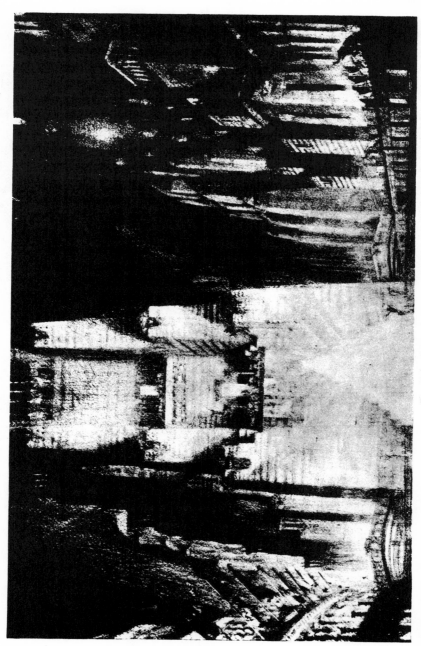

FIG. 374.   A Drawing by Hugh Ferriss.

374

sance which will probably be regarded in future histories as a great architectural epoch. If our study has brought home only a small portion of the variegated interest, the taste, the skill, the imagination, the vibrant energy, and the exuberant vitality of American architecture to-day, it will not have been in vain.

BIBLIOGRAPHY

A SELECTED BIBLIOGRAPHY

The reader should note that the bibliography is not intended in any sense to be complete. Its references are chiefly to articles which concern buildings mentioned in the text. In a number of cases, however, these lists have been amplified to include buildings not so mentioned, in order to give useful leads to readers who want to study some special type. In the beginning there is included a heading "Architects and Architectural Firms." This contains monographs on the work of certain famous American architects, but does not imply that there are no other architects as worthy and as famous whose works are not so published. There is also a brief list of works on the history and theory of architecture, not necessarily American, which will be an aid to the student in the study of American architecture.

BIBLIOGRAPHY

ABBREVIATIONS USED FOR PERIODICALS LISTED IN BIBLIOGRAPHY

Am. Arch.: The American Architect. Published bi-monthly by the Architectural and Building Press, New York.

Amer. Soc. of Civil Eng., Proceedings. Published in New York.

Arch. and Eng.: The Architect and Engineer. Published monthly by the Architect and Engineer, Inc., San Francisco, Calif.

Arch. Forum: Architectural Forum, N. Y. Published monthly by Rogers & Manson Company, New York.

Arch. Rec.: Architectural Record. Published monthly by the F. W. Dodge Corporation, New York.

Arch. Rev., N. Y. Now combined with *The American Architect.*

Arch.: Architecture. Published monthly by Charles Scribner's Sons, New York.

Arts and Decoration. Published monthly by Arts and Decoration Publishing Company, New York.

Brickbuilder. Now the *Architectural Forum.*

Journal, Amer. Inst. of Archs.: Journal of the American Institute of Architects. Published monthly by the Press of the American Institute of Architects, New York.

Lond. Mer.: The London Mercury. Published monthly in London, England.

The Nation. Published monthly in New York.

Suburban Life. Ceased publication.

West. Arch.: The Western Architect. Published monthly in Chicago, Ill.

World's Work. Published monthly by Doubleday, Page and Company, Garden City, N. Y.

ARCHITECTS AND ARCHITECTURAL FIRMS

DWIGHT JAMES BAUM.

    Matlack Price—The Work of Dwight James Baum, Architect. New York, William Helburn, Inc., 1927. Illus.

DANIEL H. BURNHAM AND CO.

    D. H. Burnham and Co.—Great American Architects Series. Part II. (*Arch. Rec.,* Dec. 1895, v. 5, pp. 49–72. Illus.)

    Charles Moore—Daniel H. Burnham, Architect Planner of Cities. 2 vols. Boston, Houghton, Mifflin Co., 1921. Illus.

    Peter B. Wrigh—Daniel Hudson Burnham and His Associates. (*Arch. Rec.,* July 1915, v. 38, pp. 1–168. Illus.)

CARRÈRE AND HASTINGS.

    The Work of Carrère and Hastings. This article includes a complete list of the clients of this firm up to 1910. (*Arch. Rec.,* Jan. 1910, v. 27, pp. 1–120. Illus.)

HENRY IVES COBB.

    Henry Ives Cobb—Great American Architects Series. Part III. (*Arch. Rec.,* Dec. 1895, v. 5, pp. 73–110. Illus.)

COPE AND STEWARDSON.
   Ralph Adams Cram—The Work of Messrs. Cope and Stewardson. (*Arch. Rec.*, Nov. 1904, v. 16, pp. 407–438. Illus.

DELANO AND ALDRICH.
   William Lawrence Bottomley—A Selection from the Works of Delano and Aldrich. (*Arch. Rec.*, July 1923, v. 54, pp. 2–71.
   Portraits of ten country houses, designed by Delano and Aldrich, drawn by Chester B. Price, with an introduction by Royal Cortissoz. Garden City, N. Y., Doubleday, Page & Company, 1924.

BERTRAM GROSVENOR GOODHUE.
   Charles Harris Whitaker, editor—Bertram Grosvenor Goodhue, Architect and Master of Many Arts. New York, Press of the American Institute of Architects, 1925. Illus.

RICHARD M. HUNT.
   The Works of the Late Richard M. Hunt. (*Arch. Rec.*, Oct.–Dec. 1895, v. 5, pp. 97–180. Illus.)

KILHAM AND HOPKINS.
   Herbert Croly—The Work of Kilham and Hopkins. (*Arch. Rec.*, Feb. 912, v. 31, pp. 97–128. Illus.)

LEBRUN AND SONS.
   Work of N. LeBrun and Sons. (*Arch. Rec.*, May 1910, v. 27, pp. 365–380. Illus.)

GUY LOWELL.
   The Works of Guy Lowell. (*Arch. Rev.*, N. Y., Feb. 1906, v. 13, pp. 13–40. Pl. 8.)

McKIM, MEAD AND WHITE.
   Henry W. Desmond—The Work of McKim, Mead and White. (*Arch. Rec.*, Sept. 1906, v. 20, pp. 153–268. Illus.)
   A Monograph of the Work of McKim, Mead and White, 1879–1915. 4 vols. New York, Architectural Book Pub. Co., 1915. Illus.
   Alfred H. Granger—Charles Follen McKim. Boston, Houghton, Mifflin Co., 1913. Illus.
   Lionel Moses—McKim, Mead and White, A History. (*Amer. Arch.* and *Arch. Rev.*, May 24, 1922, v. 121, pp. 413–424, with plates.)
   C. H. Reilly—McKim, Mead and White. London, Ernest Benn, Ltd., 1924. Illus.
   Sketches and Designs by Stanford White: with an introduction of his career by his son, Lawrence Grant White. New York, The Architectural Book Pub. Co., 1920.

MAGINNIS AND WALSH.
   Sylvester Baxter—A Selection from the Works of Maginnis and Walsh. (*Arch. Rec.*, Feb. 1923, v. 53, pp. 92–115. Illus.)

MELLOR, MEIGS AND HOWE.
   Monograph of the Work of Mellor, Meigs and Howe. New York, The Architectural Book Pub. Co., 1923. Illus.

PARKER, THOMAS AND RICE.
Notes on the Work of Parker, Thomas and Rice of Boston and Baltimore. (*Arch. Rec.*, Aug. 1913, v. 34, pp. 97–184. Illus.)

PEABODY AND STEARNS.
Great American Architects Series. Part II. Work of Peabody and Stearns. (*Arch. Rec.*, July 1896, v. 6, pp. 53–94. Illus.)

CHARLES ADAMS PLATT.
Monograph of the Work of Charles A. Platt, with an introduction by Royal Cortissoz. New York, The Architectural Book Pub. Co., 1913. Illus.

JOHN RUSSELL POPE.
Herbert Croly—Recent Works of John Russell Pope. (*Arch. Rec.*, June 1911, v. 29, pp. 441–511. Illus.)

Royal Cortissoz—Architecture of John Russell Pope. New York, William Helburn Inc., 1925– Illus. (Vol. 1 complete, to be finished in 3 vols.)

HENRY HOBSON RICHARDSON.
Mariana Griswold Van Rensselaer—Henry Hobson Richardson and His Works. Boston, Houghton, Mifflin, 1888. Illus.

JOHN WELBURN ROOT.
Harriet Monroe—John Welburn Root. Boston, Houghton, Mifflin Company, 1896. Illus.

ELIEL SAARINEN.
Irving K. Pond—Eliel Saarinen and His Work. (*West. Arch.*, July 1923, v. 32, pp. 75–77, pl. 1–16.)

HOWARD SHAW.
Herbert D. Croly—Recent Work of Howard Shaw. Chiefly residential. (*Arch. Rec.* April 1913, v. 33, pp. 284–331. Illus.)

SHEPLEY, RUTAN AND COOLIDGE.
Great American Architects Series. Part I. Work of Shepley, Rutan and Coolidge. (*Arch. Rec.*, July 1896, v. 6, pp. 1–52. Illus.)

LOUIS H. SULLIVAN.
The Young Man in Architecture. (*West. Arch.*, Jan. 1925, v. 34, pp. 4–10, pl. 1–6. Illus.)

Great American Architects. Part I. Adler and Sullivan. Architecture in Chicago. (*Arch. Rec.*, Dec. 1895, v. 5, pp. 1–48. Illus.)

Fiske Kimball—Louis Sullivan, an Old Master. (*Arch. Rec.*, April 1925, v. 57, pp. 289–304. Illus.)

L. H. Sullivan—Autobiography of an idea, with a foreword by Claude Bragdon. New York, Press of the American Institute of Architects, 1924.

FRANK LLOYD WRIGHT.
Wendingen—Frank Lloyd Wright. The Life Work of the American Architect, F. L. Wright, with contributions by F. L. Wright, an introduction by H. T. Wijdeveld, and many articles by famous European architects and American writers. Santpoort, Holland, C. A. Mees, 1925. Illus.

YORK AND SAWYER.
The Recent Work of York and Sawyer. (*Arch. Rev.*, N. Y., Aug. 1909, v. 16, pp. 97–116, pls. 61–70. Illus.)

THEORY AND HISTORY

Stanley D. Adshead—A Comparison of Modern American Architecture with that of European Cities. (*Arch. Rec.*, Feb. 1911, v. 29, pp. 113–125. Illus.)

American Architect—Fifty Years of American Architecture. Illustrated articles by Royal Cortissoz, George C. Nimmons, Alfred C. Bossom, Myron Hunt, and others. (*Am. Arch.*, Jan. 5, 1926, v. 129, pp. 1–168.)

Alfred C. Bossom—American National Architecture. An interesting suggestion of modern adaptation of Mayan architecture. (*Am. Arch.*, July 29, 1925, v. 128, pp. 77–83. Illus.)

Claude Bragdon—Architecture in the United States. I. The Birth of Taste. II. The Growth of Taste. III. The Skyscraper. (Illus. articles, *Arch. Rec.*, June–Aug. 1909, v. 25, pp. 426–433; v. 26, pp. 38–45, pp. 85–96.)

Barr Ferree—An "American Style" of Architecture. (*Arch. Rec.*, July–Sept. 1891, v. 1, pp. 39–45.)

Leo Friedlander—The New Architecture and the Master Sculptor. (*Arch. Forum*, Jan. 1927, v. 46, pp. 1–8.)

H. S. Goodhart-Rendel—What Architecture Can Give to the Layman. (*London Mercury*, April 1924, v. 9, pp. 628–657.)

Jacques Gréber—L'architecture aux États-Unis preuve de la force d'éxpansion du génie français. 2 vols. Paris, Payot et Cie, 1920. Illus.

A. D. F. Hamlin—Twenty-five Years of American Architecture. With illustrations of the Library of Congress, Boston Public Library, Masonic Temple of Chicago, Pennsylvania Station of N. Y., and other buildings. (*Arch. Rec.*, July 1916, v. 40, pp. 1–14.)

Talbot Faulkner Hamlin—The American Spirit in Architecture. Vol. 13 of the Pageant of America. New Haven, Yale University Press, 1926. Illus.

Werner Hegemann and Albert Peets—The American Vitruvius: An Architect's Handbook of Civic Art. New York, The Architectural Book Pub. Co., 1922. Illus. (There is a German edition of this publication.)

Fiske Kimball—Domestic Architecture of the American Colonies and of the Early Republic. New York, Charles Scribner's Sons, 1922. Illus.

Fiske Kimball—What is Modern Architecture? (*The Nation*, N. Y., July 30, 1924, v. 119, pp. 128–129.)
Recent Architecture in the South. (Illus. article, *Arch. Rec.*, March 1924, v. 55, pp. 209–271.)

Le Corbusier—Towards a New Architecture. Translated by Frederick Etchella. N. Y., Payson and Clarke, 1927. Illus.

Howard Major—The Domestic Architecture of the Early American Republic. The Greek Revival. Philadelphia, J. B. Lippincott Co., 1926. Illus.

Erich Mendelsohn—Amerika, bilderbuch eines Architekten. Berlin, Rudolf Mosse, 1926. Illus.

Lewis Mumford—Sticks and Stones, A Study of American Architecture and Civilization. New York, Boni and Liveright, 1924.

Charles Matlack Price—The Practical Book of Architecture. Philadelphia, J. B. Lippincott Co., 1915.

Oliver Reagan, editor—American Architecture of the Twentieth Century, a series of photographs and measured drawings of modern, civic, commercial and industrial buildings. New York, Architectural Book Publishing Co. Part I, II, 1927. (In process of publication.)

Montgomery Schuyler—The Romanesque Revival in New York. (Illus. articles, *Arch. Rec.*, July–Sept., and Oct.–Dec. 1891, v. 1, pp. 7–38, pp. 151–198.)

Geoffrey Scott—The Architecture of Humanism. London, Constable and Co., Ltd., 1924.

Russell Clipston Sturgis—How to Judge Architecture. New York, Baker and Taylor, 1903. Illus.

Robert C. Sweatt—Architecture of the Pacific Northwest. (Illus. article, *Arch. Rec.*, v. 26, pp. 166–175, Sept. 1909.)

Thomas E. Tallmadge—The Story of Architecture in America. New York, W. W. Norton and Co., 1927. Illus.

SPECIAL TYPES

APARTMENT HOUSES

Architectural Forum—Apartment House Reference Number, Sept. 1925, v. 43, pp. 121–184, pls. 33–56. Plans, exts., ints.

R. A. Sexton, Editor—American Apartment Houses of To-day, illustrating plans, details, exteriors, and interiors of modern city and suburban apartment houses throughout the United States. New York, Architectural Book Publishing Company, 1926.

NEW YORK CITY, TURTLE BAY GARDENS. Edward C. Dean and William Lawrence Bottomley, Associate Architects. (*Arch. Rec.*, Dec. 1920, v. 48, pp. 466–493. Plans, exts., ints.)

NEW YORK CITY. NO. 277 PARK AVE. AN APARTMENT HOTEL. McKim, Mead & White, Architects. (*Arch. Forum*, July 1925, v. 43, pls. 9–11. Plans, exts.)

AUTOMOTIVE BUILDINGS

Architectural Forum—Automotive Buildings Reference Number, March 1927, v. 46, pp. 201–312. Plans, exts., ints.

Alexander G. Guth—The Automobile Service Station. (*Arch. Forum*, July 1926, v. 45, pp. 33–56. Illus.)

BANKS

Architectural Forum—Special Number on Banks, June 1923, v. 38, pp. 253–312, pls. 65–88. Plans, exts., ints.

NEW YORK CITY. BOWERY SAVINGS BANK. York and Sawyer, Architects. (*Am. Arch.* and *Arch. Rev.*, Aug. 1, 1923, v. 124, pls. p. 138 + exts., details.)

Six Modern Banks, by Dennison and Hirons, Architects. (*Arch. Forum*, May 1925, v. 42, pp. 299–304. Plans, sketches.)

BRIDGES

Claude Bragdon—Abstract Thoughts on Concrete Bridges. (*Arch. Rec.*, Jan. 1923, v. 53, pp. 3–10. Illus.)

Wilbur J. Watson—Bridge Architecture, containing two hundred illustrations of the notable bridges of the world, ancient and modern . . . New York, William Helburn, Inc., 1927. Illus.

HUDSON RIVER, N. Y. PROPOSED MEMORIAL BRIDGE. Alfred C. Bossom, Architect. (*Amer. Arch.*, April 6, 1921, v. 119, pp. 423–425. Plan, sketches.)

Montgomery Schuyler—Our Four Big Bridges. THE OLD EAST RIVER BRIDGE; QUEENSBOROUGH BRIDGE; MANHATTAN BRIDGE; WILLIAMSBURG BRIDGE. (*Arch. Rec.*, Mar. 1909, v. 25, pp. 147–160. Illus.)

PHILADELPHIA, THE DELAWARE RIVER BRIDGE between Philadelphia and Camden. Paul P. Cret, Architect. Ralph Modjeski, Engineer. Illus. article by Harold Donaldson Eberlein. (*Arch. Rec.*, Jan. 1927, v. 61, pp. 1–12.)

WASHINGTON, D. C. ARLINGTON MEMORIAL BRIDGE. Rendered drawings of plan, elev., perspective sketch. McKim, Mead and White, Architects. (*Journal, Amer. Inst. of Archs.*, Feb. 1924, v. 12, pp. 65–71.)

WILMINGTON, DEL. WASHINGTON MEMORIAL BRIDGE. Vance W. Torbert, Architect. (*Arch. Forum*, Dec. 1923, v. 39, pp. 295–298, pls. 102–103. Plan, elev., views.)

CAPITOLS

Architectural Forum—Public Buildings Reference Number, Part I, June 1927, v. 46, pp. 505–616. Part II, Sept. 1927, v. 47, pp. 193–304. Plans, exts., ints.

ALBANY, N. Y. CAPITOL BUILDING. (*Arch. Rec.*, Oct. 1899, v. 9, pp. 142–157. Illus.)

HARRISBURG, PA. CAPITOL PARK. Scale model of the buildings, grounds and approach. Plan, sketches of capitol building during construction. Arnold W. Brunner, Architect. (*Arch. Rec.*, April 1923, v. 53, pp. 286–306.)

LINCOLN, NEB. STATE CAPITOL. Competition drawings of designs submitted for the Nebraska State Capitol. Plans and elevs. of designs by Bertram G. Goodhue;

John R. Pope; McKim, Mead and White; Tracy and Swartwout; Paul P. Cret and Zantzinger. (*Amer. Arch.*, July 21, 1920, v. 118, pp. 79–80, and plates.)

——. SAME. The Architectural Sculpture of the Nebraska State Capitol by Charles Harris Whitaker and Hartley Burr Alexander. New York, Press of the American Institute of Architects, Inc., 1926. Illus.

——. SAME. Plan, Sketches, Models for Reliefs by Bertram G. Goodhue, Architect; Lee Lawrie, Sculptor. (*West. Arch.*, Oct. 1923, v. 32, pp. 113–116, pls. 1–6.)

MADISON, WIS. STATE CAPITOL. George B. Post and Sons, Architects. (*Arch. Rec.*, Sept. 1917, v. 42, pp. 194–233. Plan, exts., ints., section.)

PROVIDENCE, R. I. STATE CAPITOL. McKim, Mead and White, Architects. (*Amer. Arch.*, Oct. 10, 17, 24, 1903, v. 82, exts., ints.)

CHURCHES

Architectural Forum—Church Reference Number, April 1924, v. 40, pp. 133–188, pls. 49–64. Illus.

Aaron G. Alexander—American Church Architecture. (*Arch. Forum*, May 1926, v. 44, pp. 313–336. Plans, exts.)

Sylvester Baxter—A Selection from the Works of Maginnis and Walsh. (*Arch. Rec.*, Feb. 1923, v. 53, pp. 92–115. Illus.)

Ralph Adams Cram—American Churches. A series of authoritative articles on designing, planning, heating, ventilating, lighting, and general equipment of churches as demonstrated by the best practice in the United States. New York, The American Architect, 1915. 2 vols. Illus.

Montgomery Schuyler—The Work of Cram, Goodhue, and Ferguson. A record of the firm's representative structures, 1892–1910. (*Arch. Rec.*, Jan. 1911, v. 29, pp. 1–41. Illus.)

BOSTON, MASS. LESLIE LINDSEY MEMORIAL CHAPEL, EMMANUEL CHURCH. Allen and Collens, Architects. (*Arch.*, Dec. 1924, v. 50, pp. 393–398. Plan, exts., ints.)

CHICAGO. ISAIAH TEMPLE. Alfred S. Alschuler, Architect. (*West. Arch.*, June, 1925, v. 34, pls. 1–8. Plans, exts., ints.)

NEW YORK CITY. CATHEDRAL OF ST. JOHN THE DIVINE. A Study of the Designs for the Cathedral of St. John the Divine, by Alfred D. Hamlin. New York, published at The Cathedral, March 1924. Illus. pamphlet.

——. THE NAVE OF THE CATHEDRAL OF ST. JOHN THE DIVINE. Ralph Adams Cram, Architect. (*Arch.*, Aug. 1917, v. 36, pp. 145–150. Plan, sketch of int., interiors of model.)

NEW YORK CITY. CHURCH OF ST. JOHN NEPOMUK. John Van Pelt, Architect. (*Arch. Rec.*, Dec. 1925, v. 58, pp. 517–529. Exts., ints.)

NEW YORK CITY. ST. THOMAS' CHURCH. The Story of St. Thomas' Church, by H. L. Bottomley. Cram, Goodhue and Ferguson, Architects. (*Arch. Rec.*, Feb. 1914, v. 35, pp. 101–131. Plan, elev., exts., ints.)

NEW YORK CITY. THIRD CHURCH OF CHRIST, SCIENTIST, Park Avenue. Delano and Aldrich, Architects. (*Arch. Forum*, Feb. 1924, v. 40, p. 85, pls. 17–21. Plans, exts., ints.)

NEWBURYPORT, MASS. ST. PAUL'S CHURCH. Perry, Shaw and Hepburn, Architects. (*Arch. Forum*, Aug. 1924, v. 41, p. 87, pls. 29–30.) Plans, exts., int.)

PETERBOROUGH, N. H. ALL SAINTS CHURCH. Illus. article by Howard Donaldson Eberlein. Cram and Ferguson, Architects. (*Arch. Rec.*, Sept. 1925, v. 58, pp. 278–288. Plans, exts., ints., sec.)

PITTSBURGH, PA. FIRST BAPTIST CHURCH. Cram, Goodhue and Ferguson, Architects. (*Arch. Rec.*, Sept. 1912, v. 32, pp. 193–208. Plans, exts., ints.)

VALLEY FORGE, PA. WASHINGTON MEMORIAL CHAPEL. Zantzinger, Borie and Medary, Architects. (*Arch. Rev.*, N. Y., Sept. 1919, v. 9 (new series); pp. 69–74, pls. 41–45. Exts., ints.)

WASHINGTON, D. C. CATHEDRAL OF ST. PETER AND ST. PAUL. Frohman, Robb and Little, Architects. Plans, exts., during construction, apse end, sketches of exterior and interior completed. (*Amer. Arch.*, April 22, 1925, v. 127, pp. 355–368, pls. 97–107. Illus.)

WASHINGTON, D. C. THE NATIONAL SHRINE OF THE IMMACULATE CONCEPTION. Maginnis and Walsh, Architects. (*Arch. Rec.*, July 1922, v. 51, pp. 2–15. Plans, sketches, models.)

COLLEGES AND UNIVERSITIES

Architectural Forum—University Buildings Reference Number, Part I, Dec. 1925, v. 43, pp. 321–384, pls. 89–104. Part II, June 1926, v. 44, pp. 345–408, pls. 97–112. Plans, exts., ints.

Brickbuilder—Recent Collegiate Architecture, as Exemplified in the Work of Messrs. Shepley, Rutan and Coolidge at Harvard University; Messrs. Cram, Goodhue and Ferguson at Richmond College; and Palmer, Hornbostel and Jones at Northwestern University. (*Brickbuilder*, Nov. 1914, v. 23, pp. 259–273, pls. 161–176.)

Montgomery Schuyler—Architecture of American Colleges. Illus. Series in *Arch. Rec.*, as below:

    I. Harvard University. (Oct. 1909, v. 26, pp. 243–269.)
    II. Yale. (Dec. 1909, v. 26, pp. 393–416.)
    III. Princeton. (Feb. 1910, v. 27, pp. 129–160.)
    IV. New York City Colleges. (June 1910, v. 27, pp. 443–469.)
    V. Univ. of Penn., Girard, Haverford, Lehigh and Bryn Mawr Colleges. (Sept. 1910, v. 28, pp. 182–211.)
    VI. Dartmouth, Williams and Amherst. (Dec. 1910, v. 28, pp. 424–442.)
    VII. Brown, Bowdoin, Trinity and Wesleyan. (Feb. 1911, v. 29, pp. 145–166.)
    VIII. The southern colleges: William and Mary, St. John's College, Univ. of Georgia, Vanderbilt Univ., Maryville College, etc. (July 1911, v. 30, pp. 57–84.)
    IX. Union, Hamilton, Hobart, Cornell and Syracuse. (Dec. 1911, v. 30, pp. 549–573.)

——. Architecture of American Colleges. Three women's colleges: Vassar, Wellesley, and Smith. (*Arch. Rec.*, May 1912, v. 31, pp. 513–537. Illus.)

BALTIMORE CITY COLLEGE COMPETITION. Group plan, plans of buildings, elevation of main building of winning design. Buckler and Fenhagen, Architects. (*Amer. Arch.* and *Arch. Rev.*, Aug. 13, 1924, v. 126, pp. 133–138.)

DENISON UNIVERSITY, GRANVILLE, OHIO. Group plan, perspective sketches, etc. Arnold W. Brunner, Architect; Frederick Law Olmsted, Landscape Architect. (*Arch. Rec.*, Oct. 1923, v. 54, pp. 298–320.)

HARVARD UNIVERSITY, CAMBRIDGE, MASS. Business School Competition. Group perspective, plan, elevation of library and dining hall of winning design. McKim, Mead and White, Architects. Other designs by Ludlow and Peabody with Harold F. Kellogg associated; J. J. Haffner with Perry, Shaw and Hepburn associated; Raymond M. Hood; Walker and Gillette; Coolidge, Shepley, Bulfinch and Abbott; Parker, Thomas and Rice; Egerton Swartwout; Aymar Embury II; Benjamin W. Morris with Eric Gugler, associated; Hewitt and Brown; Guy Lowell. (*Arch.*, March, April, May, June 1925, v. 51, pp. 131, 132, 193, 194, 227–230, pls. 33–36.)

JOHNS HOPKINS UNIVERSITY, BALTIMORE, MD. The New Home of Johns Hopkins University. Parker, Thomas and Rice, Architects. (*Arch. Rec.*, June 1915, v. 37, pp. 481–492. Illus.)

MASS. INSTITUTE OF TECHNOLOGY, CAMBRIDGE, MASS. Building the "New Technology," by H. E. Kebbon. William Welles Bosworth, Architect. (*Arch. Rev.*, New York, June 1916, v. 4 (New Series), pp. 85–92, pls. 57–70. Plans, elev., sections, exts., ints.)

NEW YORK STATE COLLEGE OF AGRICULTURE, ITHACA, N. Y. The State Architect and His Works: II. The State Agricultural College and other Institutions. Plans and sketches of the New York State College of Agriculture, Cornell University, Ithaca, N. Y. Lewis F. Pilcher, Architect. (*Arch. Rec.*, Sept. 1923, v. 54, pp. 265–276.)

PHILADELPHIA DIVINITY SCHOOL. Zantzinger, Borie & Medary, Architects. Exteriors of library; plan, elevations, and sections of St. Andrew's Chapel; model of group. (*Arch. Rec.*, Aug. 1923, v. 54, pp. 106–120.)

PRINCETON UNIVERSITY, PRINCETON, N. J. Graduate College and Cleveland Memorial Tower. Cram, Goodhue and Ferguson, Architects. (*Amer. Arch.*, Nov. 26, 1913, pp. 205–208, v. 104, plates of exts., ints.)

UNIVERSITY OF CALIFORNIA, BERKELEY, CALIF. Greek amphitheater, revised group model, exterior of California Hall, Hearst Mining Building. John Galen Howard, Architect. (*Arch. Rec.*, April 1908, v. 23, pp. 269–293. Illus.)

UNIVERSITY OF MICHIGAN, ANN ARBOR, MICH. Law Courts Buildings. York and Sawyer, Architects. (*Arch.*, July 1925, v. 52, pp. 237–242, pls. 97–102. Exts., ints., details.)

UNIVERSITY OF PITTSBURGH, PA. The Cathedral of Learning. Illus. pamphlet by John G. Bowman. Published by the University of Pittsburgh, February 1925.

WEST POINT MILITARY ACADEMY, WEST POINT, N. Y. The New West Point. Bird's-eye sketch, views and plans of the Chapel, Post Headquarters. Cram, Goodhue and Ferguson, Architects. (*Arch. Rec.*, Jan. 1911, v. 29, pp. 86–112.)

YALE UNIVERSITY, NEW HAVEN, CONN. Peabody Museum of Natural History.
Day and Klauder, Architects. (*Arch.*, Nov. 1925, v. 52, pls. 165–168. Plans, exts.,
ints.)

——. Sterling Hall of Medicine. Day and Klauder, Architects. (*Arch.*, Aug. 1925, v.
52, pls. 117–122. Plan, exts., ints.)

——. Yale University, A Plan for its Future Building. John Russell Pope, Architect.
Illus. by O. R. Eggers. New York, Cheltenham Press, 1919. (Proposed, not followed.)

——. Harkness Memorial. James G. Rogers, Architect. (*Arch.*, October 1921, v. 44,
pp. 287–310, pls. 141–156. Plans, exts., ints., details, sections.)

——. Harkness Memorial. James G. Rogers, Architect. (*Arch. Rec.*, Sept. 1921, v. 50,
pp. 163–182, plan, exts.)

COUNTRY CLUBS

Architectural Forum—Golf and Country Club Reference Number, March 1925, v. 42, pp.
129–212, pls. 17–40. Illus.

BAYSIDE, N. Y. OAKLAND GOLF CLUB. Roger H. Bullard, Architect. (*Arch.
Forum*, Dec. 1923, v. 39, pls. 97–101. Plans, exts., ints.)

LOCUST VALLEY, LONG ISLAND, N. Y. PIPING ROCK COUNTRY CLUB.
Guy Lowell, Architect. (*Suburban Life*, July 1914, v. 19, pp. 8–11. Illus.) *Amer.
Arch.*, Dec. 25, 1912, v. 102, plates.)

LONG BRANCH, N. J. NORWOOD GOLF CLUB. Harry Allan Jacobs, Architect.
(*Arch.*, Aug. 1922, v. 46, pls. 117–119. Plans, exts., ints.)

MAMARONECK, N. Y. WINGED FOOT GOLF CLUB. Clifford C. Wendehack,
Architect. (*Arch. Rec.*, Jan. 1926, v. 59, pp. 7–17. Plans, exts., ints.)

PASADENA, CALIF. FLINTRIDGE COUNTRY CLUB. Myron Hunt, Architect.
(*Arch. Rec.*, Aug. 1921, v. 50, pp. 93–101. Plans, exts., ints.)

SAN ANTONIO, TEXAS. SAN ANTONIO COUNTRY CLUB. George Willis, Architect. (*Arch. Rec.*, Jan. 1921, v. 49, pp. 48–55. Plans, exts., ints.)

TENAFLY, N. J. KNICKERBOCKER COUNTRY CLUB. Aymar Embury II, Architect. (*Arch.*, Feb. 1917, v. 35, pls. 27–30. Plans, exts., ints.)

COURT HOUSES

NEW YORK CITY. COURT HOUSE. Guy Lowell, Architect. (*Arch.*, April 1927,
v. 55, pp. 189–192. Plan, exts., ints.)

(For illustrations of other court houses, see Public Buildings Reference Numbers, compiled
by the *Architectural Forum* and listed under CAPITOLS.)

EXPOSITIONS

BUFFALO, N. Y. PAN-AMERICAN EXPOSITION OF 1901.
C. D. Arnold—Official Views of Pan-American Exposition. Buffalo, 1901.

Walter H. Page and others—Pan-American Exposition. (*World's Work*, Aug. 1901,
v. 2, pp. 1015–1096. Illus.)

CHICAGO, ILL. WORLD'S COLUMBIAN EXPOSITION OF 1893.

The Dream City. A Portfolio of Photographic Views of the World's Columbian Exposition. With an introduction by Professor Halsey C. Ives, St. Louis, Mo. N. D. Thompson Pub. Co., 1893.

Lessons of the Chicago World's Fair. An interview with the late Daniel H. Burnham. (*Arch. Rec.*, Jan. 1913, v. 33, pp. 34–44. Illus.)

Portfolio of Views Issued by the Department of Photography. C. D. Arnold, Chief. Chicago National Chemigraph Co., 1893.

Portfolio of Photographs of the World's Fair. Chicago, Werner Co., 1893. Plates.

OMAHA, NEB. TRANS–MISSISSIPPI AND INTERNATIONAL EXPOSITION, 1898.

James B. Haynes—History of the Trans-Mississippi and International Exposition. Omaha, Neb. St. Louis, Woodward and Tiernan Printing Co., 1910. Illus.

PHILADELPHIA, PA. CENTENNIAL EXHIBITION OF 1876.

James D. McCabe—Illustrated History of the Centennial Exhibition. Philadelphia, National Publishing Co., 1876.

PHILADELPHIA, PA. SESQUI–CENTENNIAL EXPOSITION OF 1926.

How the Sesqui-Centennial was Designed. John Molitor, Supervising Architect. (*Am. Arch.*, v. 130, pp. 377–384, pls. 265–280, Nov. 5, 1926. Plans, exts., ints., sketches.)

ST. LOUIS, MO. LOUISIANA PURCHASE EXPOSITION, 1904.

The Greatest of Expositions Illustrated. Official publication. St. Louis, Official Photograph Co., 1904.

SAN DIEGO, CALIF. PANAMA–CALIFORNIA EXPOSITION, 1915.

C. Matlack Price—Panama-California Exposition. Bertram G. Goodhue and the Renaissance of Spanish-Colonial Architecture. (*Arch. Rec.*, March 1915, v. 37, pp. 229–251. Illus.)

C. M. Winslow—The Architecture and the Gardens of San Diego Exposition. Illus. San Francisco, P. Elder and Company, 1916.

SAN FRANCISCO, CALIF. PANAMA–PACIFIC EXPOSITION OF 1915.

The Architecture and Landscape Gardening of the Exposition, a Pictorial Survey of the Most Beautiful of the Architectural Compositions of the Panama-Pacific International Exposition. Described by M. W. Raymond. With an introduction by L. C. Mullgardt, Architect. San Francisco, P. Elder and Company, 1915.

Paul E. Denivelle—Texture and Color at the Panama-Pacific Exposition. (*Arch. Rec.*, Nov. 1915, v. 38, pp. 562–570. Illus.)

Ben Macomber—The Jewel City, its Planning and Achievement; its Architecture, Sculpture, Symbolism, and Music; its Gardens, Palaces, and Exhibits. With colored frontispiece and more than seventy-five other illustrations. San Francisco, John H. Williams, 1915.

Louis C. Mullgardt—Panama-Pacific Exposition at San Francisco. (*Arch. Rec.*, March 1915, v. 37, pp. 193–227. Illus.)

W. L. Woollett—Color in Architecture at the Panama-Pacific Exposition. (*Arch. Rec.*, May 1915, v. 37, pp. 437–444. Illus.)

SEATTLE, WASH. ALASKA–YUKON–PACIFIC EXPOSITION OF 1909.

Our Exposition in Seattle. (*Arch. Rec.*, July 1909, v. 26, pp. 24–32. Group plan, exts.)

HOSPITALS

Architectural Forum—Hospital Reference Number, Dec. 1922, v. 37, pp. 245–314. Plans, exts., ints.

William J. Sayward—Planning of College Infirmaries. (*Arch. Forum*, June 1926, v. 44, pp. 373–376. Illus.)

Edward F. Stevens—The American Hospital of the Twentieth Century. New York, Architectural Record Publishing Co., revised edition, 1921.

Edward F. Stevens—The Small Hospital. (*Arch. Forum*, October 1926, v. 45, pp. 229–248. Plans, exts., ints.)

HOTELS

Architectural Forum—Hotel Reference Number, Nov. 1923, v. 39, pp. 195–274. Illus.

Frederick Jennings—Recent Hotel Architecture in California. (*Arch. and Eng.*, Jan. 1925, v. 80, pp. 51–111. Plans, exts., ints.)

William L. Stoddart—Designing the Small City Hotel. (*Arch. Forum*, Feb. 1926, v. 44, pp. 109–128. Illus.)

ALBUQUERQUE, NEW MEXICO. HOTEL FRANCISCAN. Trost and Trost, Architects. (*Arch.*, Dec. 1923, v. 48, pls. 191, 192. Ext.)

ATLANTIC CITY, N. J. TRAYMORE HOTEL. Price & McLanahan, Architects. (*Arch. Forum*, Nov. 1917, v. 27, pp. 119–124. Plans, exts., ints.)

LOS ANGELES, CALIF. BILTMORE HOTEL. Schultze & Weaver, Architects. (*Arch. Forum*, Nov. 1923, v. 39, pls. 73–79. Plans, exts., ints.)

NEW YORK CITY. BILTMORE HOTEL. Warren & Wetmore, Architects. (*Arch.*, Feb. 1914, v. 29, pls. 24–29, pp. 41–45. Plans, exts., ints.)

NEW YORK CITY. HOTEL COMMODORE. Warren & Wetmore, Architects. (*Amer. Arch.*, March 5, 1919, v. 115, pls. 69–77. Plans, exts., ints.)

NEW YORK CITY. THE SHELTON HOTEL. (*Arch.*, April 1924, v. 49, pp. 101–110, pls. 49–58. Plans, exts., ints.)

——. SAME. Arthur Loomis Harmon, Architect. (*Arch. Rec.*, July 1925, v. 58, pp. 1–18. Plans, exts., ints.)

——. SAME. Evolution of an Architectural Design, by Leon V. Solon. (*Arch. Rec.*, April 1926, v. 59, pp. 367–375. Illus.)

TOKIO, JAPAN. IMPERIAL HOTEL. Frank Lloyd Wright, Architect. (*Arch. Rec.*, April 1923, v. 53, pp. 332–352. Plans, exts., ints.)

BIBLIOGRAPHY

HOUSES, COUNTRY

American Country Houses of To-day. Edited by B. W. Close. New York, Architectural Book Pub. Co., 1922. Illus.

Architectural Forum—Small House Reference Number, March 1926, v. 44, pp. 137–216, pls. 34–64. Illus.

Atlantic Monthly Company—House Beautiful Building Annual 1927. A comprehensive and practical manual of procedure, materials, and methods of construction for all who contemplate building or remodelling a home. Boston, 1927. Illus.

Adrian Bentley—An English Tudor Country House. The Residence of George Marshall Allen, Esq., Morristown, N. J. Charles I. Berg, Architect. (*Arch. Forum*, Dec. 1918, v. 29, pp. 145–150, pls. 81–92. Illus.)

A. Lawrence Kocher—The American Country House. (*Arch. Rec.*, Nov. 1925, v. 58, pp. 401–512. Illus., plans, exts., ints.)

A. Lawrence Kocher—The Country House. Are we developing an American Style? (*Arch. Rec.*, Nov. 1926, pp. 385–502. Illus.)

Ralph Rodney Root—Country Place Types of the Middle West. (*Arch. Rec.*, Jan. 1924, v. 55, pp. 1–32. Illus.)

Russell T. Whitehead—Current Country House Architecture. (*Arch. Rec.*, Nov. 1924, v. 56, pp. 385–488. Illus.)

CALIFORNIA

BEVERLY HILLS, CALIF. "DIAS DORADOS," RESIDENCE FOR MR. THOMAS H. INCE. Roy Seldon Price, Architect. (*West. Arch.*, May 1924, v. 33, pls. 8–16. Plans, exts., ints.)

Giles Edgerton—"Dias Dorados," a Beautiful California Estate. A well designed Spanish ranch, the home of Thomas H. Ince. (*Arts and Dec.*, June 1924, v. 21, pp. 16–18. Plans, exts., ints.)

Arthur C. David—An Architect of Bungalows in California: Greene and Greene. (*Arch. Rec.*, Oct. 1906, v. 20, pp. 306–315. Illus.)

Irving F. Morrow—A Dialogue which Touches upon Mr. Smith's Architecture. Plans, ints., exts., of houses by George Washington Smith, Architect. (*Arch. and Eng.*, July 1924, v. 78, pp. 53–97. Illus.)

CONNECTICUT

FARMINGTON, CONN. HOUSE OF MRS. R. M. BISSELL. E. S. Dodge, Architect. (*Arch. Forum*, March 1924, v. 40, pls. 39–42. Plans, exts., ints.)

DELAWARE

WILMINGTON, DEL. THE A. I. DU PONT RESIDENCE. Carrère and Hastings, Architects. (*Arch. Rec.*, Oct. 1913, v. 34, pp. 337–347. Exts., ints.)

FLORIDA

Rexford Newcomb—Recent Architecture in Florida: house for George A. McKinlock, Palm Beach. (*West. Arch.*, Dec. 1925, v. 34, pp. 119–121, pls. 1–16. Plans, exts., ints.)

MIAMI, FLA. "VIZCAYA," THE VILLA AND GROUNDS. F. Burrall Hoffman, Jr., and Paul Chalfin, Associate Architects. (*Arch. Rev.*, New York, July 1917, v. 5 (New Series), pp. 121–167. Illus.)

Matlack Price—Mediterranean Architecture in Florida. (*Arch. Forum*, Jan. 1926, v. 44, pp. 33–40. Illus.)

ILLINOIS

LAKE FOREST, ILL. HOUSE OF HAROLD F. McCORMICK. Charles A. Platt, Architect. (*Arch. Rec.*, March 1912, v. 31, pp. 201–225. Plans, exts., ints.)

NEW YORK

Charles Downing Lay—Style and Expression in Landscape Architecture. Air Views of Long Island Estates. (*Arch. Forum*, July 1924, v. 41, pp. 1–8. Illus.)

PLEASANTVILLE, N. Y. HOUSE OF H. EDWARD MANVILLE. Donn Barber, Architect. (*Arch. Rec.*, Jan. 1926, v. 59, pp. 39–49. Plans, exts.)

NORTH CAROLINA

Russell T. Whitehead—Some Work of Aymar Embury II in the Sand Hills of North Carolina. (*Arch. Rec.*, June 1924, v. 55, pp. 505–568. Plans, exts., ints.)

PENNSYLVANIA

Harold D. Eberlein—Examples of the Work of Mellor and Meigs. (*Arch. Rec.*, March 1916, v. 39, pp. 213–246. Illus.)

Arthur J. Meigs—An American Country House, the Property of Arthur E. Newbold, Jr., Laverock, Pa. New York, Architectural Book Pub. Co., 1925. Illus.

ST. MARTIN'S PA. HOUSES ON NAVAJO STREET. Edmund B. Gilchrist, Architect. (*Amer. Arch.*, July 29, 1925, v. 128, pls. 209–211. Plans, exts., ints.)

HOUSES, CITY

NEW YORK CITY. HOUSE OF MAURICE BRILL. Frederick Sterner, Architect. (*Arch. Forum*, Jan. 1924, v. 40, pls. 10–13. Plans, exts., ints.)

NEW YORK CITY. OFFICE AND RESIDENCE OF FREDERICK STERNER. Frederick Sterner, Architect. (*Arch. Forum*, Oct. 1922, v. 37, pls. 57–61. Plans, exts., ints.)

NEW YORK CITY. RESIDENCE OF MRS. WILLARD STRAIGHT. Delano and Aldrich, Architects. (*Arch.*, Mar. 1920, v. 41, pls. 33–38. Plans, exts., ints.)

NEW YORK CITY. TWO NOTABLE HOUSES ON SUTTON PLACE. The homes of Mrs. W. K. Vanderbilt and Miss Anne Morgan. Mott B. Schmidt, Architect. (*Arch. Forum*, Aug. 1924, v. 41, pp. 49–60, pls. 17–24. Illus.)

INDUSTRIAL BUILDINGS

Architectural Forum—Industrial Building Reference Number, Sept. 1923, v. 39, pp. 83–151. Illus.

George C. Nimmons—Modern Industrial Plants. (*Arch. Rec.*, Nov., Dec., 1918, Jan.—June, 1919; v. 44, pp. 414–421, 532–549; v. 45, pp. 26–43, 148–168, 262–282, 343–365, 450–470, 506–525. Illus.)

Moritz Kahn—The Design of Industrial Buildings. The Detroit *Evening News*, Hudson Motor Co. Albert Kahn, Inc., Architects. (*West. Arch.*, Aug. 1925, v. 34, p. 80, pls. 1–16. Plans, exts., ints.)

Arthur J. McEntee—Recent Development in the Architectural Treatment of Concrete Industrial Buildings. (*Arch.*, Jan. 1921, v. 43, pp. 18–21. Illus.)

INTERNATIONAL BUILDINGS

WASHINGTON, D. C. PAN AMERICAN UNION and its annex: A Study in Plan and Detail. Albert Kelsey and Paul P. Cret, Associate Architects. (*Arch. Rec.*, Nov. 1913, v. 34, pp. 385–457. Plans, exts., ints.)

LIBRARIES

Chalmers Hadley—Library Buildings, Notes, and Plans. Chicago, American Library Association, 1924. Illus.

Snead and Company Iron Works, Inc.—Library Planning, Bookstacks and Shelving with Contributions from the Architects' and Librarians' Points of View. Jersey City, N. J., Snead and Company Iron Works, Inc., 1915. Illus.

BOSTON, MASS. PUBLIC LIBRARY. McKim, Mead and White, Architects. (*American Architect and Building News*, April 6, 1895, v. 48, p. 3 text and plates. Exts., ints.) (*Brickbuilder*, Feb. 1910, v. 19, pp. 32–37. Plans, exts., ints.)

DETROIT, MICH. PUBLIC LIBRARY. Cass Gilbert, Architect. (*Arch.*, July 1921, v. 44, pp. 203–212, pls. 93–105. Plans, exts., ints., sections.)

LA JOLLA, CALIF. PUBLIC LIBRARY. William Templeton Johnson, Architect. (*Arch. Rec.*, July 1924, v. 56, pp. 33–37. Plan, ext., int.)

LOS ANGELES, CALIF. PUBLIC LIBRARY. Carleton M. Winslow, Architect, and Bertram G. Goodhue Associates. (*West. Arch.*, Feb. 1927, v. 36, pp. 19–22, pls. 19–26. Plans, exts., ints.)

NEW YORK. PUBLIC LIBRARY. Carrère and Hastings, Architects. (*Arch. Rec.*, Sept. 1910, v. 28, pp. 145–172. Plans, exts., ints., details.)

ST. PAUL, MINN. THE JAMES J. HILL REFERENCE LIBRARY AND THE ST. PAUL PUBLIC LIBRARY. Electus D. Litchfield, Architect. (*Arch. Rec.*, Jan. 1920, v. 47, pp. 3–24. Plans, exts., ints.)

SAN MARINO, CALIF. LIBRARY OF HENRY E. HUNTINGTON. Myron Hunt, Architect. (*Arch. Forum*, March 1922, v. 36, pp. 95–96, pls. 33–34. Plans, exts., ints.)

WALTHAM, MASS. PUBLIC LIBRARY. Leland and Loring, Architects. (*Amer. Arch.*, Oct. 29, 1919, v. 116, pls. 149–152. Exts., ints.)

WASHINGTON, D. C. THE LIBRARY OF CONGRESS. Smithmeyer, Pelz and Casey, Architects. (*Arch. Rec.*, Jan.–March 1898, v. 7, pp. 295–332. Plans, exts., ints.)

MEMORIALS

Architectural Forum—Memorial Buildings and Monuments Reference Number, Dec. 1926, v. 45, pp. 321–368. Plans, exts, ints.

INDIANAPOLIS, IND. WAR MEMORIAL. Group plan, elev. Walker and Weeks, Architects. (*Arch. Rec.*, June 1923, v. 53, pp. 573–575.)

KANSAS CITY, MO. KANSAS CITY MEMORIAL. Plan, elev., perspective sketch. H. Van Buren Magonigle, Architect. (*Journal, Amer. Inst. of Archs.*, Aug. 1921, v. 9, pp. 266–270.)

——. SAME. Plan, elev., perspective sketch. Exteriors and sculptured frieze. H. Van Buren Magonigle, Architect. (*Arch.*, Jan. 1927, v. 55, pp. 1–8.)

NEW YORK STATE. THEODORE ROOSEVELT MEMORIAL. Design Winning the Competition for the Selection of an Architect. Plan, elev., section by John Russell Pope. Also designs submitted by Helmle and Corbett; Trowbridge and Livingston (*Amer, Arch.*, July 1, 1925, p. 14, v. 128, pls. 168–178.)

WASHINGTON, D. C. LINCOLN MEMORIAL. Henry Bacon, Architect. (*Journal, Amer. Inst. of Archs.*, May 1923, v. 11, pls. opp. p. 190. Plan, exts.)

——. SAME. (*Arch. Rec.*, June 1923, v. 53, pp. 478–508. Exts., ints.)

WASHINGTON, D. C. THEODORE ROOSEVELT MEMORIAL. Views of Model of Prize Winning Design by John Russell Pope, Architect. (*Amer. Arch.*, May 20, 1926, v. 129, pls. 105–108.)

——. SAME. Designs Submitted in the Competition for a Monumental Memorial in Washington, D. C. to Theodore Roosevelt. Plans and elevs., by Pond and Pond; Egerton Swartwout; Charles A. Platt; John Mead Howells; McKim, Mead and White; Delano and Aldrich; C. Grant LaFarge; Albert Randolph Ross. (*Amer. Arch.*, Feb. 5, 1926, v. 129, pls. 13–20)

——. SAME. Prize Winning Designs in Competition for a Memorial to Theodore Roosevelt. John Russell Pope, Architect. (*Amer. Arch.*, Jan. 20, 1926, v. 129, pls. 7–11. Plan, elev., detail, perspective.)

MUSEUMS

Architectural Forum—Library and Museum Reference Number, Dec. 1927, v. 47, pp. 497–608, pls. 97–128. Plans, exts., ints.

Benjamin Ives Gilman—Museum Ideals of Purpose and Method. Cambridge, Printed by Order of the Trustees of the Museum at the Riverside Press, 1918. Illus.

BOSTON, MASS. MUSEUM OF FINE ARTS. Guy Lowell, Architect. (*Arch.*, Jan. 1910, v. 21, pp. 1–2, 4, pl. 51. Exts., ints.)

CAMBRIDGE, MASS. HARVARD UNIVERSITY. FOGG MUSEUM OF ART. Coolidge, Shepley, Bulfinch and Abbott, Architects. (*Arch. Rec.*, June 1927, v. 61, pp. 465–477. Plans, exts., ints.)

CHICAGO, ILL. FIELD MUSEUM OF NATURAL HISTORY. Graham, Anderson, Probst and White, Architects. (*Arch. Rec.*, July 1924, v. 56, pp. 1–15. Plan, exts., ints.)

CLEVELAND, O. MUSEUM OF ART. Hubbell and Benes, Architects. (*Arch. Rec.*, Sept. 1916, v. 40, pp. 194–211. Plans, exts., ints.)

DETROIT, MICH. MUSEUM OF THE INSTITUTE OF ARTS. Paul P. Cret and Zantzinger, Borie and Medary, Architects. (*Amer. Arch.*, June 3, 1925, v. 127, p. 494. Plan, elev.)

MINNEAPOLIS, MINN. MUSEUM OF FINE ARTS. McKim, Mead and White, Architects. (*Amer. Arch.*, April 21, 1915, v. 107, pp. 245–248, and plates.)

NEW YORK CITY. METROPOLITAN MUSEUM. R. M. Hunt, Architect. (*Arch. Rec.*, Aug. 1902, v. 12, pp. 304–310. Exts.)

PHILADELPHIA, PA. MUSEUM OF ART. Borie, Trumbauer, Zantzinger, Architects. Plans, exts., ints., elev., section. (*Arch. Rec.*, Aug. 1926, v. 60, pp. 97–111. Exteriors under construction and polychrome detail.)

SAN DIEGO, CALIF. FINE ARTS BUILDING. W. T. Johnson and Robert W. Snyder, Architects. (*Arch. Forum*, Oct. 1926, v. 45, pp. 193–198. Plans, exts., ints.)

SAN FRANCISCO, CALIF. MEMORIAL MUSEUM. Louis C. Mullgardt, Architect. (*Arch. Rev.*, New York, Feb. 1921, v. 12 (New Series), pls. 19–20. Exts.)

SANTA FÉ, NEW MEXICO. ART MUSEUM. Rapp and Rapp and Hendrickson, Architects. (Illus. article, *Arch. Rev.*, New York, Feb. 1918, v. 6 (New Series), pp. 17–18, pls. 10–14. Plan, exts., ints., sections.)

WASHINGTON, D. C. FREER GALLERY OF ART. Charles A. Platt, Architect. (*Arch.*, Sept. 1923, v. 48, pp. 293–297, pls. 129–134. Plans, elev., exts., ints.)

OFFICE BUILDINGS

Architectural Forum—Office Building Reference Number, Sept. 1924, v. 41, pp. 89–160, pls. 33–48. Plans and exts. of Bush Bldg., New York; Standard Oil, San Francisco; London Guarantee and Accident Building, Chicago, etc.

Walter Curt Behrendt—Skyscrapers in Germany (includes remarks on American skyscrapers.) (*Journal, Amer. Inst. of Archs.*, Sept. 1923, v. 11, pp. 365–370. Illus.)

John Taylor Boyd, Jr.—The New York Zoning Resolution and its Influence upon Design. (*Arch. Rec.*, Sept. 1920, v. 48, pp. 193–217. Illus.)

——. A new emphasis in Skyscraper Design, Exemplified in the Recent Work of Starrett and Van Vleck. (*Arch. Rec.*, Dec. 1922, v. 52, pp. 496–509. Illus.)

Harvey W. Corbett—High Buildings on Narrow Streets. (*Amer. Arch.*, June 8, 1921, v. 119, pp. 603–608, 617. Illus.)

Leonard Cox—This Cinematerial Age. (*Journal, Amer. Inst. of Archs.*, March, May 1926, v. 14, pp. 96–98, 222–223.)

Herbert D. Croly—The Skyscraper in the Service of Religion. (Speculative Comment on Donn Barber's Broadway Temple, New York City.) (*Arch. Rec.*, Feb. 1924, v. 55, pp. 203–204.)

Aymar Embury II—New York's New Architecture. The Effect of the Zoning Law on High Buildings. Plans, exts., of Heckscher Building, New York; Fisk Building and

Wrigley Building, Chicago, etc. (*Arch. Forum*. Oct. 1921, v. 35, pp. 119–124, pls. 47–55. Illus.)

W. J. Fryer—New York Building Law. (*Arch. Rec.*, July–Sept. 1891, v. 1, pp. 69–82.)

Bassett Jones—The Modern Building is a Machine. (*Amer. Arch.*, Jan. 30, 1924, v. 125, pp. 93–98.)

Irving F. Morrow—Recent San Francisco Skyscrapers. (*Arch. and Eng.*, Nov. 1923, v. 75, pp. 51–84. Illus.)

Lewis Mumford—Is the Skyscraper Tolerable? (*Arch.*, Feb. 1927, v. 55, pp. 67–69. Illus.)

Lewis Mumford—High Buildings, an American View. (*Amer. Arch.*, Nov. 5, 1924, v. 126, pp. 423–424.)

Rexford Newcomb—The Trend of Skyscraper Design. (*West. Arch.*, Mar. 1926, v. 35, pp. 31–33.)

George C. Nimmons—Skyscrapers in America. (*Journal, Amer. Inst. of Archs.*, Sept. 1923, v. 11, pp. 370–372.)

Arthur J. Penty—Architecture in the United States. (*Journal, Amer. Inst. of Archs.*, Nov. 1924, v. 12, pp. 473–478.)

Leon V. Solon—Passing of the Skyscraper Formula for Design. (*Arch. Rec.*, Feb. 1924, v. 55, pp. 135–144. Illus.)

Herbert S. Swan—Making the New York Zoning Ordinance Better. A Program of improvement. (*Arch. Forum*, Oct. 1921, v. 35, pp. 125–130. Illus.)

CHICAGO

The Chicago *Tribune*—International Competition for a New Administration Building for the Chicago *Tribune*, 1922; containing all the designs submitted in response to the Chicago *Tribune's* $100,000 offer commemorating its seventy-fifth anniversary, June 10, 1922. Chicago: Chicago *Tribune*, 1923.

CHICAGO TRIBUNE BUILDING. Winning designs by John Mead Howells and Raymond M. Hood, Associate Architects. (*Amer. Arch.*, Oct. 5, 1925, v. 128, pls. 264–271. Plans, exts., details.)

——. SAME. (*West. Arch.*, Nov. 1925, v. 34, pp. 111–115, pls. 1–16. Plans, exts., details.)

——. SAME. The Evolution of an Architectural Design—Tribune Building Tower, Chicago. (*Arch. Rec.*, March 1926, v. 59, pp. 215–225. Illus.)

——. SAME. High Buildings and Beauty, Part 1 and 2. Illus. with competition drawings of the Chicago *Tribune* Tower. (*Arch. Forum*, Feb., April 1923, v. 38, pp. 41–44, 179–182.)

MONADNOCK BUILDING. Burnham & Root, Architects. (*Arch. Rec.*, July 1915, v. 38, p. 39. Ext.)

ROOKERY BUILDING. Burnham & Root, Architects. (*Arch. Rec.*, July 1915, v. 38, p. 42. Ext.)

BUHL BUILDING.   Smith, Hinchman and Grylls, Architects.   (*Arch. Forum*, July 1926, v. 45, pp. 30–32, pls. 9–14.   Plans, exts., ints.)

AMERICAN RADIATOR BUILDING.   Raymond M. Hood, Architect.   (*Amer. Arch.*, Nov. 19, 1924, v. 126, pp. 467–484, pls. 161–168.   Plans, exts., ints., model.)

BARCLAY–VESEY TELEPHONE BUILDING.   McKenzie, Voorhees & Gmelin, Architects.   (*Amer. Arch.*, Nov. 20, 1926, v. 130, pp. 387–428, pls. 281–296.)

CHICKERING BUILDING.   Cross & Cross, Architects.   (*Arch.*, Jan. 1925, v. 51, pls. 2–6.   Exts., ints.)

CUNARD BUILDING.   Benjamin W. Morris, Architect; Carrère and Hastings, Consulting Architects.   (*Arch. Forum*, July 1921, v. 35, pp. 1–24, pls. 1–15.   Plans, exts., ints., details.)

FULLER BUILDING (Flatiron).   D. H. Burnham & Co., Architects.   (*Arch. Rec.*, Aug. 1909, v. 26, p. 93.   Ext.)

METROPOLITAN LIFE INSURANCE BUILDING.   N. LeBrun and Sons, Architects.   (*Arch. Rec.*, Aug. 1909, v. 26, p. 95.   Ext.)

SINGER BUILDING.   Ernest Flagg, Architect.   (*Arch. Rec.*, Aug. 1909, v. 26, p. 95.   Ext.)

WOOLWORTH BUILDING.   Cass Gilbert, Architect.   (*Arch.*, Jan., June 1913, v. 27, pp. 3, 8–10, pls. 1–4, 52–59.   Exts., ints, plans.)

——.   SAME.   The Towers of Manhattan and Notes on the Woolworth Building.   Cass Gilbert, Architect.   (*Arch. Rec.*, Feb. 1913, v. 33, pp. 98–122.   Illus.)

——.   SAME.   Notes on Gargoyles, Grotesque and Chimeras.   (*Arch. Rec.*, Feb. 1914, v. 35, pp. 132–139.   Illus.)

PACIFIC GAS AND ELECTRIC BUILDING.   Bakewell and Brown, Architects.   (*Amer. Arch.*, Nov. 20, 1925, v. 128, p. 434, pls. 304–308.   Plans, exts., ints.)

PACIFIC TELEPHONE AND TELEGRAPH BUILDING.   J. R. Miller and T. L. Pflueger, A. A. Cantin, Associate Architects.   (*Amer. Arch.*, March 20, 1926, v. 129, pp. 367–372, pls. 49–53.)

——.   SAME.   (*West. Arch.*, March 1926, v. 35, pls. 33–40.)

——.   SAME.   (*Arch. and Eng.*, Dec. 1925, v. 83, pp. 51–80.   Plans, exts., ints.)

PUEBLO ARCHITECTURE

Rose Henderson—A Primitive Basis for Modern Architecture.   (*Arch. Rec.*, Aug. 1923, v. 54, pp. 188–196.   Illus.)

Rexford Newcomb—Santa Fé, the Historic and Modern.   (*West. Arch.*, Jan. 1924, v. 33, pp. 4–6, pls. 1–16.   Illus.)

SANTE FÉ, NEW MEXICO.   (*Amer. Arch.*, May 7, 1924, v. 125, pp. 421–425.   Illus.)

RAILROAD STATIONS

W. W. Beach—Railway Stations of Moderate Size. (*Arch. Forum*, April 1926, v. 44, pp. 251–272. Plans, exts., ints.)

AJO, ARIZONA. RAILROAD DEPOT. W. M. Kenyon and Maurice F. Maine, Architects. (*Arch.*, Jan. 1919, v. 39, pls. 11–13. Exts.)

CHICAGO, ILL. UNION STATION. Graham, Anderson, Probst and White, Architects. (*Arch. Forum*, Feb. 1926, v. 44, pp. 85–88, pls. 17–24. Plan, exts., ints.)

NEW YORK CITY. GRAND CENTRAL TERMINAL. Warren and Wetmore, Architects. (*Arch.*, March 1913, v. 37, pls. 20–29. Exts., ints.)

NEW YORK CITY. PENNSYLVANIA STATION. McKim, Mead and White, Architects. (*Arch. Rec.*, June 1910, v. 27, pp. 518–521. Ext.)

RICHMOND, VA. UNION PASSENGER STATION. John Russell Pope, Architect. (*Amer. Arch.*, July 9, 1919, v. 116, pp. 31–38, pls. 10–18. Plans, elev., sections, exts. ints.)

SAN DIEGO, CALIF. SANTA FÉ STATION. Bakewell and Brown, Architects. (*Amer. Arch.*, Nov. 21, 1917, v. 112, pls. 242, 243. Plan, ext., int.)

WASHINGTON, D. C. UNION STATION. D. H. Burnham and Co., Architects. (*Arch. Rec.*, July 1915, v. 38, pp. 154–158. Plan, ext., ints.)

SCHOOLS

Grade School Buildings, Book II. New York, Rogers and Manson, 1927. Illus.

John J. Donovan—School Architecture, Principles and Practices. New York, Macmillan Company, 1921.

Guy Study—Elementary School Buildings. (*Arch. Rec.*, May 1926, v. 59, pp. 403–421. Illus.)

——. Junior and Senior High Schools. (*Arch. Rec.*, Sept. 1926, v. 60, pp. 202–224. Illus.)

BUILDINGS FOR SOCIETIES

Architectural Forum—Club and Fraternal Buildings Reference Number, September 1926, v. 45, pp. 129–192, pls. 33–48. Illus.

WASHINGTON, D. C. NATIONAL ACADEMY OF SCIENCES AND NATIONAL RESEARCH COUNCIL. Bertram G. Goodhue, Architect. (*Arch.*, Oct. 1924, v. 50, pp. 329–334, pls. 145–152. Plans, exts., ints., details.)

WASHINGTON, D. C. TEMPLE OF THE SCOTTISH RITE. John Russell Pope, Architect. (*Arch. Rev.*, New York, Jan. 1916, v. 4 (New Series), pp. 1–12, pls. 1–12. Plans, exts.)

STADIA

Roi L. Morin—Stadia: Illus. Series in the *American Architect*, as below:

    I. University of Pennsylvania, Franklin Field Stadium. (Oct. 24, 1923, v. 124, pp. 365–373.)

II. Yankee Stadium, New York City. (Nov. 7, 1923, v. 124, pp. 412–416.)
III. Los Angeles Coliseum. (May 7, 1924, v. 125, pp. 427–434.)
IV. University of Kansas Stadium. (Aug. 27, 1924, v. 126, pp. 197–205.)

H. D. Smith—Report on Trip to Princeton, College of the City of New York, Yale and Harvard, for the Purpose of Inspecting the Stadia at those Universities. (*Amer. Arch.*, July 21, Aug. 4, 18, 25, 1920, v. 118, pp. 94–96, 124–126, 160–164, 221–224, 260–262. Illus.)

ARLINGTON, VA. ARLINGTON MEMORIAL AMPHITHEATRE. Carrère and Hastings, Architects. (*Arch. Forum*, March 1921, v. 34, pp. 91–96, pls. 33–36. Plan, elev., section, views.)

BROWN UNIVERSITY, PROVIDENCE, R. I. STADIUM. Gavin Hadden, Engineer; Paul P. Cret, Consulting Architect. (*Amer. Arch.*, Feb. 20, 1926, v. 129, pp. 285–288. ·Plan, elev., section, exts.)

CHICAGO, ILL. GRANT PARK STADIUM. Holabird and Roche, Architects. (*Arch. Forum*, Feb. 1925, v. 42, pp. 79–80, pls. 9–10. Illus.)

CORNELL UNIVERSITY, ITHACA, N. Y. CORNELL CRESCENT. Gavin Hadden, Designer. (*Arch. Rec.*, March 1925, v. 57, pp. 193–203. Plans, exts., ints.)

NEW YORK, N. Y. COLLEGE OF THE CITY OF NEW YORK. STADIUM. Arnold W. Brunner, Architect. (*Amer. Arch.*, Aug. 4, 1915, v. 108, pp. 69–72, and plates. Plans, elev., section, views.)

PASADENA, CALIF. STADIUM. Myron Hunt, Architect. (*Amer. Arch.*, Oct. 20, 1925, v. 128, pp. 341–346. Plans, air views, sections, elev.)

TERRE HAUTE, IND. MEMORIAL STADIUM. Shourds-Stoner Co., Inc., Architects and Engineers. (*Amer. Arch.*, Feb. 20, 1926, v. 129, pp. 281–284. Plan, ext., elev., section.)

YALE UNIVERSITY, NEW HAVEN, CONN. THE YALE BOWL. Donn Barber, Architect. (In Proceedings of Amer. Society of Civil Eng., 1917, v. 81, pp. 249–296. Paper No. 1386. Illus., diagrs.)

STORES AND SHOPS

Architectural Forum—Shop and Store Reference Number, June 1924, v. 40, pp. 233–287, pls. 81–96. Illus.)

John Taylor Boyd—The Newer Fifth Ave. Retail Shop Fronts. (*Arch. Rec.*, June 1921. v. 49, pp. 458–487. Illus.)

NEW YORK CITY. CHILDS BUILDING, 604 Fifth Ave. Severance and William Van Alen, Architects. (*Arch. Rec.*, Jan. 1926, v. 59, pp. 59–63. Illus.)

NEW YORK CITY. GORHAM BUILDING. McKim, Mead and White, Architects. (*Arch. Rec.*, Aug. 1909, v. 26, p. 86. Ext.)

NEW YORK CITY. LORD & TAYLOR STORE. Starrett and Van Vleck, Architects. (*Arch.*, April 1914, v. 29, pls. 42–51. Exts., ints.)

NEW YORK CITY. MACMILLAN COMPANY BUILDING, Fifth Ave. Carrère and Hastings, and Shreve and Lamb, Architects. (*Amer. Arch.*, June 17, 1925, v. 127, pls. 157–161. Plans, exts., ints.)

NEW YORK CITY. ADDITION TO DEPARTMENT STORE OF R. H. MACY & CO. Robert D. Kohn and Associates, Architects. (*Amer. Arch.* and *Arch. Rev.*, June 4, 1924, v. 125, pp. 531–537 and plates. Plan, exts.)

NEW YORK CITY. WANAMAKER BUILDING. D. H. Burnham & Co., Architects. (*Arch. Rec.*, Nov. 1905, v. 18, p. 394. Ext.)

NEW YORK CITY. SHOP FOR E. WEYHE. Henry S. Churchill, Architect. (*Amer. Arch.* and *Arch. Rev.*, March 26, 1924, v. 125, plate. Ext.)

PHILADELPHIA, PA. WANAMAKER BUILDING. D. H. Burnham & Co., Architects. (*Arch. Rec.*, March 1911, v. 29, pp. 277–288. Exts., ints.)

THEATRES

Architectural Forum—Motion Picture Reference Number, June 1925, v. 42, pp. 361–432, pls. 61–92. Illus.)

Claude Bragdon—A Theatre Transformed, a Description of the Permanent Setting by Norman Bel Geddes for Max Reinhardt's spectacle "The Miracle." (*Arch. Rec.*, April 1924, v. 55, pp. 388–397. Plans, sections, details.)

——. Towards a New Theatre. Plans by Norman Bel Geddes. (*Arch. Rec.*, Sept. 1922, v. 52, 170–182. Illus.)

BOSTON, MASS. METROPOLITAN THEATRE. (*Amer. Arch.*, Aug. 5, 1926, v. 130, pls. 181–187. Plans, exts., ints.)

BOSTON, MASS. REPERTORY THEATRE OF BOSTON. J. Williams Beal Sons, Architects. (*Arch.*, Feb. 1926, v. 53, pls. 17–22. Plans, exts., ints.)

HOLLYWOOD, CALIF. GRAUMAN THEATRE. Meyer and Holler, Architects. (*Amer. Arch.*, Jan. 31, 1923, v. 123, pp. 113–116 and plates, pp. 125–127. Plan, sections, exts., ints.)

NEW YORK CITY. GUILD THEATRE. C. Howard Crane, Kenneth Franzheim and Charles Hunter Bettis, Architects. (*Arch. Forum*, July 1925, v. 43, pp. 13–16, pls. 1–4. Plans, exts., ints.)

——. SAME. (*Arch. Rec.*, Dec. 1924, v. 56, pp. 508–516. Plan, elev., sec., sketch.)

NEW YORK CITY. MANHATTAN OPERA HOUSE. Hammerstein and Denivelle, Decorators. (*Arch. Rec.*, Feb. 1907, v. 21, pp. 148–152. Ints.)

NEW YORK CITY. NEIGHBORHOOD PLAY HOUSE. Harry Creighton Ingalls and F. Burrall Hoffman, Jr., Associate Architects. (*Arch. Rec.*, Nov. 1915, v. 38, pp. 550–554. Plan, ext., ints.)

NEW YORK CITY. ZIEGFELD THEATRE. Joseph Urban and Thomas W. Lamb, Architects. (*Arch. Rec.*, May 1927, v. 61, pp. 385–393. Plans, exts., ints., details.)

——. SAME. (*Arch. Forum*, May 1927, v. 46, pp. 414–420, pl. 83. Plans, exts., ints.)

PASADENA, CALIF. PLAYHOUSE. Elmer Grey, Architect. (*Amer. Arch.*, Nov. 5, 1925, v. 128, pls. 288–293. Plan, exts., ints.)

ROCHESTER, N. Y. EASTMAN SCHOOL OF MUSIC, UNIVERSITY OF ROCHES-TER. Gordon and Kaelber, Architects; McKim, Mead and White, Associate Architects. (*Amer. Arch.* and *Arch. Rev.*, Feb. 28, 1923, v. 123, pp. 181–184, 195–199, and plates. Plans, exts., ints., sections, murals.)

TOWN AND CITY HALLS

Charles G. Loring—The Small Town Hall: Plattsburg, N. Y.; Arlington, Mass.; Tewksbury, Mass.; Weston, Mass.; Kennebunk, Me.; Peterborough, N. H. (*Arch. Forum*, Nov. 1925, v. 43, pp. 289–312. Plans, exts.)

CLEVELAND, OHIO. CITY HALL. J. Milton Dyer, Architect. (*Amer. Arch.*, July 25, 1917, v. 112, pp. 61–63, pls. 32–50. Plans, exts., ints.)

DALLAS, TEXAS. HIGHLAND PARK CITY HALL. Lang and Witchell, Architects. (*Arch.*, Dec. 1925, v. 52, pls. 182–183. Plans, exts.)

NEW YORK CITY. MUNICIPAL BUILDING. McKim, Mead & White, Architects. (*Amer. Arch.* and *Arch. Rev.*, May 24, 1922, v. 121, pp. 426a, 433. Ext.)

OAKLAND, CALIF. CITY HALL. Palmer, Hornbostel & Jones, Architects. (*Brickbuilder*, July 1914, v. 23, pp. 159–162, pls. 97–100. Plans, exts., details.)

SAN FRANCISCO, CALIF. CITY HALL. Bakewell & Brown, Architects. (*Arch.* and *Eng.*, Aug. 1916, v. 46, pp. 39–84. Plans, exts., ints.)